The Essential
Franklin Delano Roosevelt

───── ★ ─────

LIBRARY OF FREEDOM

The Essential Franklin Delano Roosevelt

──★──

EDITED, WITH AN INTRODUCTION, BY
John Gabriel Hunt

GRAMERCY BOOKS
NEW YORK • AVENEL

A NOTE ON THE TEXT

All selections in *The Essential Franklin Delano Roosevelt* are complete and unabridged, except for: the fireside chats on reorganization of the judiciary, national defense, and conservation of natural resources; all of the Annual Messages to Congress; the radio addresses to the 1940 Democratic National Convention and announcing an unlimited national emergency; the messages to Congress on the embargo provisions of the Neutrality Act and the progress of the war; the "quarantine" speech in Chicago; and the address on the Yalta Conference. The text has been edited to modernize punctuation and spelling, but Roosevelt's language remains unaltered. The location for the delivery of speeches and broadcast addresses, unless otherwise indicated, is Washington, D.C.

This 1995 edition is published by Gramercy Books,
distributed by Random House Value Publishing, Inc.,
40 Engelhard Avenue, Avenel, New Jersey 07001.

Random House
New York • Toronto • London • Sydney • Auckland

Printed and bound in the United States of America

Library of Congress Cataloging-in-Publication Data
Roosevelt, Franklin D. (Franklin Delano), 1882–1945.
The essential Franklin Delano Roosevelt / [edited by John Gabriel Hunt].
p. cm.—(Library of freedom)
ISBN 0-517-12289-8
1. United States—Politics and government—1993–1945—Sources.
2. World War, 1939–1945—United States—Sources.
3. New York (State)—Politics and government—1865–1950—Sources.
I. Hunt, John Gabriel, 1952–   . II. Title. III. Series.
E742.5.R65   1994
973.917—dc20   94-40318
                                                                          CIP

8 7 6 5 4 3 2 1

CONTENTS

INTRODUCTION

FOR TWELVE YEARS, President Franklin Delano Roosevelt talked to the people of America as if he were sitting with them in their living rooms. Every significant program and piece of legislation, every important event in the nation and the world was presented to an audience of millions in a way that was accessible and reassuring. Roosevelt's success as president was in large part due to his personal style—his ability to act decisively, to inspire confidence, to radiate warmth and cheerfulness, to make ordinary Americans feel that they were partners in his decisions.

Roosevelt's twenty-eight fireside chats, during which he spoke directly and informally to enormous audiences, were broadcast over the radio, as were many of his other addresses—from political-convention and inaugural speeches to messages in support of the National Foundation for Infantile Paralysis. A gifted speaker, he communicated his own optimism and hope to men, women, and children battered by the Great Depression, and later he imparted a spirit of sacrifice and resolve to people whose lives were forever changed by a formidable world war.

Franklin Delano Roosevelt, the only child of James and Sara Delano Roosevelt, was born on January 30, 1882, on his patrician family's estate in Hyde Park, New York. He was educated by private tutors until, at the age of fourteen, he entered the prestigious Groton School. Groton's headmaster, Endicott Peabody, was an Episcopal minister who instilled in his students the conviction that they were an elite class, destined for greatness. Four years later, Franklin entered Harvard, where he joined the football and crew teams, edited the *Harvard Crimson,* and was president of his senior class. On March 17, 1905, he married his fifth cousin, Anna Eleanor Roosevelt, the niece of President Theodore Roosevelt, who gave the bride away.

Franklin Roosevelt's early years and rise to the presidency almost directly parallel those of Teddy Roosevelt. Both men were born into affluent families, traveled in Europe during their childhoods, attended Groton and Harvard, studied law (unlike Teddy, Franklin became a lawyer), began their political careers in the New York State legislature, and attained the positions of assistant secretary of the navy and governor of New York before becoming president. In addition to the belief that those in a privileged position must devote themselves to public service, they shared an ability to communicate their ideas in plain and memorable language. Both had an infectious cheerfulness and took great delight in the job of being president. All of the similarities were by no means coincidental. Before he entered politics, Franklin had confided in friends that his plan was to eventually become president—by following exactly the steps of the cousin he so admired.

As a New York State senator, Franklin Roosevelt supported Woodrow Wilson for president in the 1912 election, although Teddy himself was a candidate. Franklin was rewarded with an appointment as assistant secretary of the navy, a position that took on greater significance with the entry of the United States into the First World War.

At the Democratic National Convention of 1920, Roosevelt was chosen to run as the vice-presidential candidate on the ticket with party standard-bearer James M. Cox; he campaigned hard and became a shining star of the party and a political figure known throughout the country. Cox was defeated by Warren G. Harding, ushering in twelve years of Republican political dominance. Roosevelt returned to New York to practice law.

Then, in August 1921, during a vacation at the family's summer home on Campobello, an island off the coast of Maine, Franklin Roosevelt suddenly contracted poliomyelitis. As a result, he was paralyzed from the waist down. Over the next decade, Roosevelt gradually rebuilt his strength and attained robust health, although for the rest of his life he was never able to stand or walk without leg braces and the strong supporting arm of another person.

Roosevelt was treated in the thermal waters at Warm Springs in Georgia. By 1927 he had established, using much of his personal fortune, the Georgia Warm Springs Foundation as a treatment center for victims of infantile paralysis. Throughout the twenties Roosevelt retained his ties to state and national Democratic party politics—he nominated Al Smith at the national convention in 1924—but for the most part his energies were devoted to his own rehabilitation and to running the successful foundation at Warm Springs.

Franklin Roosevelt's illness and paralysis radically changed the relationship between him and his wife. Since the beginning of their marriage, Eleanor had been a submissive, dutiful wife and mother, subservient to the will and financial control of her mother-in-law, Sara. Eleanor's early years had been difficult. Her own mother, Anna Hall Roosevelt, a charming and graceful beauty, was clearly disappointed in her awkward, plain-looking, and serious daughter. She died when Eleanor was eight, and two years later the girl's adored father, Elliott Roosevelt, an alcoholic who had left home when Eleanor was six, also died. Eleanor spent the next few years in her grandmother's dreary and depressing household with her younger brother Hall (a second brother died shortly after arriving there), her alcoholic uncle, and her suicidal aunt.

At fifteen, Eleanor finally escaped to Allenswood, a finishing school near London. There, under the kind tutelage of the headmistress, Marie Souvestre, she gained self-confidence and an appreciation of liberal causes. Soon after her return to New York three years later, she met her fifth cousin Franklin and within a year they were married. During the next decade, the couple had six children—one died in infancy—and Eleanor played the role of a society wife.

As assistant secretary of the navy, Franklin felt he had found his metier in Washington political life. A charming extrovert, he enjoyed the liveliness of the District's social scene, which Eleanor disliked; she spent more and more time at Campobello. Then, in 1918, she learned of Franklin's love affair with Lucy Mercer, her personal secretary. Franklin contemplated divorce, but the urging of the family and of his close friend and political advisor Louis Howe persuaded him to end the affair. The breach was irreparable. For the rest of their marriage, the relationship between Eleanor and Franklin was based on mutual political and social commitments and, later, mutual respect and affection.

Throughout the twenties, Eleanor developed her own political interests and social relationships, and was particularly active in the Women's Division of the New York Democratic State Committee. She became an effective lecturer and wrote articles for mass-circulation publications. She was also a key member of New York governor Al Smith's staff.

At the 1928 Democratic National Convention in Houston, Smith finally won his party's nomination, and Roosevelt repeated the pattern of the 1924 convention by referring to Smith as the Happy Warrior when he again placed his name in nomination. Smith wanted Roosevelt to be his successor in New York, but Roosevelt was reluctant to run, since he was heavily involved with his foundation and his own rehabilitation and felt that 1928 would not be a good election year for the Democrats. It was Eleanor who convinced her husband that he had a responsibility to his party and to his own career to accede to the wishes of Smith and the other state Democratic leaders. After Franklin Roosevelt became president, Eleanor traveled all over the country to investigate local situations and social conditions and then reported back to him. And, beginning in 1936, she wrote a daily newspaper column called "My Day."

Roosevelt won the New York governorship in 1928 by a slim margin. When he ran again and won, two years later, the country had slid into a severe depression. Under the passive presidency of Herbert Hoover, unemployment reached 25 percent, almost half of the country's farmers faced foreclosure, and breadlines were everywhere; hopelessness and fear pervaded the nation.

At the 1932 Democratic National Convention, Roosevelt battled Al Smith for the nomination and finally won on the fourth ballot. His acceptance speech, broadcast over the radio, introduced the New Deal and repeated his previous insistence that government must not forget the ordinary citizen—the "forgotten man." He campaigned energetically, in large part to show that his paralysis would not prevent him from being a vigorous president.

Between Roosevelt's landslide election victory over Hoover on November 8, 1932, and his inauguration on March 4, thousands of banks closed their doors as panicky depositors sought to remove their savings. Roosevelt himself was the victim of an even harsher reality, when Giuseppe Zangara, an unemployed bricklayer, tried to assassinate him as he spoke from his car to a crowd in Miami. Instead he shot Chicago mayor Anton Cermak, who stood nearby; Cermak died three weeks later. Media reports of Roosevelt's calmness and poise in the days following the incident greatly enhanced the nation's confidence in his leadership.

In this climate of despair and tragedy, Franklin Delano Roosevelt, grinning ebulliantly and waving his top hat, rode to the inauguration in an open car with the dour Hoover. His inaugural address, broadcast to the nation, was like a cannon blast of hope. Roosevelt, in a resonant and confident voice, announced that "this nation asks for action, and action now," and told Americans that "the only thing we have to fear is fear itself." Within days he gave the first of his almost one thousand presidential press conferences—immediately setting a tone of informality and good humor by eliminating presubmitted written questions. His first fireside chat soon followed: he explained why he had declared a bank holiday and assured people of access to their savings. "We had a bad banking situation," he stated. "It was the government's job to straighten out this situation and do it as quickly as possible. And the job is being performed."

Millions of Americans soon began making bank deposits again. In the subsequent months, known as the Hundred Days, the president sent Congress an impressive array of new legislation, designed to put the country back to work and reestablish economic confidence. Congress quickly passed the Emergency Banking Relief Act, the National Industrial Recovery Act, and legislation creating the Tennessee Valley Authority, the Agricultural Adjustment Administration, and the Civilian Conservation Corps.

The visible symbol of the early New Deal was the emblem of the National Recovery Administration, the federal agency whose purpose it was to stimulate economic recovery and reduce unemployment through a system of industrial codes regulating production, prices, trade practices, and labor relations. Businesses all over the nation began displaying the signs of the NRA, with its blue eagle grasping lightning bolts and the gears of industry in its talons, and which proclaimed, "We Do Our Part." In his fireside chat about the new agency, Roosevelt expressed what could be considered a theme for his entire domestic policy: "I have no faith in 'cure-alls,' but I believe we can greatly influence economic forces." By the end of 1935, the spirit of the American people had changed from gloom to optimism. One important element was the end of Prohibition, which the president gladly announced on December 5, 1933, in the proclamation repealing the Eighteenth Amendment.

In 1935 Roosevelt crowned the accomplishments of his first term with more landmark social legislation. The Social Security Act, said the president, would "give some measure of protection to the average citizen and to his family against the loss of a job and against poverty-ridden old age." In addition, during the next decade the Works Progress Administration's government projects, from road repair to murals in public buildings, provided jobs for millions of Americans.

Roosevelt was nominated by acclamation at the 1936 Democratic National Convention in Philadelphia, where the candidate's acceptance speech pictured a nation that had "a rendezvous with destiny." In the November presidential election, Republican candidate Alf Landon received the electoral votes of only two states, Vermont and Maine. Roosevelt's second inaugural address pointed to the important work yet to be done to raise the nation's standard of living and defeat poverty. He stated: "I see a third of a nation ill-housed, ill-clothed, ill-fed. . . . It is not in despair that I paint you that picture. I paint it for you in hope—because the nation, seeing and understanding the injustice in it, proposes to paint it out."

Since the early days of the New Deal, Roosevelt had increasingly faced opposition from those who felt his programs were giving the federal government too much control over the economy. Indeed, in 1935 the U.S. Supreme Court declared the acts creating the National Recovery Administration and the Agricultural Adjustment Administration unconstitutional. Early in 1937, Roosevelt asked Congress to add six more justices to the Court and to set a mandatory retirement age for all federal judges. Speaking to the nation in a fireside chat about this controversial proposal, the president declared that his plan would "save our national Constitution from hardening of the judicial arteries." This effort to "pack the Court" turned out to be one of the major mistakes of Roosevelt's administration, and, in the wake of strident opposition, he abandoned it. The Court's subsequent decisions were, however, more liberal, and from 1937 to 1941, several conservative justices stepped down.

Despite the difficulties with the Supreme Court, massive labor unrest, a recession in 1937, and the unprecedented pursuit by a president of a third term, Franklin Delano Roosevelt easily won the election of 1940, defeating Wendell Willkie by about five million votes. It was obvious that the nation wanted the forceful and decisive leader to continue in office during the period of international conflict that was threatening to engulf even the United States.

Roosevelt had addressed the issue of world peace as early as 1933, when he sent a message on disarmament to the nations of the world. Since then, with each passing year, the march of aggressor nations became stronger and more threatening. In October 1935 Italy invaded the African kingdom of Abyssinia. In April 1936 Hitler sent troops into the Rhineland. In July 1937 Japan, which was already occupying Manchuria and Inner Mongolia, attacked central China. In 1938 Hitler annexed the Sudetenland and Austria, and in March 1939 took over the rest of an already dismembered Czechoslovakia. On September 1, 1939, the Nazis marched into Poland, and two days later Great Britain and France declared war on Germany. In his fireside chat of September 3, 1939, President Roosevelt addressed the nation on these alarming events. He warned that "when peace has been broken anywhere, the peace of all countries everywhere is in danger."

Roosevelt's desire to support the countries that were victims of the aggression met with consistent opposition from America's isolationists. But as a result of the European declarations of war in fall 1939, however, Roosevelt was able to begin assembling elements of a foreign policy that would aid Great Britain and other beleaguered nations while building up the defense capabilities of the United States. The president first mustered support to revoke the embargo provisions of the 1935 Neutrality Act, so that arms could be sold on a "cash and carry" basis to "belligerent" nations. In September 1940, Roosevelt signed the Selective Service Act, establishing mandatory registration for the nation's first peacetime draft. And the Lend-Lease program, passed by Congress on March 11, 1941, gave the president the power to "sell, transfer title to, exchange, lease, lend, or otherwise dispose of" arms and supplies to any nation whose self-defense was linked to U.S. national security. In August 1941, President Roosevelt and Prime Minister Winston Churchill of

England met for three days on their anchored naval vessels off the coast of Newfoundland. The result was the Atlantic Charter, a joint statement of war aims and common principles.

During 1941, the United States and Japan were engaged in negotiations for peace and security in the Pacific. But even as the meetings with Japanese envoys progressed, the U.S. government intercepted ominous Japanese coded messages. The Roosevelt administration's worst fears were realized on December 7, 1941, when Japanese bombers attacked the U.S. Pacific fleet berthed at Pearl Harbor, Hawaii. The following day, President Roosevelt appeared before Congress to ask for a declaration of war between Japan and the United States, calling December 7 "a date which will live in infamy." In a fireside chat on December 9, the president prepared the nation for the long road ahead. "Every single man, woman, and child," he said, "is a partner in the most tremendous undertaking of our American history." Within two more days, a state of war also existed between the United States and Germany and Italy.

For the rest of his presidency, Roosevelt traveled extensively: first across the nation, to personally show his support for the war effort and the sacrifices of millions of Americans, and then all over the world to meet with Allied leaders and plot war strategy. On January 11, 1943, he flew to Casablanca in North Africa to meet with Churchill, and for ten days they set strategic goals. Then, late in 1943, Soviet leader Joseph Stalin joined Churchill and Roosevelt at the Teheran Conference. At Cairo, Roosevelt met with China's leader, Generalissimo Chiang Kai-shek, and in a stopover in Sicily, with General Dwight D. Eisenhower, who was to command the Allied armies' invasion of Europe. When that operation began, on June 6, 1944, Roosevelt read a special D-Day prayer to the nation.

There was no doubt that Franklin Roosevelt would run again for president in 1944. Although he announced that it would be inappropriate to campaign extensively, he did make a number of trips and speeches, mostly to show that he still had the stamina to campaign and to allay fears about his health.

(Early in 1943 his physician had found that he had a weakened heart and hardening of the arteries.) Roosevelt, whose new vice-president would be Missouri senator Harry S. Truman, soundly defeated Governor Thomas E. Dewey of New York in the November election.

In February, President Roosevelt flew to the Crimea to meet with Stalin and Churchill at the Yalta Conference. There the three leaders mapped out a political structure for a postwar world. Roosevelt was satisfied that a broad and fair agreement had been reached. On March 1, 1945, he reported to Congress on the results of the talks. It was obvious to everyone that the president was a tired and ailing man. He began his speech, which was broadcast, by apologizing for sitting down. His delivery was halting, and radio listeners could not see how haggard he looked. In this speech, the last of his career, he pointed to the future and especially to the United Nations Conference that was to open in San Francisco two months later. "We propose . . . a universal organization in which all peace-loving nations will finally have a chance to join," he said. He described the results of the Yalta Conference as "the beginnings of a permanent structure of peace upon which we can begin to build, under God, that better world in which our children and grandchildren . . . must live, and can live."

At the end of March, Roosevelt went to Warm Springs. There his spirits were raised and his health seemed to be improving. Then, on April 12, 1945, he complained of a severe headache. Within moments he was dead. He had had a cerebral hemorrhage. The man who had served longer than any other president of the United States, the beloved and respected leader who had brought the American people through a devastating depression and a world war with confidence, optimism, and hope, was gone.

JOHN GABRIEL HUNT

New York
1995

FIRST GUBERNATORIAL INAUGURAL ADDRESS

Albany, New York, January 1, 1929

Governor and Mrs. Smith, Mr. Secretary of State, My Friends: This day is notable not so much for the inauguration of a new governor as that it marks the close of the term of a governor who has been our chief executive for eight years.

I am certain that no governor in the long history of the state has accomplished more than he in definite improvement of the structure of our state government, in the wise, efficient, and honorable administration of its affairs, and finally in his possession of that vibrant, understanding heart attuned to the needs and hopes of the men, the women, and the children who form the sovereignty known as "the People of the State of New York."

To Alfred E. Smith, a public servant of true greatness, I extend on behalf of our citizens our affectionate greetings, our wishes for his good health and happiness, and our prayer that God will watch over him and his in the years to come.

It is a proud thing to be a citizen of the state of New York, not because of our great population and our natural resources, nor on account of our industries, our trade, or our agricultural development, but because the citizens of this state, more than any other state in the Union, have grown to realize the interdependence on each other which modern civilization has created.

Under the leadership of the great governor whose place you have selected me to fill has come a willingness on our part to give as well as to receive, to aid, through the agency of the state, the well-being of the men and women who, by their toil, have made our material prosperity possible.

I object to having this spirit of personal civil responsibility to the state and to the individual, which has placed New York in the lead as a progressive commonwealth, described as "humanitarian." It is far more than that. It is the recognition that our civilization cannot endure unless we, as individuals, realize our personal responsibility to and dependence on the rest of the world. For it is literally true that the "self-supporting" man or woman has become as extinct as the man of the stone age. Without the help of thousands of others, any one of us would die, naked and starved. Consider the bread upon our table, the clothes upon our backs, the luxuries that make life pleasant; how many men worked in sunlit fields, in dark mines, in the fierce heat of molten metal, and among the looms and wheels of countless factories, in order to create them for our use and enjoyment.

I am proud that we of this state have grown to realize this dependence, and, what is more important, have also come to know that we, as individuals, in our turn must give our time and our intelligence to help those who have helped us. To secure more of life's pleasures for the farmer; to guard the toilers in the factories and to insure them a fair wage and protection from the dangers of their trades; to compensate them by adequate insurance for injuries received while working for us; to open the doors of knowledge to their children more widely; to aid those who are crippled and ill; to pursue with strict justice all evil persons who prey upon their fellow men; and at the same time, by intelligent and helpful sympathy, to lead wrongdoers into right paths—all of these great aims of life are more fully realized here than in any other state in the Union. We have but started on the road, and we have far to go; but during the last six years in particular, the people of this state have shown their impatience of those who seek to make such things a football of politics or by blind, unintelligent obstruction attempt to bar the road to progress.

Most gratifying of all, perhaps, is the practical way in which we have set about to take the first step toward this higher civilization, for, first of all, has been the need to set our machinery of government in order. If we are to reach these aims efficiently without needless waste of time or money we must continue the efforts to simplify and modernize. You cannot build a modern dynamo with the ancient forge and bellows of the medieval blacksmith. The modernization of our administrative procedure, not alone that of the state, but also of those other vital units of counties, of cities, of towns and of villages, must be accomplished; and while in the unit of the state we have almost reached our goal, I want to emphasize that in other units we have a long road to travel.

Each one of us must realize the necessity of our personal interest, not only toward our fellow citizens, but in the government itself. You must watch, as a public duty, what is done and what is not done at Albany. You must understand the issues that arise in the legislature, and the recommendations made by your governor, and judge for yourselves if they are right or wrong. If you find them right it is your duty as citizens on next election day to repudiate those who oppose, and to support by your vote those who strive for their accomplishment.

I want to call particularly on the public press of this state, in whose high standards I have the greatest confidence, to devote more space to the explanation and consideration of such legislation as may come up this year, for no matter how willing the individual citizen may be to support wise and progressive measures, it is only through the press—and I mean not only our great dailies but their smaller sisters in the rural districts—that our electorate can learn and understand what is going on.

There are many puzzling problems to be solved. I shall here mention but three. In the brief time that I have been speaking to you, there has run to waste on their paths toward the sea enough power from our rivers to have turned the wheels of a thousand factories, to have lit a million farmers' homes—power which nature has supplied us through the gift of God. It is intolerable that the utilization of this stupendous heritage should be longer delayed by petty squabbles and partisan dispute. Time will not solve the problem; it will be more difficult as time goes on to reach a fair conclusion. It must be solved now.

I should like to state clearly the outstanding features of the problem itself. First, it is agreed, I think, that the water power of the state should belong to all the people. There was, perhaps, some excuse for careless legislative gift of power sites in the days when it was of no seemingly great importance. There can be no such excuse now. The title to this power must vest forever in the people of this state. No commission—no, not the legislature itself—has any right to give, for any consideration whatever, a single potential kilowatt in virtual perpetuity to any person or corporation whatsoever. The legislature in this matter is but the trustee of the people, and it is its solemn duty to administer such heritage so as most greatly to benefit the whole people. On this point there can be no dispute.

It is also the duty of our legislative bodies to see that this power, which belongs to all the people, is transformed into usable electrical energy and distributed to them at the lowest possible cost. It is our power; and no inordinate profits must be allowed to those who act as the people's agents in bringing this power to their homes and workshops. If we keep these two fundamental facts before us, half of the problem disappears.

There remains the technical question as to which of several methods will bring this power to our doors with the least expense. Let me here make clear the three divisions of this technical side of the question.

First, the construction of the dams, the erection of power houses and the installation of the turbines necessary to convert the force of the falling water into electricity;

Second, the construction of many thousands of miles of transmission lines to bring the current so produced to the smaller distributing centers throughout the state; and

Third, the final distribution of this power into thousands of homes and factories.

How much of this shall be undertaken by the state, how much of this carried out by properly regulated private enterprises, how much of this by some combination of the two, is the practical question that we have before us. And in the consideration of the question I want to warn the people of this state against too hasty assumption that mere regulation by public service commissions is, in itself, a sure guarantee of protection of the interest of the consumer.

The questionable taking of jurisdiction by federal courts, the gradual erection of a body of court-made law, the astuteness of our legal brethren, the possible temporary capitulation of our public servants and even of a dormant public opinion itself, may, in the future, as in the past, nullify the rights of the public.

I, as your governor, will insist—and I trust with the support of the whole people—that there be no alienation of our possession of and title to our power sites, and that whatever method of distribution be adopted, there be no possible legal thwarting of the protection of the people themselves from excessive profits on the part of anybody.

On another matter I tread perhaps a new path. The phrase "rich man's justice" has become too common nowadays. So complicated has our whole legal machinery become through our attempt to mend antiquated substructures by constant patching of the legal procedure and the courts that justice is our most expensive commodity. That rich criminals too often escape punishment is a general belief of our people. The difficulty with which our citizens maintain their civil rights before the courts has not been made a matter of such public notice but is equally serious. It is my hope that within the next two years we shall have begun to simplify and to cheapen justice for the people.

Lastly, I want to refer to the difficult situation to which in recent years a large part of the rural population of our state has come. With few exceptions it has not shared in the prosperity of the urban centers.

It is not enough to dismiss this problem with the generality that it is the result of changing economic conditions. It is time to take practical steps to relieve our farm population of unequal tax burdens, to install economies in the methods of local government, to devise sounder marketing to stabilize what has been too much a speculative industry, and finally to encourage the use of each acre of our state for the purpose to which it is by nature most suited. I am certain that the cities will cooperate to this end, and that, more and more, we as citizens shall become state-minded.

May I, as your newly elected governor, appeal for your help, for your advice, and, when you feel it is needed, for your criticism? No man may be a successful governor without the full assistance of the people of his own commonwealth.

Were I as wise as Solomon, all that I might propose or decide would be mere wasted effort, unless I have your constant support. On many of the great state questions that confront us, the platforms and the public pledges of candidates of both parties are substantially agreed. We have passed through a struggle against old-time political ideas, against antiquated conservatism, against ignorance of modern conditions, marked by serious disagreements between the legislative and the executive branches of the government. As I read the declarations of both parties in asking the support of the people at the polls, I can see little reason for further controversies of this kind.

There is a period in our history known in all our school books as the Era of Good Feeling. It is my hope that we stand on the threshold of another such era in this state. For my part, I pledge that the business of the state will not be allowed to become involved in partisan politics and that I shall not attempt to claim unfair advantage for my party or for myself, for the accomplishing of those things on which we are all agreed.

You have honored me greatly by selecting me as your chief executive. It is my hope that I shall not fail you in this critical period of our history. I wish that you may have a continuance of good government and the happiest of New Years.

Second Gubernatorial Inaugural Address

Albany, New York, January 1, 1931

To all of you who are here today and to all the people of the state of New York I extend New Year's Greetings. May 1931 be a year of happiness, a year of greater well-being, a year in which all of us may dedicate ourselves more unselfishly and more truly to the good of our commonwealth and of our fellow men.

Twenty years ago today I first entered into public service, and on this anniversary it is not unnatural that I should think of the progress of government during that period. On January 1, 1911, the people of New York were experiencing for the first time in many decades a sustained public interest in their state government, an interest first stimulated by the fine insistence of Governor Hughes and later translated into action at several legislative sessions. At that time were laid the foundations for the continuing general attention of our citizens toward state government which has followed through all these years.

With this awakening of interest followed logically the studies of the structure and functioning of the state government itself, which culminated in the Constitutional Convention of 1915 and eventually resulted in the reorganization of the departments and the creation of the present businesslike budget system under the leadership of Governor Smith.

As a summing up of this quarter century I think that we can well say that we have made great strides in modernizing the government of the state and in vastly increasing both its honesty and its efficiency; in bringing this government into a sound and responsible relationship to the social needs and the welfare of the citizens themselves; and at the same time in avoiding the pitfalls of paternalism.

This noteworthy and continuing improvement in the theory and practice of state government has come in part from progressive leadership, but most of all from a genuine public interest backed up by the willingness of thousands of citizens to give practical and unselfish service. Therefore while properly we recognize the many tasks, the many new problems which lie ahead, still I think we can take genuine pride and satisfaction in the structure and functioning of that instrumentality of our sovereignty known as the government of the state of New York.

But this gratifying modernization and perfecting of our state government serve at the same time to accentuate by contrast our lack of progress in improving local government. Not long ago I received a letter from an eminent editor, telling me tearfully that all local government had broken down, and begging me as governor—note the unconscious willingness to accept a Tsar or absolute dictator in the governor's chair in Albany—to usurp and assume the functions of the officials duly elected by the communities themselves. He ended with the suggestion that if I did not do so, the alternative would be to call out the militia and establish martial law.

I cite this as an illustration of the present dangerous tendency to forget a fundamental of American democracy, which rests on the right of a locality to manage its local affairs—the tendency to encourage concentration of power at the top of a governmental structure alien to our system and more closely akin to a dictatorship or the central committee of a communistic regime.

Now my friend was right about one thing. Local government as a whole is open to severe criticism, and this applies to the cities, to the towns, to the counties, and to the multiplicity of other local agencies. During this century the problem of local government has been complicated by three new factors—the unparalleled growth of city populations, the birth of a new type of community known as the suburban area, and, piled on top of these, a wholly new series of human physical needs such as highways, pavements, water, sewers, lighting, bridges, tunnels, schools, which affect every inhabited area of the state. We have shifted and shuffled our population by the millions, we have made more physical changes in 25 years than in the previous 250, and we have expected the old machinery of local government without any redesigning to carry the new load. The only real wonder is that the inefficiency is not worse, and that public honesty is probably on a higher general plane among the rank and file than it was a generation ago.

But why are our local governments archaic in design, unsuited for the purpose for which they are established, unsatisfactory in their functioning, and profligate in the spending of the taxpayers' contributions? The answer is not hard to find. It is because the individual citizen is indifferent to his local government problems. The stress of business competition in this hectic twentieth century of ours, the even more feverish pursuit of pleasure to compensate for our strenuous business days—these so occupy the time and thought of our average taxpayer as to leave no inclination either to study or assist in the conduct of the community in which he lives. We do not trust our personal business affairs to strangers; we do not take our pleasures vicariously; but when it comes to running our local communities we gladly let John Doe do it. We do not even take the trouble to inquire what manner of person John Doe may be when he is nominated by a political party for a responsible local office. We do not know enough about the machinery of our local government to find out after he is elected whether he has been an efficient official or not. We know neither what his job is nor how he has performed it. We grumble at the taxes, but have not the slightest idea what could be done to lower them, because we do not know for what they are spent. We are occasionally aroused into driving out the grafter and the crook but we allow complacently a hundred times the amount of their peculations to be frittered away for needless and costly duplication of governmental functions under a system designed originally for the simple needs of our colonial forefathers. We are far more familiar with the structure of our national government at Washington and of our state government at Albany than we are with the government of our own town, village, city, or county. Our criticism is seldom valuable because we have no clear idea of what is wrong and not the faintest real conception of any practical remedy.

It would be appalling to compute the millions of dollars which our local taxpayers needlessly pay as the price of their indifference. Our state government has been reformed because of the ability of great leaders to awaken public interest in the affairs of state. Our local communities, alas, only in rare instances, have aroused themselves to an interest in local government extending down to the average citizen.

Too often reform associations, preachers, editors, committees of eminent citizens have, with the best intentions, come forward for a few months only to right an emergency evil, or else they have represented one angle only in a many-sided problem, or else they have had an ulterior motive of mere partisanship. It is impossible to get better government locally if only 5 percent of the electorate participate in civic affairs two months of the year while the other 95 percent remain uninterested all twelve months of the year.

Let us get this picture clearly before us. We have three main divisions of government: first, the federal, operating, at least in theory, in the national field and in accordance with strictly limited powers of control ceded to it by the sovereign states; second, the state, moving only in the statewide field and careful not to confuse state with local functions; third, the several divisions of local government, authorized to be sure by the state, but based on the centuries-old conception of the town meeting.

When states become indifferent to their duties, the natural tendency is for the national government to grasp for more power. In like manner if community government becomes slipshod and lax, the way of opportunism is to carry the problem to Albany and get the local legislators to introduce a bill.

Some of us for many years have striven against the multiplicity of local laws passed each year by complacent legislatures. During the past two years I have the record of having vetoed more bills of this character than any previous governor. Back of the immediate reason in the individual case has been the fundamental thought that the elimination of piecemeal legislation might to some degree make people think along broader lines and come back another year with a well-thought-out comprehensive plan to cover the subject as a whole. This is, of course, in direct line with what is commonly called the home rule principle. The principle is right. We have started to apply it. But at the same time its success must depend on local interest on the part of the 95 percent of the citizens as well as of the 5 percent if we are not to slip back into the system of a generation ago when even the number of dog catchers in a community was made the subject of state legislation.

How often do people stop to realize the relative influence which the three great branches of government play in their daily lives? What daily contact has the average man or woman with the activities, the machinery, or the administration of the government in Washington? What personal touch has the average man or woman with the government in Albany except when traveling over a state highway or visiting a state park? If you own a piece of real estate, whether it be a business property or a home or a farm, do you ever stop to realize that when you pay the taxes on it not one cent goes to Albany or to Washington?

Much has been said of the mounting burden of taxation; yet lack of thought leads most of us to forget that by far the greater part of the increase has been caused during this generation by mounting local expenditures. And this is further emphasized by the fact that over half of all the tax money collected by the state of New York is spent not by the state, but is returned by the state to the counties and communities for local expenditure.

It is my ardent hope that in the twenty years to come the people of New York will be able to accomplish as much for the cause of improved local government along American lines as we have accomplished for our state government in the past twenty years. This can come only through leadership and through a greater dedication on the part of the individual, giving more generously of his time and thought and personal service.

First, we need to plan, to go to the root of the problem in order that specific remedies may be offered. When this is done I am very certain that the legislature and the administration of this state will lend their aid and sympathy to the granting of the necessary authority.

I have spent two happy years in Albany and today I look forward to 1931 and 1932 as giving me, because of the experience which I have had, a greater opportunity for usefulness to the people of the state. The older I grow the more insistent I am that the average of the citizenship of the state will respond to the presentation of problems of government if the fundamentals of the issues are presented to them clearly and honorably. I am convinced, too, that the electorate has a sense of proportion and, given the facts, will of its own accord recognize them in the order of their importance.

That is why on this New Year's Day I have taken occasion to speak somewhat at length on government. One part at least of our government we can be proud of—the state is functioning well. Another part, the one which enters more closely than any other into our daily affairs, needs our attention, our interest, and our earnest efforts to improve.

The vitality of our American institutions has been amply proven in the past. We have met difficulties before this and have solved them in accordance with the basic theories of a representative democracy. Let us not at this time pursue the easy road of centralization of authority lest someday we discover too late that our liberties have disappeared. Let us pause in our pursuit of materialism and pleasure and devote greater efforts to retain these liberties within the communities in which we dwell.

That is the New Year's message from the governor of your state who pledges himself anew to devote the best that is in him to the wholehearted service of the men and women and children of the state of New York.

Radio Address on the National Economic Emergency

April 7, 1932

The Forgotten Man

Although I understand that I am talking under the auspices of the Democratic National Committee, I do not want to limit myself to politics. I do not want to feel that I am addressing an audience of Democrats or that I speak merely as a Democrat myself. The present condition of our national affairs is too serious to be viewed through partisan eyes for partisan purposes.

Fifteen years ago my public duty called me to an active part in a great national emergency, the World War. Success then was due to a leadership whose vision carried beyond the timorous and futile gesture of sending a tiny army of 150,000 trained soldiers and the regular navy to the aid of our allies. The generalship of that moment conceived of a whole nation mobilized for war: economic, industrial, social, and military resources gathered into a vast unit capable of and actually in the process of throwing into the scales 10 million men equipped with physical needs and sustained by the realization that behind them were the united efforts of 110 million human beings. It was a great plan because it was built from bottom to top and not from top to bottom.

In my calm judgment, the nation faces today a more grave emergency than in 1917.

It is said that Napoleon lost the battle of Waterloo because he forgot his infantry—he staked too much upon the more spectacular but less substantial cavalry. The present administration in Washington provides a close parallel. It has either forgotten or it does not want to remember the infantry of our economic army.

These unhappy times call for the building of plans that rest upon the forgotten, the unorganized but the indispensable units of economic power, for plans like those of 1917 that build from the bottom up and not from the top down, that put their faith once more in the forgotten man at the bottom of the economic pyramid.

Obviously, these few minutes tonight permit no opportunity to lay down the ten or a dozen closely related objectives of a plan to meet our present emergency, but I can draw a few essentials, a beginning in fact, of a planned program.

It is the habit of the unthinking to turn in times like this to the illusions of economic magic. People suggest that a huge expenditure of public funds by the federal government and by state and local governments will completely solve the unemployment problem. But it is clear that even if we could raise many billions of dollars and find definitely useful public works to spend these billions on, even all that money would not give employment to the seven million or ten million people who are out of work. Let us admit frankly that it would be only a stopgap. A real economic cure must go to the killing of the bacteria in the system rather than to the treatment of external symptoms.

How much do the shallow thinkers realize, for example, that approximately one-half of our whole population, fifty or sixty million people, earn their living by farming or in small towns whose existence immediately depends on farms. They have today lost their purchasing power. Why? They are receiving for farm products less than the cost to them of growing these farm products. The result of this loss of purchasing power is that many other millions of people engaged in industry in the cities cannot sell industrial products to the farming half of the nation. This brings home to every city worker that his own employment is directly tied up with the farmer's dollar. No nation can long endure half bankrupt. Main Street, Broadway, the mills, the mines will close if half the buyers are broke.

I cannot escape the conclusion that one of the essential parts of a national program of restoration must be to restore purchasing power to the farming half of the country. Without this the wheels of railroads and of factories will not turn.

Closely associated with this first objective is the problem of keeping the home-owner and the farm-owner where he is, without being dispossessed through the foreclosure of his mortgage. His relationship to the great banks of Chicago and New York is pretty remote. The $2 billion fund which President Hoover and the Congress have put at the disposal of the big banks, the railroads, and the corporations of the nation is not for him.

His is a relationship to his little local bank or local loan company. It is a sad fact that even though the local lender in many cases does not want to evict the farmer or home-owner by foreclosure proceedings, he is forced to do so in order to keep his bank or company solvent. Here should be an objective of government itself, to provide at least as much assistance to the little fellow as it is now giving to the large banks and corporations. That is another example of building from the bottom up.

One other objective closely related to the problem of selling American products is to provide a tariff policy based upon economic common sense rather than upon politics, hot air, and pull. This country during the past few years, culminating with the Hawley-Smoot Tariff in 1929, has compelled the world to build tariff fences so high that world trade is decreasing to the vanishing point. The value of goods internationally exchanged is today less than half of what it was three or four years ago.

Every man and woman who gives any thought to the subject knows that if our factories run even 80 percent of capacity, they will turn out more products than we as a nation can possibly use ourselves. The answer is that if they run on 80 percent of capacity, we must sell some goods abroad. How can we do that if the outside nations cannot pay us in cash? And we know by sad experience that they cannot do that. The only way they can pay us is in their own goods or raw materials, but this foolish tariff of ours makes that impossible.

What we must do is this: revise our tariff on the basis of a reciprocal exchange of goods, allowing other nations to buy and to pay for our goods by sending us such of their goods as will not seriously throw any of our industries out of balance, and incidentally making impossible in this country the continuance of pure monopolies which cause us to pay excessive prices for many of the necessities of life.

Such objectives as these three—restoring farmers' buying power, relief to the small banks and home-owners, and a reconstructed tariff policy—are only a part of ten or a dozen vital factors. But they seem to be beyond the concern of a national administration which can think in terms only of the top of the social and economic structure. It has sought temporary relief from the top down rather than permanent relief from the bottom up. It has totally failed to plan ahead in a comprehensive way. It has waited until something has cracked and then at the last moment has sought to prevent total collapse.

It is high time to get back to fundamentals. It is high time to admit with courage that we are in the midst of an emergency at least equal to that of war. Let us mobilize to meet it.

Speech Before the 1932 Democratic National Convention

Chicago, Illinois, July 2, 1932

A New Deal

Chairman Walsh, My Friends of the Democratic National Convention of 1932: I appreciate your willingness after these six arduous days to remain here, for I know well the sleepless hours which you and I have had. I regret that I am late, but I have no control over the winds of heaven and could only be thankful for my navy training.

The appearance before a national convention of its nominee for president, to be formally notified of his selection, is unprecedented and unusual, but these are unprecedented and unusual times. I have started out on the tasks that lie ahead by breaking the absurd traditions that the candidate should remain in professed ignorance of what has happened for weeks until he is formally notified of that event many weeks later.

My friends, may this be the symbol of my intention to be honest and to avoid all hypocrisy or sham, to avoid all silly shutting of the eyes to the truth in this campaign. You have nominated me and I know it, and I am here to thank you for the honor.

Let it also be symbolic that in so doing I broke traditions. Let it be from now on the task of our party to break foolish traditions. We will break foolish traditions and leave it to the Republican leadership, far more skilled in that art, to break promises.

Let us now and here highly resolve to resume the country's

interrupted march along the path of real progress, of real justice, of real equality for all of our citizens, great and small. Our indomitable leader in that interrupted march is no longer with us, but there still survives today his spirit. Many of his captains, thank God, are still with us, to give us wise counsel. Let us feel that in everything we do there still lives with us, if not the body, the great indomitable, unquenchable, progressive soul of our commander in chief, Woodrow Wilson.

I have many things on which I want to make my position clear at the earliest possible moment in this campaign. That admirable document, the platform which you have adopted, is clear. I accept it 100 percent.

And you can accept my pledge that I will leave no doubt or ambiguity on where I stand on any question of moment in this campaign.

As we enter this new battle, let us keep always present with us some of the ideals of the party: the fact that the Democratic party by tradition and by the continuing logic of history, past and present, is the bearer of liberalism and of progress and at the same time of safety to our institutions. And if this appeal fails, remember well, my friends, that a resentment against the failure of Republican leadership—and note well that in this campaign I shall not use the words *Republican party,* but I shall use, day in and day out, the words *Republican leadership*—the failure of Republican leaders to solve our troubles may degenerate into unreasoning radicalism.

The great social phenomenon of this depression, unlike others before it, is that it has produced but a few of the disorderly manifestations that too often attend upon such times.

Wild radicalism has made few converts, and the greatest tribute that I can pay to my countrymen is that in these days of crushing want there persists an orderly and hopeful spirit on the part of the millions of our people who have suffered so much. To fail to offer them a new chance is not only to betray their hopes but to misunderstand their patience.

To meet by reaction that danger of radicalism is to invite

disaster. Reaction is no barrier to the radical. It is a challenge, a provocation. The way to meet that danger is to offer a workable program of reconstruction, and the party to offer it is the party with clean hands.

This, and this only, is a proper protection against blind reaction on the one hand and an improvised, hit-or-miss, irresponsible opportunism on the other.

There are two ways of viewing the government's duty in matters affecting economic and social life. The first sees to it that a favored few are helped and hopes that some of their prosperity will leak through, sift through, to labor, to the farmer, to the small-businessman. That theory belongs to the party of Toryism, and I had hoped that most of the Tories left this country in 1776.

But it is not and never will be the theory of the Democratic party. This is no time for fear, for reaction or for timidity. Here and now I invite those nominal Republicans who find that their conscience cannot be squared with the groping and the failure of their party leaders to join hands with us; here and now, in equal measure, I warn those nominal Democrats who squint at the future with their faces turned toward the past, and who feel no responsibility to the demands of the new time, that they are out of step with their party.

Yes, the people of this country want a genuine choice this year, not a choice between two names for the same reactionary doctrine. Ours must be a party of liberal thought, of planned action, of enlightened international outlook, and of the greatest good to the greatest number of our citizens.

Now it is inevitable—and the choice is that of the times— it is inevitable that the main issue of this campaign should revolve about the clear fact of our economic condition, a depression so deep that it is without precedent in modern history. It will not do merely to state, as do Republican leaders to explain their broken promises of continued inaction, that the depression is worldwide. That was not their explanation of the apparent prosperity of 1928. The people will not forget the claim made by them then that prosperity was only a domestic product manufactured by a Republican president and a Republican Congress. If they claim paternity for the one they cannot deny paternity for the other.

I cannot take up all the problems today. I want to touch on a few that are vital. Let us look a little at the recent history and the simple economics, the kind of economics that you and I and the average man and woman talk.

In the years before 1929 we know that this country had completed a vast cycle of building and inflation; for ten years we expanded on the theory of repairing the wastes of the war, but actually expanding far beyond that, and also beyond our natural and normal growth. Now it is worth remembering, and the cold figures of finance prove it, that during that time there was little or no drop in the prices that the consumer had to pay, although those same figures proved that the cost of production fell very greatly; corporate profit resulting from this period was enormous; at the same time little of that profit was devoted to the reduction of prices. The consumer was forgotten. Very little of it went into increased wages; the worker was forgotten, and by no means an adequate proportion was even paid out in dividends—the stockholder was forgotten.

And, incidentally, very little of it was taken by taxation to the beneficent government of those years.

What was the result? Enormous corporate surpluses piled up—the most stupendous in history. Where, under the spell of delirious speculation, did those surpluses go? Let us talk economics that the figures prove and that we can understand. Why, they went chiefly in two directions: first, into new and unnecessary plants which now stand stark and idle; and second, into the call-money market of Wall Street, either directly by the corporations, or indirectly through the banks. Those are the facts. Why blink at them?

Then came the crash. You know the story. Surpluses invested in unnecessary plants became idle. Men lost their jobs; purchasing power dried up; banks became frightened and started calling loans. Those who had money were afraid to part with it. Credit contracted. Industry stopped. Commerce declined, and unemployment mounted.

And there we are today.

Translate that into human terms. See how the events of the past three years have come home to specific groups of people: first, the group dependent on industry; second, the group dependent on agriculture; third, and made up in large part of members of the first two groups, the people who are called "small investors and depositors." In fact, the strongest possible tie between the first two groups, agriculture and industry, is the fact that the savings and to a degree the security of both are tied together in that third group—the credit structure of the nation.

Never in history have the interests of all the people been so united in a single economic problem. Picture to yourself, for instance, the great groups of property owned by millions of our citizens, represented by credits issued in the form of bonds and mortgages—government bonds of all kinds, federal, state, county, municipal; bonds of industrial companies, of utility companies; mortgages on real estate in farms and cities, and finally the vast investments of the nation in the railroads. What is the measure of the security of each of those groups? We know well that in our complicated, interrelated credit structure if any one of these credit groups collapses they may all collapse. Danger to one is danger to all.

How, I ask, has the present administration in Washington treated the interrelationship of these credit groups? The answer is clear: it has not recognized that interrelationship existed at all. Why, the nation asks, has Washington failed to understand that all of these groups, each and every one, the top of the pyramid and the bottom of the pyramid, must be considered together, that each and every one of them is dependent on every other; each and every one of them affecting the whole financial fabric?

Statesmanship and vision, my friends, require relief to all at the same time.

Just one word or two on taxes, the taxes that all of us pay toward the cost of government of all kinds.

I know something of taxes. For three long years I have been going up and down this country preaching that government—federal and state and local—costs too much. I shall not stop that preaching. As an immediate program of action we must abolish useless offices. We must eliminate unnecessary functions of government—functions, in fact, that are not definitely essential to the continuance of government. We must merge, we must consolidate subdivisions of government, and, like the private citizen, give up luxuries which we can no longer afford.

By our example at Washington itself, we shall have the opportunity of pointing the way of economy to local government, for let us remember well that out of every tax dollar in the average state in this nation, forty cents enter the Treasury in Washington, D.C., ten or twelve cents only go to the state capitals, and forty-eight cents are consumed by the costs of local government in counties and cities and towns.

I propose to you, my friends, and through you, that government of all kinds, big and little, be made solvent and that the example be set by the president of the United States and his Cabinet.

And talking about setting a definite example, I congratulate this convention for having had the courage fearlessly to write into its declaration of principles what an overwhelming majority here assembled really thinks about the Eighteenth Amendment. This convention wants repeal. Your candidate wants repeal. And I am confident that the United States of America wants repeal.

Two years ago the platform on which I ran for governor the second time contained substantially the same provision. The overwhelming sentiment of the people of my state, as shown by the vote of that year, extends, I know, to the people of many of the other states. I say to you now that from this date on the Eighteenth Amendment is doomed. When that happens, we as Democrats must and will, rightly and morally, enable the states to protect themselves against the importation of intoxicating liquor where such importation may violate their state laws. We must rightly and morally prevent the return of the saloon.

To go back to this dry subject of finance, because it all ties in together—the Eighteenth Amendment has something to do with finance, too—in a comprehensive planning for the reconstruction of the great credit groups, including government credit, I list an important place for that prize statement of principle in the platform here adopted calling for the letting in of the light of day on issues of securities, foreign and domestic, which are offered for sale to the investing public.

My friends, you and I as common-sense citizens know that it would help to protect the savings of the country from the dishonesty of crooks and from the lack of honor of some men in high financial places. Publicity is the enemy of crookedness.

And now one word about unemployment, and incidentally about agriculture. I have favored the use of certain types of public works as a further emergency means of stimulating employment and the issuance of bonds to pay for such public works, but I have pointed out that no economic end is served if we merely build without building for a necessary purpose. Such works, of course, should insofar as possible be self-sustaining if they are to be financed by the issuing of bonds. So as to spread the points of all kinds as widely as possible, we must take definite steps to shorten the working day and the working week.

Let us use common sense and business sense. Just as one example, we know that a very hopeful and immediate means of relief, both for the unemployed and for agriculture, will come from a wide plan of the converting of many millions of acres of marginal and unused land into timberland through reforestation. There are tens of millions of acres east of the Mississippi River alone in abandoned farms, in cut-over land, now growing up in worthless brush. Why, every European nation has a definite land policy, and has had one for generations. We have none. Having none, we face a future of soil erosion and timber famine. It is clear that economic foresight and immediate employment march hand in hand in the call for the reforestation of these vast areas.

In so doing, employment can be given to a million men. That is the kind of public work that is self-sustaining, and therefore capable of being financed by the issuance of bonds which are made secure by the fact that the growth of tremendous crops will provide adequate security for the investment.

Yes, I have a very definite program for providing employment by that means. I have done it, and I am doing it today in the state of New York. I know that the Democratic party can do it successfully in the nation. That will put men to work, and that is an example of the action that we are going to have.

Now as a further aid to agriculture, we know perfectly well —but have we come out and said so clearly and distinctly?— we should repeal immediately those provisions of law that compel the federal government to go into the market to purchase, to sell, to speculate in farm products in a futile attempt to reduce farm surpluses. And they are the people who are talking of keeping government out of business. The practical way to help the farmer is by an arrangement that will, in addition to lightening some of the impoverishing burdens from his back, do something toward the reduction of the surpluses of staple commodities that hang on the market. It should be our aim to add to the world prices of staple products the amount of a reasonable tariff protection, to give agriculture the same protection that industry has today.

And in exchange for this immediately increased return I am sure that the farmers of this nation would agree ultimately to such planning of their production as would reduce the surpluses and make it unnecessary in later years to depend on dumping those surpluses abroad in order to support domestic prices. That result has been accomplished in other nations; why not in America, too?

Farm leaders and farm economists, generally, agree that a plan based on that principle is a desirable first step in the reconstruction of agriculture. It does not in itself furnish a complete program, but it will serve in great measure in the long run to remove the pall of a surplus without the continued perpetual threat of world dumping. Final voluntary reduction of surplus is a part of our objective, but the long continuance and the present burden of existing surpluses make it necessary to repair great damage of the present by immediate emergency measures.

Such a plan as that, my friends, does not cost the government any money, nor does it keep the government in business or in speculation.

As to the actual wording of a bill, I believe that the Democratic party stands ready to be guided by whatever the responsible farm groups themselves agree on. That is a principle that is sound; and again I ask for action.

One more word about the farmer, and I know that every delegate in this hall who lives in the city knows why I lay emphasis on the farmer. It is because one-half of our population, over fifty million people, are dependent on agriculture; and, my friends, if those fifty million people have no money, no cash, to buy what is produced in the city, the city suffers to an equal or greater extent.

That is why we are going to make the voters understand this year that this nation is not merely a nation of independence, but it is, if we are to survive, bound to be a nation of interdependence—town and city, and North and South, East and West. That is our goal, and that goal will be understood by the people of this country no matter where they live.

Yes, the purchasing power of that half of our population dependent on agriculture is gone. Farm mortgages reach nearly ten billions of dollars today and interest charges on that alone are $560 million a year. But that is not all. The tax burden caused by extravagant and inefficient local government is an additional factor. Our most immediate concern should be to reduce the interest burden on these mortgages.

Rediscounting of farm mortgages under salutary restrictions must be expanded and should, in the future, be conditioned on the reduction of interest rates. Amortization payments, maturities should likewise in this crisis be extended before rediscount is permitted where the mortgagor is sorely pressed. That, my friends, is another example of practical, immediate relief: action.

I aim to do the same thing, and it can be done, for the small home-owner in our cities and villages. We can lighten his burden and develop his purchasing power. Take away, my friends, that specter of too high an interest rate. Take away that specter of the due date just a short time away. Save homes; save homes for thousands of self-respecting families, and drive out that specter of insecurity from our midst.

Out of all the tons of printed paper, out of all the hours of oratory, the recriminations, the defenses, the happy-thought plans in Washington and in every state, there emerges one great, simple, crystal-pure fact that during the past ten years a nation of 120 million people has been led by the Republican leaders to erect an impregnable barbed wire entanglement around its borders through the instrumentality of tariffs which have isolated us from all the other human beings in all the rest of the round world. I accept that admirable tariff statement in the platform of this convention. It would protect American business and American labor. By our acts of the past we have invited and received the retaliation of other nations. I propose an invitation to them to forget the past, to sit at the table with us, as friends, and to plan with us for the restoration of the trade of the world.

Go into the home of the businessman. He knows what the tariff has done for him. Go into the home of the factory worker. He knows why goods do not move. Go into the home of the farmer. He knows how the tariff has helped to ruin him.

At last our eyes are open. At last the American people are ready to acknowledge that Republican leadership was wrong and that the democracy is right.

My program, of which I can only touch on these points, is based upon this simple moral principle: the welfare and the soundness of a nation depend first upon what the great mass of the people wish and need; and second, whether or not they are getting it.

What do the people of America want more than anything else? To my mind, they want two things: work, with all the moral and spiritual values that go with it; and with work, a reasonable measure of security—security for themselves and for their wives and children. Work and security—these are more than words. They are more than facts. They are the spiritual values, the true goal toward which our efforts of reconstruction should lead. These are the values that this program is intended to gain; these are the values we have failed to achieve by the leadership we now have.

Our Republican leaders tell us economic laws—sacred, inviolable, unchangeable—cause panics which no one could prevent. But while they prate of economic laws, men and women are starving. We must lay hold of the fact that economic laws are not made by nature. They are made by human beings.

Yes, when—not if—when we get the chance, the federal government will assume bold leadership in distress relief. For years Washington has alternated between putting its head in the sand and saying there is no large number of destitute people in our midst who need food and clothing, and then saying the states should take care of them, if there are. Instead of planning two and a half years ago to do what they are now trying to do, they kept putting it off from day to day, week to week, and month to month, until the conscience of America demanded action.

I say that while primary responsibility for relief rests with localities now, as ever, yet the federal government has always had and still has a continuing responsibility for the broader public welfare. It will soon fulfill that responsibility.

And now, just a few words about our plans for the next four months. By coming here instead of waiting for a formal notification, I have made it clear that I believe we should eliminate expensive ceremonies and that we should set in motion at once, tonight, my friends, the necessary machinery for an adequate presentation of the issues to the electorate of the nation.

I myself have important duties as governor of a great state, duties which in these times are more arduous and more grave than at any previous period. Yet I feel confident that I shall be able to make a number of short visits to several parts of the nation. My trips will have as their first objective the study at first hand, from the lips of men and women of all parties and all occupations, of the actual conditions and needs of every part of an interdependent country.

One word more: out of every crisis, every tribulation, every disaster, mankind rises with some share of greater knowledge, of higher decency, of purer purpose. Today we shall have come through a period of loose thinking, descending morals, an era of selfishness, among individual men and women and among nations. Blame not governments alone for this. Blame ourselves in equal share. Let us be frank in acknowledgment of the truth that many amongst us have made obeisance to Mammon, that the profits of speculation, the easy road without toil, have lured us from the old barricades. To return to higher standards we must abandon the false prophets and seek new leaders of our own choosing.

Never before in modern history have the essential differences between the two major American parties stood out in such striking contrast as they do today. Republican leaders not only have failed in material things, they have failed in national vision, because in disaster they have held out no hope, they have pointed out no path for the people below to climb back to places of security and of safety in our American life.

Throughout the nation, men and women, forgotten in the political philosophy of the government of the last years, look to us here for guidance and for more equitable opportunity to share in the distribution of national wealth.

On the farms, in the large metropolitan areas, in the smaller cities and in the villages, millions of our citizens cherish the hope that their old standards of living and of thought have not gone forever. Those millions cannot and shall not hope in vain.

I pledge you, I pledge myself, to a New Deal for the American people. Let us all here assembled constitute ourselves prophets of a new order of competence and of courage. This is more than a political campaign; it is a call to arms. Give me your help, not to win votes alone, but to win in this crusade to restore America to its own people.

First Inaugural Address

March 4, 1933

The Only Thing We Have to Fear Is Fear Itself

I am certain that my fellow Americans expect that on my induction into the presidency I will address them with a candor and a decision which the present situation of our nation impels. This is preeminently the time to speak the truth, the whole truth, frankly and boldly. Nor need we shrink from honestly facing conditions in our country today. This great nation will endure as it has endured, will revive and will prosper. So, first of all, let me assert my firm belief that the only thing we have to fear is fear itself—nameless, unreasoning, unjustified terror which paralyzes needed efforts to convert retreat into advance. In every dark hour of our national life a leadership of frankness and vigor has met with that understanding and support of the people themselves which is essential to victory. I am convinced that you will again give that support to leadership in these critical days.

In such a spirit on my part and on yours we face our common difficulties. They concern, thank God, only material things. Values have shrunken to fantastic levels; taxes have risen; our ability to pay has fallen; government of all kinds is faced by serious curtailment of income; the means of exchange are frozen in the currents of trade; the withered leaves of industrial enterprise lie on every side; farmers find no markets for their produce; the savings of many years in thousands of families are gone.

More important, a host of unemployed citizens face the grim problem of existence, and an equally great number toil with little return. Only a foolish optimist can deny the dark realities of the moment.

Yet our distress comes from no failure of substance. We are stricken by no plague of locusts. Compared with the perils which our forefathers conquered because they believed and were not afraid, we have still much to be thankful for. Nature still offers her bounty and human efforts have multiplied it. Plenty is at our doorstep, but a generous use of it languishes in the very sight of the supply. Primarily this is because rulers of the exchange of mankind's goods have failed through their own stubbornness and their own incompetence, have admitted their failure, and have abdicated. Practices of the unscrupulous money changers stand indicted in the court of public opinion, rejected by the hearts and minds of men.

True, they have tried, but their efforts have been cast in the pattern of an outworn tradition. Faced by failure of credit they have proposed only the lending of more money. Stripped of the lure of profit by which to induce our people to follow their false leadership, they have resorted to exhortations, pleading tearfully for restored confidence. They know only the rules of a generation of self-seekers. They have no vision, and when there is no vision the people perish.

The money changers have fled from their high seats in the temple of our civilization. We may now restore that temple to the ancient truths. The measure of the restoration lies in the extent to which we apply social values more noble than mere monetary profit.

Happiness lies not in the mere possession of money; it lies in the joy of achievement, in the thrill of creative effort. The joy and moral stimulation of work no longer must be forgotten in the mad chase of evanescent profits. These dark days will be worth all they cost us if they teach us that our true destiny is not to be ministered unto but to minister to ourselves and to our fellow men.

Recognition of the falsity of material wealth as the standard of success goes hand in hand with the abandonment of the false belief that public office and high political position are to be valued only by the standards of pride of place and personal profit; and there must be an end to a conduct in banking and in business which too often has given to a sacred trust the likeness of callous and selfish wrongdoing. Small wonder that confidence languishes, for it thrives only on honesty, on honor, on the sacredness of obligations, on faithful protection, on unselfish performance; without them it cannot live.

Restoration calls, however, not for changes in ethics alone. This nation asks for action, and action now.

Our greatest primary task is to put people to work. This is no unsolvable problem if we face it wisely and courageously. It can be accomplished in part by direct recruiting by the government itself, treating the task as we would treat the emergency of a war, but at the same time, through this employment, accomplishing greatly needed projects to stimulate and reorganize the use of our natural resources.

Hand in hand with this we must frankly recognize the over-balance of population in our industrial centers and, by engaging on a national scale in a redistribution, endeavor to provide a better use of the land for those best fitted for the land. The task can be helped by definite efforts to raise the values of agricultural products and with this the power to purchase the output of our cities. It can be helped by preventing realistically the tragedy of the growing loss through foreclosure of our small homes and our farms. It can be helped by insistence that the federal, state, and local governments act forthwith on the demand that their cost be drastically reduced. It can be helped by the unifying of relief activities which today are often scattered, uneconomical, and unequal. It can be helped by national planning for and supervision of all forms of transportation and of communications and other utilities which have a definitely public character. There are many ways in which it can be helped, but it can never be helped merely by talking about it. We must act and act quickly.

Finally, in our progress toward a resumption of work we require two safeguards against a return of the evils of the old order: there must be a strict supervision of all banking and

credits and investments, so that there will be an end to speculation with other people's money; and there must be provision for
an adequate but sound currency.

These are the lines of attack. I shall presently urge upon a
new Congress, in special session, detailed measures for their
fulfillment, and I shall seek the immediate assistance of the
several states.

Through this program of action we address ourselves to
putting our own national house in order and making income
balance outgo. Our international trade relations, though vastly
important, are in point of time and necessity secondary to the
establishment of a sound national economy. I favor as a practical policy the putting of first things first. I shall spare no effort
to restore world trade by international economic readjustment,
but the emergency at home cannot wait on that accomplishment.

The basic thought that guides these specific means of national recovery is not narrowly nationalistic. It is the insistence,
as a first consideration, upon the interdependence of the various
elements in and parts of the United States—a recognition of the
old and permanently important manifestation of the American
spirit of the pioneer. It is the way to recovery. It is the immediate
way. It is the strongest assurance that the recovery will endure.

In the field of world policy I would dedicate this nation to
the policy of the Good Neighbor—the neighbor who resolutely
respects himself and, because he does so, respects the rights of
others—the neighbor who respects his obligations and respects
the sanctity of his agreements in and with a world of neighbors.

If I read the temper of our people correctly, we now realize
as we have never realized before our interdependence on each
other; that we cannot merely take but we must give as well; that
if we are to go forward, we must move as a trained and loyal
army willing to sacrifice for the good of a common discipline,
because without such discipline no progress is made, no leadership becomes effective. We are, I know, ready and willing to
submit our lives and property to such discipline, because it

makes possible a leadership which aims at a larger good. This I propose to offer, pledging that the larger purposes will bind upon us all as a sacred obligation with a unity of duty hitherto evoked only in time of armed strife.

With this pledge taken, I assume unhesitatingly the leadership of this great army of our people dedicated to a disciplined attack upon our common problems.

Action in this image and to this end is feasible under the form of government which we have inherited from our ancestors. Our Constitution is so simple and practical that it is possible always to meet extraordinary needs by changes in emphasis and arrangement without loss of essential form. That is why our constitutional system has proved itself the most superbly enduring political mechanism the modern world has produced. It has met every stress of vast expansion of territory, of foreign wars, of bitter internal strife, of world relations.

It is to be hoped that the normal balance of executive and legislative authority may be wholly adequate to meet the unprecedented task before us. But it may be that an unprecedented demand and need for undelayed action may call for temporary departure from that normal balance of public procedure.

I am prepared under my constitutional duty to recommend the measures that a stricken nation in the midst of a stricken world may require. These measures, or such other measures as the Congress may build out of its experience and wisdom, I shall seek, within my constitutional authority, to bring to speedy adoption.

But in the event that the Congress shall fail to take one of these two courses, and in the event that the national emergency is still critical, I shall not evade the clear course of duty that will then confront me. I shall ask the Congress for the one remaining instrument to meet the crisis—broad executive power to wage a war against the emergency, as great as the power that would be given to me if we were in fact invaded by a foreign foe.

For the trust reposed in me I will return the courage and the devotion that befit the time. I can do no less.

We face the arduous days that lie before us in the warm courage of national unity; with the clear consciousness of seeking old and precious moral values; with the clean satisfaction that comes from the stern performance of duty by old and young alike. We aim at the assurance of a rounded and permanent national life.

We do not distrust the future of essential democracy. The people of the United States have not failed. In their need they have registered a mandate that they want direct, vigorous action. They have asked for discipline and direction under leadership. They have made me the present instrument of their wishes. In the spirit of the gift I take it.

In this dedication of a nation we humbly ask the blessing of God. May He protect each and every one of us. May He guide me in the days to come.

PROCLAMATION OF A BANK HOLIDAY

March 6, 1933

Whereas there have been heavy and unwarranted withdrawals of gold and currency from our banking institutions for the purpose of hoarding; and

Whereas continuous and increasingly extensive speculative activity abroad in foreign exchange has resulted in severe drains on the nation's stocks of gold; and

Whereas those conditions have created a national emergency; and

Whereas it is in the best interests of all bank depositors that a period of respite be provided with a view to preventing further hoarding of coin, bullion, or currency or speculation in foreign exchange and permitting the application of appropriate measures to protect the interests of our people; and

Whereas it is provided in Section 5(b) of the act of October 6, 1917 (40 Stat. L. 411), as amended, "That the president may investigate, regulate, or prohibit, under such rules and regulations as he may prescribe, by means of licenses or otherwise, any transactions in foreign exchange and the export, hoarding, melting, or earmarkings of gold or silver coin or bullion or currency . . ."; and

Whereas it is provided in Section 16 of the said act, "That whoever shall willfully violate any of the provisions of this act or of any license, rule, or regulation issued thereunder, and whoever shall willfully violate, neglect, or refuse to comply with any order of the president issued in compliance with the provisions of this act, shall, upon conviction, be fined not more than ten thousand dollars, or, if a natural person, imprisoned for not more than ten years, or both . . .";

Now, therefore, I, Franklin D. Roosevelt, President of the United States of America, in view of such national emergency and by virtue of the authority vested in me by said act and in order to prevent the export, hoarding, or earmarking of gold or silver coin or bullion or currency, do hereby proclaim, order, direct, and declare that from Monday, the sixth day of March, to Thursday, the ninth day of March, nineteen hundred and thirty-three, both dates inclusive, there shall be maintained and observed by all banking institutions and all branches thereof located in the United States of America, including the territories and insular possessions, a bank holiday, and that during said period all banking transactions shall be suspended. During such holiday, excepting as hereinafter provided, no such banking institution or branch shall pay out, export, earmark, or permit the withdrawal or transfer in any manner or by any device whatsoever, of any gold or silver coin or bullion or currency or take any other action which might facilitate the hoarding thereof; nor shall any such banking institution or branch pay out deposits, make loans or discounts, deal in foreign exchange, transfer credits from the United States to any place abroad, or transact any other banking business whatsoever.

During such holiday, the secretary of the Treasury, with the approval of the president and under such regulations as he may prescribe, is authorized and empowered: (a) to permit any or all of such banking institutions to perform any or all of the usual banking functions; (b) to direct, require or permit the issuance of clearinghouse certificates or other evidences of claims against assets of banking institutions; and (c) to authorize and direct the creation in such banking institutions of special trust accounts for the receipt of new deposits which shall be subject to withdrawal on demand without any restriction or limitation and shall be kept separately in cash or on deposit in Federal Reserve Banks or invested in obligations of the United States.

As used in this order the term *banking institutions* shall

include all Federal Reserve Banks, national banking associations, banks, trust companies, savings banks, building and loan associations, credit unions, or other corporations, partnerships, associations, or persons engaged in the business of receiving deposits, making loans, discounting business paper, or transacting any other form of banking business.

FIRESIDE CHAT ON
THE BANKING CRISIS

March 12, 1933

I want to talk for a few minutes with the people of the United States about banking—with the comparatively few who understand the mechanics of banking but more particularly with the overwhelming majority who use banks for the making of deposits and the drawing of checks. I want to tell you what has been done in the last few days, why it was done, and what the next steps are going to be. I recognize that the many proclamations from state capitols and from Washington, the legislation, the Treasury regulations, etc., couched for the most part in banking and legal terms, should be explained for the benefit of the average citizen. I owe this in particular because of the fortitude and good temper with which everybody has accepted the inconvenience and hardships of the banking holiday. I know that when you understand what we in Washington have been about I shall continue to have your cooperation as fully as I have had your sympathy and help during the past week.

First of all, let me state the simple fact that when you deposit money in a bank the bank does not put the money into a safe deposit vault. It invests your money in many different forms of credit—bonds, commercial paper, mortgages, and many other kinds of loans. In other words, the bank puts your money to work to keep the wheels of industry and of agriculture turning around. A comparatively small part of the money you put into the bank is kept in currency—an amount which in normal times is wholly sufficient to cover the cash needs of the average citizen. In other words, the total amount of all the currency in the country is only a small fraction of the total deposits in all of the banks.

What, then, happened during the last few days of February

and the first few days of March? Because of undermined confidence on the part of the public, there was a general rush by a large portion of our population to turn bank deposits into currency or gold—a rush so great that the soundest banks could not get enough currency to meet the demand. The reason for this was that on the spur of the moment it was, of course, impossible to sell perfectly sound assets of a bank and convert them into cash except at panic prices far below their real value.

By the afternoon of March third scarcely a bank in the country was open to do business. Proclamations temporarily closing them in whole or in part had been issued by the governors in almost all the states.

It was then that I issued the proclamation providing for the nationwide bank holiday, and this was the first step in the government's reconstruction of our financial and economic fabric.

The second step was the legislation promptly and patriotically passed by the Congress confirming my proclamation and broadening my powers so that it became possible in view of the requirement of time to extend the holiday and lift the ban of that holiday gradually. This law also gave authority to develop a program of rehabilitation of our banking facilities. I want to tell our citizens in every part of the nation that the national Congress—Republicans and Democrats alike—showed by this action a devotion to public welfare and a realization of the emergency and the necessity for speed that it is difficult to match in our history.

The third stage has been the series of regulations permitting the banks to continue their functions to take care of the distribution of food and household necessities and the payment of payrolls.

This bank holiday, while resulting in many cases in great inconvenience, is affording us the opportunity to supply the currency necessary to meet the situation. No sound bank is a dollar worse off than it was when it closed its doors last Monday. Neither is any bank which may turn out not to be in a position for immediate opening. The new law allows the twelve

Federal Reserve Banks to issue additional currency on good assets and thus the banks which reopen will be able to meet every legitimate call. The new currency is being sent out by the Bureau of Engraving and Printing in large volume to every part of the country. It is sound currency because it is backed by actual, good assets.

A question you will ask is this: Why are all the banks not to be reopened at the same time? The answer is simple. Your government does not intend that the history of the past few years shall be repeated. We do not want and will not have another epidemic of bank failures.

As a result, we start tomorrow, Monday, with the opening of banks in the twelve Federal Reserve Bank cities—those banks which on first examination by the Treasury have already been found to be all right. This will be followed on Tuesday by the resumption of all their functions by banks already found to be sound in cities where there are recognized clearinghouses. That means about 250 cities of the United States.

On Wednesday and succeeding days banks in smaller places all through the country will resume business, subject, of course, to the government's physical ability to complete its survey. It is necessary that the reopening of banks be extended over a period in order to permit the banks to make applications for necessary loans, to obtain currency needed to meet their requirements and to enable the government to make common sense checkups.

Let me make it clear to you that if your bank does not open the first day you are by no means justified in believing that it will not open. A bank that opens on one of the subsequent days is in exactly the same status as the bank that opens tomorrow.

I know that many people are worrying about state banks not members of the Federal Reserve System. These banks can and will receive assistance from member banks and from the Reconstruction Finance Corporation. These state banks are following the same course as the national banks except that they get their licenses to resume business from the state authorities, and these authorities have been asked by the secretary of the treasury to permit their good banks to open up on the same schedule as the national banks. I am confident that the state banking departments will be as careful as the national government in the policy relating to the opening of banks and will follow the same broad policy.

It is possible that when the banks resume a very few people who have not recovered from their fear may again begin withdrawals. Let me make it clear that the banks will take care of all needs—and it is my belief that hoarding during the past week has become an exceedingly unfashionable pastime. It needs no prophet to tell you that when the people find that they can get their money—that they can get it when they want it for all legitimate purposes—the phantom of fear will soon be laid. People will again be glad to have their money where it will be safely taken care of and where they can use it conveniently at any time. I can assure you that it is safer to keep your money in a reopened bank than under the mattress.

The success of our whole great national program depends, of course, upon the cooperation of the public—on its intelligent support and use of a reliable system.

Remember that the essential accomplishment of the new legislation is that it makes it possible for banks more readily to convert their assets into cash than was the case before. More liberal provision has been made for banks to borrow on these assets at the Reserve Banks and more liberal provision has also been made for issuing currency on the security of these good assets. This currency is not flat currency. It is issued only on adequate security, and every good bank has an abundance of such security.

One more point before I close. There will be, of course, some banks unable to reopen without being reorganized. The new law allows the government to assist in making these reorganizations quickly and effectively and even allows the government to subscribe to at least a part of new capital which may be required.

I hope you can see from this elemental recital of what your

government is doing that there is nothing complex, or radical, in the process.

We had a bad banking situation. Some of our bankers had shown themselves either incompetent or dishonest in their handling of the people's funds. They had used the money entrusted to them in speculations and unwise loans. This was, of course, not true in the vast majority of our banks, but it was true in enough of them to shock the people for a time into a sense of insecurity and to put them into a frame of mind where they did not differentiate, but seemed to assume that the acts of a comparative few had tainted them all. It was the government's job to straighten out this situation and do it as quickly as possible. And the job is being performed.

I do not promise you that every bank will be reopened or that individual losses will not be suffered, but there will be no losses that possibly could be avoided; and there would have been more and greater losses had we continued to drift. I can even promise you salvation for some at least of the sorely pressed banks. We shall be engaged not merely in reopening sound banks but in the creation of sound banks through reorganization.

It has been wonderful to me to catch the note of confidence from all over the country. I can never be sufficiently grateful to the people for the loyal support they have given me in their acceptance of the judgment that has dictated our course, even though all our processes may not have seemed clear to them.

After all, there is an element in the readjustment of our financial system more important than currency, more important than gold, and that is the confidence of the people. Confidence and courage are the essentials of success in carrying out our plan. You people must have faith; you must not be stampeded by rumors or guesses. Let us unite in banishing fear. We have provided the machinery to restore our financial system; it is up to you to support and make it work.

It is your problem no less than it is mine. Together we cannot fail.

Message to Congress on the Creation of the Tennessee Valley Authority

April 10, 1933

The continued idleness of a great national investment in the Tennessee Valley leads me to ask the Congress for legislation necessary to enlist this project in the service of the people.

It is clear that the Muscle Shoals development is but a small part of the potential public usefulness of the entire Tennessee River. Such use, if envisioned in its entirety, transcends mere power development; it enters the wide fields of flood control, soil erosion, afforestation, elimination from agricultural use of marginal lands, and distribution and diversification of industry. In short, this power development of war days leads logically to national planning for a complete river watershed involving many states and the future lives and welfare of millions. It touches and gives life to all forms of human concerns.

I, therefore, suggest to the Congress legislation to create a Tennessee Valley Authority, a corporation clothed with the power of government but possessed of the flexibility and initiative of a private enterprise. It should be charged with the broadest duty of planning for the proper use, conservation, and development of the natural resources of the Tennessee River drainage basin and its adjoining territory for the general social and economic welfare of the nation. This authority should also be clothed with the necessary power to carry these plans into effect. Its duty should be the rehabilitation of the Muscle Shoals development and the coordination of it with the wider plan.

Many hard lessons have taught us the human waste that results from lack of planning. Here and there a few wise cities and counties have looked ahead and planned. But our nation has "just grown." It is time to extend planning to a wider field, in this instance comprehending in one great project many states directly concerned with the basin of one of our greatest rivers.

This in a true sense is a return to the spirit and vision of the pioneer. If we are successful here we can march on, step by step, in a like development of other great natural territorial units within our borders.

ADDRESS TO THE
GOVERNING BOARD OF THE
PAN-AMERICAN UNION

April 12, 1933

THE GOOD NEIGHBOR POLICY

I rejoice in this opportunity to participate in the celebration of Pan-American Day and to extend on behalf of the people of the United States a fraternal greeting to our sister American republics. The celebration of Pan-American Day in this building, dedicated to international goodwill and cooperation, exemplifies a unity of thought and purpose among the peoples of this hemisphere. It is a manifestation of the common ideal of mutual helpfulness, sympathetic understanding, and spiritual solidarity.

There is inspiration in the thought that on this day the attention of the citizens of the twenty-one republics of America is focused on the common ties—historical, cultural, economic, and social—which bind them to one another. Common ideals and a community of interest, together with a spirit of cooperation, have led to the realization that the well-being of one nation depends in large measure upon the well-being of its neighbors. It is upon these foundations that Pan-Americanism has been built.

This celebration commemorates a movement based upon the policy of fraternal cooperation. In my inaugural address I stated that I would "dedicate this nation to the policy of the Good Neighbor—the neighbor who resolutely respects himself and, because he does so, respects the rights of others—the neighbor who respects his obligations and respects the sanctity of his agreements in and with a world of neighbors." Never before has the significance of the words *good neighbor* been so manifest in international relations. Never have the need and benefit of neighborly cooperation in every form of human activity been so evident as they are today.

Friendship among nations, as among individuals, calls for constructive efforts to muster the forces of humanity in order that an atmosphere of close understanding and cooperation may be cultivated. It involves mutual obligations and responsibilities, for it is only by sympathetic respect for the rights of others and a scrupulous fulfillment of the corresponding obligations by each member of the community that a true fraternity can be maintained.

The essential qualities of a true Pan-Americanism must be the same as those which constitute a good neighbor, namely, mutual understanding, and, through such understanding, a sympathetic appreciation of the other's point of view. It is only in this manner that we can hope to build up a system of which confidence, friendship, and goodwill are the cornerstones.

In this spirit the people of every republic on our continent are coming to a deep understanding of the fact that the Monroe Doctrine, of which so much has been written and spoken for more than a century, was and is directed at the maintenance of independence by the peoples of the continent. It was aimed and is aimed against the acquisition in any manner of the control of additional territory in this hemisphere by any non-American power.

Hand in hand with this Pan-American doctrine of continental self-defense, the peoples of the American republics understand more clearly, with the passing years, that the independence of each republic must recognize the independence of every other republic. Each one of us must grow by an advancement of civilization and social well-being and not by the acquisition of territory at the expense of any neighbor.

In this spirit of mutual understanding and of cooperation on this continent you and I cannot fail to be disturbed by any armed strife between neighbors. I do not hesitate to say to you, the distinguished members of the Governing Board of the Pan-American Union, that I regard existing conflicts between four of our sister republics as a backward step.

Your Americanism and mine must be a structure built of confidence, cemented by a sympathy which recognizes only equality and fraternity. It finds its source and being in the hearts of men and dwells in the temple of the intellect.

We, all of us, have peculiar problems, and, to speak frankly, the interest of our own citizens must, in each instance, come first. But it is equally true that it is of vital importance to every nation of this continent that the American governments, individually, take, without further delay, such action as may be possible to abolish all unnecessary and artificial barriers and restrictions which now hamper the healthy flow of trade between the peoples of the American republics.

I am glad to deliver this message to you, gentlemen of the Governing Board of the Pan-American Union, for I look upon the Union as the outward expression of the spiritual unity of the Americas. It is to this unity which must be courageous and vital in its element that humanity must look for one of the great stabilizing influences in world affairs.

In closing, may I refer to the ceremony which is to take place a little later in the morning at which the government of Venezuela will present to the Pan-American Union the bust of a great American leader and patriot, Francisco de Miranda. I join with you in this tribute.

FIRESIDE CHAT ON
NEW ECONOMIC POLICIES

May 7, 1933

On a Sunday night a week after my inauguration I used the radio to tell you about the banking crisis and the measures we were taking to meet it. I think that in that way I made clear to the country various facts that might otherwise have been misunderstood and in general provided a means of understanding which did much to restore confidence.

Tonight, eight weeks later, I come for the second time to give you my report; in the same spirit and by the same means to tell you about what we have been doing and what we are planning to do.

Two months ago we were facing serious problems. The country was dying by inches. It was dying because trade and commerce had declined to dangerously low levels; prices for basic commodities were such as to destroy the value of the assets of national institutions such as banks, savings banks, insurance companies, and others. These institutions, because of their great needs, were foreclosing mortgages, calling loans, refusing credit. Thus there was actually in process of destruction the property of millions of people who had borrowed money on that property in terms of dollars which had had an entirely different value from the level of March 1933. That situation in that crisis did not call for any complicated consideration of economic panaceas or fancy plans. We were faced by a condition and not a theory.

There were just two alternatives. The first was to allow the foreclosures to continue, credit to be withheld, and money to go into hiding, thus forcing liquidation and bankruptcy of banks, railroads, and insurance companies and a recapitalizing of all business and all property on a lower level. This alternative meant a continuation of what is loosely called "deflation," the net result of which would have been extraordinary hardships on all property owners and, incidentally, extraordinary hardships on all persons working for wages through an increase in unemployment and a further reduction of the wage scale.

It is easy to see that the result of this course would have not only economic effects of a very serious nature, but social results that might bring incalculable harm. Even before I was inaugurated I came to the conclusion that such a policy was too much to ask the American people to bear. It involved not only a further loss of homes, farms, savings, and wages, but also a loss of spiritual values—the loss of that sense of security for the present and the future so necessary to the peace and contentment of the individual and of his family. When you destroy these things you will find it difficult to establish confidence of any sort in the future. It was clear that mere appeals from Washington for confidence and the mere lending of more money to shaky institutions could not stop this downward course. A prompt program applied as quickly as possible seemed to me not only justified but imperative to our national security. The Congress —and when I say Congress I mean the members of both political parties—fully understood this and gave me generous and intelligent support. The members of Congress realized that the methods of normal times had to be replaced in the emergency by measures which were suited to the serious and pressing requirements of the moment. There was no actual surrender of power, Congress still retained its constitutional authority, and no one has the slightest desire to change the balance of these powers. The function of Congress is to decide what has to be done and to select the appropriate agency to carry out its will. To this policy it has strictly adhered. The only thing that has been happening has been to designate the president as the agency to carry out certain of the purposes of the Congress. This was constitutional and in keeping with the past American tradition.

The legislation which has been passed or is in the process of enactment can properly be considered as part of a well-grounded plan.

First, we are giving opportunity of employment to one-quarter of a million of the unemployed, especially the young men who have dependents, to go into the forestry and flood-prevention work. This is a big task because it means feeding, clothing, and caring for nearly twice as many men as we have in the regular army itself. In creating this Civilian Conservation Corps we are killing two birds with one stone. We are clearly enhancing the value of our natural resources, and we are relieving an appreciable amount of actual distress. This great group of men has entered upon its work on a purely voluntary basis; no military training is involved and we are conserving not only our natural resources, but our human resources. One of the great values to this work is the fact that it is direct and requires the intervention of very little machinery.

Second, I have requested the Congress and have secured action upon a proposal to put the great properties owned by our government at Muscle Shoals to work after long years of wasteful inaction, and with this a broad plan for the improvement of a vast area in the Tennessee Valley. It will add to the comfort and happiness of hundreds of thousands of people and the incident benefits will reach the entire nation.

Next, the Congress is about to pass legislation that will greatly ease the mortgage distress among the farmers and the home-owners of the nation, by providing for the easing of the burden of debt now bearing so heavily upon millions of our people.

Our next step in seeking immediate relief is a grant of half a billion dollars to help the states, counties, and municipalities in their duty to care for those who need direct and immediate relief.

The Congress also passed legislation authorizing the sale of beer in such states as desired it. This has already resulted in considerable reemployment and incidentally has provided much-needed tax revenue.

We are planning to ask the Congress for legislation to enable the government to undertake public works, thus stimulating directly and indirectly the employment of many others in well-considered projects.

Further legislation has been taken up which goes much more fundamentally into our economic problems. The Farm Relief Bill seeks by the use of several methods, alone or together, to bring about an increased return to farmers for their major farm products, seeking at the same time to prevent in the days to come disastrous overproduction, which so often in the past has kept farm commodity prices far below a reasonable return. This measure provides wide powers for emergencies. The extent of its use will depend entirely upon what the future has in store.

Well-considered and conservative measures will likewise be proposed which will attempt to give to the industrial workers of the country a more fair wage return, prevent cutthroat competition and unduly long hours for labor, and at the same time encourage each industry to prevent overproduction.

Our railroad bill falls into the same class because it seeks to provide and make certain definite planning by the railroads themselves, with the assistance of the government, to eliminate the duplication and waste that is now resulting in railroad receiverships and continuing operating deficits.

I am certain that the people of this country understand and approve the broad purposes behind these new governmental policies relating to agriculture and industry and transportation. We found ourselves faced with more agricultural products than we could possibly consume ourselves and with surpluses which other nations did not have the cash to buy from us except at prices ruinously low. We found our factories able to turn out more goods than we could possibly consume, and at the same time we were faced with a falling export demand. We found ourselves with more facilities to transport goods and crops than there were goods and crops to be transported. All of this has been caused in large part by a complete lack of planning and a complete failure to understand the danger signals that have been flying ever since the close of the World War. The people of this country have been erroneously encouraged to believe that they could keep on increasing the output of farm and factory indefinitely and that some magician would find ways and means for that increased output to be consumed with reasonable profit to the producer.

Today we have reason to believe that things are a little better than they were two months ago. Industry has picked up, railroads are carrying more freight, farm prices are better, but I am not going to indulge in issuing proclamations of overenthusiastic assurance. We cannot ballyhoo ourselves back to prosperity. I am going to be honest at all times with the people of the country. I do not want the people of this country to take the foolish course of letting this improvement come back on another speculative wave. I do not want the people to believe that because of unjustified optimism we can resume the ruinous practice of increasing our crop output and our factory output in the hope that a kind Providence will find buyers at high prices. Such a course may bring us immediate and false prosperity but it will be the kind of prosperity that will lead us into another tailspin.

It is wholly wrong to call the measures that we have taken government control of farming, industry, and transportation. It is rather a partnership between government and farming and industry and transportation, not partnership in profits, for the profits still go to the citizens, but rather a partnership in planning, and a partnership to see that the plans are carried out.

Let me illustrate with an example. Take the cotton-goods industry. It is probably true that 90 percent of the cotton manufacturers would agree to eliminate starvation wages, would agree to stop long hours of employment, would agree to stop child labor, would agree to prevent an overproduction that would result in unsalable surpluses. But, what good is such an agreement if the other 10 percent of cotton manufacturers pay starvation wages, require long hours, employ children in their mills, and turn out burdensome surpluses? The unfair 10 percent could produce goods so cheaply that the fair 90 percent would be compelled to meet the unfair conditions. Here is where government comes in. Government ought to have the right and will have the right, after surveying and planning for an industry, to prevent, with the assistance of the overwhelming majority of that industry, unfair practices and to enforce this agreement by the authority of government. The so-called antitrust laws were intended to prevent the creation of monopolies and to forbid unreasonable profits to those monopolies. That purpose of the antitrust laws must be continued, but these laws were never intended to encourage the kind of unfair competition that results in long hours, starvation wages, and overproduction.

The same principle applies to farm products and to transportation and every other field of organized private industry.

We are working toward a definite goal, which is to prevent the return of conditions which came very close to destroying what we call modern civilization. The actual accomplishment of our purpose cannot be attained in a day. Our policies are wholly within purposes for which our American constitutional government was established 150 years ago.

I know that the people of this country will understand this and will also understand the spirit in which we are undertaking this policy. I do not deny that we may make mistakes of procedure as we carry out the policy. I have no expectation of making a hit every time I come to bat. What I seek is the highest possible batting average, not only for myself but for the team. Theodore Roosevelt once said to me: "If I can be right 75 percent of the time I shall come up to the fullest measure of my hopes."

Much has been said of late about federal finances and inflation, the gold standard, etc. Let me make the facts very simple and my policy very clear. In the first place, government credit and government currency are really one and the same thing. Behind government bonds there is only a promise to pay. Behind government currency we have, in addition to the promise to pay, a reserve of gold and a small reserve of silver. In this connection it is worthwhile remembering that in the past the government has agreed to redeem nearly thirty billions of its debts and its currency in gold, and private corporations in this country have agreed to redeem another sixty or seventy billions of securities and mortgages in gold. The government and private corporations were making these agreements when they knew full well that all of the gold in the United States amounted to only between three and four billions and that all of the gold in all of the world amounted to only about eleven billions.

If the holders of these promises to pay started in to demand gold the first-comers would get gold for a few days and they would amount to about one-twenty-fifth of the holders of the securities and the currency. The other twenty-four people out of twenty-five, who did not happen to be at the top of the line, would be told politely that there was no more gold left. We have decided to treat all twenty-five in the same way in the interest of justice and the exercise of the constitutional powers of this government. We have placed everyone on the same basis in order that the general good may be preserved.

Nevertheless, gold, and to a partial extent silver, are perfectly good bases for currency, and that is why I decided not to let any of the gold now in the country go out of it.

A series of conditions arose three weeks ago which very readily might have meant, first, a drain on our gold by foreign countries, and second, as a result of that, a flight of American capital, in the form of gold, out of our country. It is not exaggerating the possibility to tell you that such an occurrence might well have taken from us the major part of our gold reserve and resulted in such a further weakening of our government and private credit as to bring on actual panic conditions and the complete stoppage of the wheels of industry.

The administration has the definite objective of raising commodity prices to such an extent that those who have borrowed money will, on the average, be able to repay that money in the same kind of dollar which they borrowed. We do not seek to let them get such a cheap dollar that they will be able to pay back a great deal less than they borrowed. In other words, we seek to correct a wrong and not to create another wrong in the opposite direction. That is why powers are being given to the administration to provide, if necessary, for an enlargement of credit, in order to correct the existing wrong. These powers will be used when, as, and if it may be necessary to accomplish the purpose.

Hand in hand with the domestic situation, which of course is our first concern, is the world situation, and I want to emphasize to you that the domestic situation is inevitably and deeply tied in with the conditions in all of the other nations of the world. In other words, we can get, in all probability, a fair measure of prosperity to return in the United States, but it will not be permanent unless we get a return to prosperity all over the world.

In the conferences which we have held and are holding with the leaders of other nations, we are seeking four great objectives: first, a general reduction of armaments and through this the removal of the fear of invasion and armed attack, and, at the same time, a reduction in armament costs, in order to help in the balancing of government budgets and the reduction of taxation; second, a cutting down of the trade barriers, in order to restart the flow of exchange of crops and goods between nations; third, the setting up of a stabilization of currencies, in order that trade can make contracts ahead; fourth, the reestablishment of friendly relations and greater confidence between all nations.

Our foreign visitors these past three weeks have responded to these purposes in a very helpful way. All of the nations have suffered alike in this great depression. They have all reached the conclusion that each can best be helped by the common action of all. It is in this spirit that our visitors have met with us and discussed our common problems. The international conference that lies before us must succeed. The future of the world demands it and we have each of us pledged ourselves to the best joint efforts to this end.

To you, the people of this country, all of us, the members of the Congress and the members of this administration, owe a profound debt of gratitude. Throughout the depression you have been patient. You have granted us wide powers; you have encouraged us with a widespread approval of our purposes. Every ounce of strength and every resource at our command we have devoted to the end of justifying your confidence. We are encouraged to believe that a wise and sensible beginning has been made. In the present spirit of mutual confidence and mutual encouragement we go forward.

Message to the Nations of the World on Disarmament

May 16, 1933

A profound hope of the people of my country impels me, as the head of their government, to address you and, through you, the people of your nation. This hope is that peace may be assured through practical measures of disarmament and that all of us may carry to victory our common struggle against economic chaos.

To these ends the nations have called two great world conferences. The happiness, the prosperity, and the very lives of the men, women, and children who inhabit the whole world are bound up in the decisions which their governments will make in the near future. The improvement of social conditions, the preservation of individual human rights, and the furtherance of social justice are dependent upon these decisions.

The World Economic Conference will meet soon and must come to its conclusions quickly. The world cannot await deliberations long drawn out. The conference must establish order in place of the present chaos by a stabilization of currencies, by freeing the flow of world trade, and by international action to raise price levels. It must, in short, supplement individual domestic programs for economic recovery, by wise and considered international action.

The Disarmament Conference has labored for more than a year and, as yet, has been unable to reach satisfactory conclusions. Confused purposes still clash dangerously. Our duty lies in the direction of bringing practical results through concerted action based upon the greatest good to the greatest number.

Before the imperative call of this great duty, petty obstacles must be swept away and petty aims forgotten. A selfish victory is always destined to be an ultimate defeat. The furtherance of durable peace for our generation in every part of the world is the only goal worthy of our best efforts.

If we ask what are the reasons for armaments, which, in spite of the lessons and tragedies of the World War, are today a greater burden on the peoples of the earth than ever before, it becomes clear that they are twofold: first, the desire, disclosed or hidden, on the part of governments to enlarge their territories at the expense of a sister nation, and I believe that only a small minority of governments or of peoples harbor such a purpose; second, the fear of nations that they will be invaded. I believe that the overwhelming majority of peoples feel obliged to retain excessive armaments because they fear some act of aggression against them and not because they themselves seek to be aggressors.

There is justification for this fear. Modern weapons of offense are vastly stronger than modern weapons of defense. Frontier forts, trenches, wire entanglements, coast defenses—in a word, fixed fortifications—are no longer impregnable to the attack of war planes, heavy mobile artillery, land battleships called tanks, and poison gas.

If all nations will agree wholly to eliminate from possession and use the weapons which make possible a successful attack, defenses automatically will become impregnable, and the frontiers and independence of every nation will become secure.

The ultimate objective of the Disarmament Conference must be the complete elimination of all offensive weapons. The immediate objective is a substantial reduction of some of these weapons and the elimination of many others.

This government believes that the program for immediate reduction of aggressive weapons, now under discussion at Geneva, is but a first step toward our ultimate goal. We do not believe that the proposed immediate steps go far enough. Nevertheless, this government welcomes the measures now proposed and will exert its influence toward the attainment of further successive steps of disarmament.

Stated in the clearest way, there are three steps to be agreed upon in the present discussions:

First, to take, at once, the first definite step toward this objective, as broadly outlined in the MacDonald Plan.

Second, to agree upon time and procedure for taking the following steps.

Third, to agree that while the first and the following steps are being taken, no nation shall increase its existing armaments over and above the limitations of treaty obligations.

But the peace of the world must be assured during the whole period of disarmament and I, therefore, propose a fourth step concurrent with and wholly dependent on the faithful fulfillment of these three proposals and subject to existing treaty rights:

That all the nations of the world should enter into a solemn and definite pact of nonaggression; that they should solemnly reaffirm the obligations they have assumed to limit and reduce their armaments, and, provided these obligations are faithfully executed by all signatory powers, individually agree that they will send no armed force of whatsoever nature across their frontiers.

Common sense points out that if any strong nation refuses to join with genuine sincerity in these concerted efforts for political and economic peace, the one at Geneva and the other at London, progress can be obstructed and ultimately blocked. In such event the civilized world, seeking both forms of peace, will know where the responsibility for failure lies. I urge that no nation assume such a responsibility, and that all the nations joined in these great conferences translate their professed policies into action. This is the way to political and economic peace.

I trust that your government will join in the fulfillment of these hopes.

FIRESIDE CHAT ON THE NATIONAL RECOVERY ADMINISTRATION

July 24, 1933

After the adjournment of the historical special session of the Congress five weeks ago I purposely refrained from addressing you for two very good reasons.

First, I think that we all wanted the opportunity of a little quiet thought to examine and assimilate in a mental picture the crowding events of the hundred days which had been devoted to the starting of the wheels of the New Deal.

Secondly, I wanted a few weeks in which to set up the new administrative organization and to see the first fruits of our careful planning.

I think it will interest you if I set forth the fundamentals of this planning for national recovery; and this I am very certain will make it abundantly clear to you that all of the proposals and all of the legislation since the fourth day of March have not been just a collection of haphazard schemes, but rather the orderly component parts of a connected and logical whole.

Long before Inauguration Day I became convinced that individual effort and local effort and even disjointed federal effort had failed and of necessity would fail and, therefore, that a rounded leadership by the federal government had become a necessity both of theory and of fact. Such leadership, however, had its beginning in preserving and strengthening the credit of the United States government, because without that no leadership was a possibility. For years the government had not lived within its income. The immediate task was to bring our regular expenses within our revenues. That has been done.

It may seem inconsistent for a government to cut down its regular expenses and at the same time to borrow and to spend billions for an emergency. But it is not inconsistent because a large portion of the emergency money has been paid out in the form of sound loans which will be repaid to the Treasury over a period of years; and to cover the rest of the emergency money we have imposed taxes to pay the interest and the installments on that part of the debt.

So you will see that we have kept our credit good. We have built a granite foundation in a period of confusion. That foundation of the federal credit stands there broad and sure. It is the base of the whole recovery plan.

Then came the part of the problem that concerned the credit of the individual citizens themselves. You and I know of the banking crisis and of the great danger to the savings of our people. On March 6 every national bank was closed. One month later 90 percent of the deposits in the national banks had been made available to the depositors. Today only about 5 percent of the deposits in national banks are still tied up. The condition relating to state banks, while not quite so good on a percentage basis, is showing a steady reduction in the total of frozen deposits—a result much better than we had expected three months ago.

The problem of the credit of the individual was made more difficult because of another fact. The dollar was a different dollar from the one with which the average debt had been incurred. For this reason large numbers of people were actually losing possession of and title to their farms and homes. All of you know the financial steps which have been taken to correct this inequality. In addition the Home Loan Act, the Farm Loan Act, and the Bankruptcy Act were passed.

It was a vital necessity to restore purchasing power by reducing the debt and interest charges upon our people, but while we were helping people to save their credit it was at the same time absolutely essential to do something about the physical needs of hundreds of thousands who were in dire straits at that very moment. Municipal and state aid were being stretched to the limit. We appropriated half a billion dollars to supplement their efforts and in addition, as you know, we have put three hundred thousand young men into practical and useful work in our forests and to prevent flood and soil erosion. The wages they earn are going in greater part to the support of the nearly one million people who constitute their families.

In this same classification we can properly place the great public works program running to a total of over $3 billion—to be used for highways and ships and flood prevention and inland navigation and thousands of self-sustaining state and municipal improvements. Two points should be made clear in the allotting and administration of these projects: first, we are using the utmost care to choose labor-creating, quick-acting, useful projects, avoiding the smell of the pork barrel; and second, we are hoping that at least half of the money will come back to the government from projects which will pay for themselves over a period of years.

Thus far I have spoken primarily of the foundation stones —the measures that were necessary to reestablish credit and to head people in the opposite direction by preventing distress and providing as much work as possible through governmental agencies. Now I come to the links which will build us a more lasting prosperity. I have said that we cannot attain that in a nation half boom and half broke. If all of our people have work and fair wages and fair profits, they can buy the products of their neighbors, and business is good. But if you take away the wages and the profits of half of them, business is only half as good. It does not help much if the fortunate half is very prosperous; the best way is for everybody to be reasonably prosperous.

For many years the two great barriers to a normal prosperity have been low farm prices and the creeping paralysis of unemployment. These factors have cut the purchasing power of the country in half. I promised action. Congress did its part when it passed the Farm and the Industrial Recovery acts. Today we are putting these two acts to work and they will work if people understand their plain objectives.

First, the Farm Act: it is based on the fact that the purchasing power of nearly half our population depends on adequate prices for farm products. We have been producing more of some crops than we consume or can sell in a depressed world market. The cure is not to produce so much. Without our help the farmers cannot get together and cut production, and the Farm Bill gives them a method of bringing their production down to a reasonable level and of obtaining reasonable prices for their crops. I have clearly stated that this method is in a sense experimental, but so far as we have gone we have reason to believe that it will produce good results.

It is obvious that if we can greatly increase the purchasing power of the tens of millions of our people who make a living from farming and the distribution of farm crops, we shall greatly increase the consumption of those goods which are turned out by industry.

That brings me to the final step—bringing back industry along sound lines.

Last autumn, on several occasions, I expressed my faith that we can make possible by democratic self-discipline in industry general increases in wages and shortening of hours sufficient to enable industry to pay its own workers enough to let those workers buy and use the things that their labor produces. This can be done only if we permit and encourage cooperative action in industry, because it is obvious that without united action a few selfish men in each competitive group will pay starvation wages and insist on long hours of work. Others in that group must either follow suit or close up shop. We have seen the result of action of that kind in the continuing descent into the economic hell of the past four years.

There is a clear way to reverse that process: If all employers in each competitive group agree to pay their workers the same wages—reasonable wages—and require the same hours—reasonable hours—then higher wages and shorter hours will hurt no employer. Moreover, such action is better for the employer than unemployment and low wages, because it makes more buyers for his product. That is the simple idea which is the very heart of the Industrial Recovery Act.

On the basis of this simple principle of everybody doing things together, we are starting out on this nationwide attack on unemployment. It will succeed if our people understand it—in the big industries, in the little shops, in the great cities, and in the small villages. There is nothing complicated about it and there is nothing particularly new in the principle. It goes back to the basic idea of society and of the nation itself that people acting in a group can accomplish things which no individual acting alone could even hope to bring about.

Here is an example. In the Cotton Textile Code and in other agreements already signed, child labor has been abolished. That makes me personally happier than any other one thing with which I have been connected since I came to Washington. In the textile industry—an industry which came to me spontaneously and with a splendid cooperation as soon as the Recovery Act was signed—child labor was an old evil. But no employer acting alone was able to wipe it out. If one employer tried it, or if one state tried it, the costs of operation rose so high that it was impossible to compete with the employers or states which had failed to act. The moment the Recovery Act was passed, this monstrous thing which neither opinion nor law could reach through years of effort went out in a flash. As a British editorial put it, we did more under a code in one day than they in England had been able to do under the common law in eighty-five years of effort. I use this incident, my friends, not to boast of what has already been done but to point the way to you for even greater cooperative efforts this summer and autumn.

We are not going through another winter like the last. I doubt if ever any people so bravely and cheerfully endured a season half so bitter. We cannot ask America to continue to face such needless hardships. It is time for courageous action, and the Recovery Bill gives us the means to conquer unemployment with exactly the same weapon that we have used to strike down child labor.

The proposition is simply this:

If all employers will act together to shorten hours and raise wages we can put people back to work. No employer will suffer, because the relative level of competitive cost will advance by the same amount for all. But if any considerable group should lag or shirk, this great opportunity will pass us by and we shall go into another desperate winter. This must not happen.

We have sent out to all employers an agreement which is the result of weeks of consultation. This agreement checks against the voluntary codes of nearly all the large industries which have already been submitted. This blanket agreement carries the unanimous approval of the three boards which I have appointed to advise in this, boards representing the great leaders in labor, in industry, and in social service. This agreement has already brought a flood of approval from every state, and from so wide a cross-section of the common calling of industry that I know it is fair for all. It is a plan—deliberate, reasonable, and just— intended to put into effect at once the most important of the broad principles which are being established, industry by industry, through codes. Naturally, it takes a good deal of organizing and a great many hearings and many months, to get these codes perfected and signed, and we cannot wait for all of them to go through. The blanket agreements, however, which I am sending to every employer will start the wheels turning now, and not six months from now.

There are, of course, men, a few men, who might thwart this great common purpose by seeking selfish advantage. There are adequate penalties in the law, but I am now asking the cooperation that comes from opinion and from conscience. These are the only instruments we shall use in this great summer offensive against unemployment. But we shall use them to the limit to protect the willing from the laggard and to make the plan succeed.

In war, in the gloom of night attack, soldiers wear a bright badge on their shoulders to be sure that comrades do not fire on comrades. On that principle, those who cooperate in this program must know each other at a glance. That is why we have provided a badge of honor for this purpose, a simple design with a legend, "We do our part," and I ask that all those who join with me shall display that badge prominently. It is essential to our purpose.

Already all the great, basic industries have come forward willingly with proposed codes, and in these codes they accept the principles leading to mass reemployment. But, important as is this heartening demonstration, the richest field for results is among the small employers, those whose contribution will be to give new work for from one to ten people. These smaller employers are indeed a vital part of the backbone of the country, and the success of our plan lies largely in their hands.

Already the telegrams and letters are pouring into the White House—messages from employers who ask that their names be placed on this special roll of honor. They represent great corporations and companies, and partnerships and individuals. I ask that even before the dates set in the agreements which we have sent out, the employers of the country who have not already done so—the big fellows and the little fellows—shall at once write or telegraph to me personally at the White House, expressing their intentions of going through with the plan. And it is my purpose to keep posted in the post office of every town, a roll of honor of all those who join with me.

I want to take this occasion to say to the twenty-four governors who are now in conference in San Francisco, that nothing thus far has helped in strengthening this great movement more than their resolutions adopted at the very outset of their meeting, giving this plan their instant and unanimous approval, and pledging to support it in their states.

To the men and women whose lives have been darkened by the fact or the fear of unemployment, I am justified in saying a word of encouragement because the codes and the agreements already approved, or about to be passed upon, prove that the plan does raise wages, and that it does put people back to work. You can look on every employer who adopts the plan as one who is doing his part, and those employers deserve well of everyone who works for a living. It will be clear to you, as it is to me, that while the shirking employer may undersell his competitor, the saving he thus makes is made at the expense of his country's welfare.

While we are making this great common effort there should be no discord and dispute. This is no time to cavil or to question the standard set by this universal agreement. It is time for patience and understanding and cooperation. The workers of this country have rights under this law which cannot be taken from them, and nobody will be permitted to whittle them away but, on the other hand, no aggression is now necessary to attain those rights. The whole country will be united to get them for you. The principle that applies to the employers applies to the workers as well, and I ask you workers to cooperate in the same spirit.

When Andrew Jackson, "Old Hickory," died, someone asked, "Will he go to heaven?" and the answer was, "He will if he wants to." If I am asked whether the American people will pull themselves out of this depression, I answer, "They will if they want to." The essence of the plan is a universal limitation of hours of work per week for any individual by common consent, and a universal payment of wages above a minimum, also by common consent. I cannot guarantee the success of this nationwide plan, but the people of this country can guarantee its success. I have no faith in "cure-alls," but I believe that we can greatly influence economic forces. I have no sympathy with the professional economists who insist that things must run their course and that human agencies can have no influence on economic ills. One reason is that I happen to know that professional economists have changed their definition of economic laws every five or ten years for a very long time, but I do have faith, and retain faith, in the strength of the common purpose, and in the strength of unified action taken by the American people.

That is why I am describing to you the simple purposes and the solid foundations upon which our program of recovery is built. That is why I am asking the employers of the nation to sign this common covenant with me—to sign it in the name of patriotism and humanity. That is why I am asking the workers to go along with us in a spirit of understanding and of helpfulness.

Proclamation on the Repeal of the Eighteenth Amendment

December 5, 1933

Whereas the Congress of the United States in second session of the Seventy-second Congress, begun at Washington on the fifth day of December in the year one thousand nine hundred and thirty-two, adopted a resolution in the words and figures following: to wit—

JOINT RESOLUTION
Proposing an amendment to the
Constitution of the United States

Resolved, by the Senate and House of Representatives of the United States of America in Congress assembled (two-thirds of each house concurring therein), That the following article is hereby proposed as an amendment to the Constitution of the United States, which shall be valid to all intents and purposes as part of the Constitution when ratified by conventions in three-fourths of the several states:

ARTICLE

Section 1. The eighteenth article of amendment to the Constitution of the United States is hereby repealed.

Section 2. The transportation or importation into any state, territory, or possession of the United States for delivery or use therein of intoxicating liquors, in violation of the laws thereof, is hereby prohibited.

Section 3. This article shall be inoperative unless it shall have been ratified as an amendment to the Constitution by conventions in the several states, as provided in the Constitution, within seven years from the date of the submission hereof to the states by the Congress.

Whereas Section 217(a) of the act of Congress entitled "An Act to Encourage National Industrial Recovery, to Foster Competition, and to Provide for the Construction of Certain Useful Public Works, and for Other Purposes," approved June 16, 1933, provides as follows:

SECTION 217(A). The president shall proclaim the date of:

(1) the close of the first fiscal year ending June 30 of any year after the year 1933, during which the total receipts of the United States (excluding public-debt receipts) exceed its total expenditures (excluding public-debt expenditures other than those chargeable against such receipts), or

(2) the repeal of the Eighteenth Amendment to the Constitution, whichever is the earlier.

Whereas it appears from a certificate issued December 5, 1933, by the acting secretary of state that official notices have been received in the Department of State that on the fifth day of December 1933, conventions in thirty-six states of the United States, constituting three-fourths of the whole number of the states, had ratified the said repeal amendment;

Now, therefore, I, Franklin D. Roosevelt, President of the United States of America, pursuant to the provisions of Section 217(a) of the said act of June 16, 1933, do hereby proclaim that the Eighteenth Amendment to the Constitution of the United States was repealed on the fifth day of December 1933.

Furthermore, I enjoin upon all citizens of the United States and upon others resident within the jurisdiction thereof, to cooperate with the government in its endeavor to restore greater respect for law and order, by confining such purchases of alcoholic beverages as they may make solely to those dealers or agencies which have been duly licensed by state or federal license.

Observance of this request, which I make personally to

every individual and every family in our nation, will result in the consumption of alcoholic beverages which have passed federal inspection, in the breakup and eventual destruction of the notoriously evil illicit liquor traffic, and in the payment of reasonable taxes for the support of the government, and thereby in the superseding of other forms of taxation.

I call specific attention to the authority given by the Twenty-first Amendment to the government to prohibit transportation or importation of intoxicating liquors into any state in violation of the laws of such state.

I ask the wholehearted cooperation of all our citizens to the end that this return of individual freedom shall not be accompanied by the repugnant conditions that obtained prior to the adoption of the Eighteenth Amendment and those that have existed since its adoption. Failure to do this honestly and courageously will be a living reproach to us all.

I ask especially that no state shall by law or otherwise authorize the return of the saloon either in its old form or in some modern guise.

The policy of the government will be to see to it that the social and political evils that have existed in the preprohibition era shall not be revived nor permitted again to exist. We must remove forever from our midst the menace of the bootlegger and such others as would profit at the expense of good government, law, and order.

I trust in the good sense of the American people that they will not bring upon themselves the curse of excessive use of intoxicating liquors, to the detriment of health, morals, and social integrity.

The objective we seek through a national policy is the education of every citizen toward a greater temperance throughout the nation.

In witness whereof, I have hereunto set my hand and caused the seal of the United States to be affixed.

First Annual Message to Congress

January 3, 1934

Mr. President, Mr. Speaker, Senators, and Representatives in Congress: I come before you at the opening of the regular session of the Seventy-third Congress not to make requests for special or detailed items of legislation; I come, rather, to counsel with you, who, like myself, have been selected to carry out a mandate of the whole people, in order that without partisanship you and I may cooperate to continue the restoration of our national well-being and, equally important, to build on the ruins of the past a new structure designed better to meet the present problems of modern civilization.

Such a structure includes not only the relations of industry and agriculture and finance to each other but also the effect which all of these three have on our individual citizens and on the whole people as a nation.

Now that we are definitely in the process of recovery, lines have been rightly drawn between those to whom this recovery means a return to old methods—and the number of these people is small—and those for whom recovery means a reform of many old methods, a permanent readjustment of many of our ways of thinking and therefore of many of our social and economic arrangements.

Civilization cannot go back; civilization must not stand still. We have undertaken new methods. It is our task to perfect, to improve, to alter when necessary, but in all cases to go forward. To consolidate what we are doing, to make our economic and social structure capable of dealing with modern life is the joint task of the legislative, the judicial, and the executive branches of the national government.

Without regard to party, the overwhelming majority of our people seek a greater opportunity for humanity to prosper and find happiness. They recognize that human welfare has not increased and does not increase through mere materialism and luxury, but that it does progress through integrity, unselfishness, responsibility, and justice.

In the past few months, as a result of our action, we have demanded of many citizens that they surrender certain licenses to do as they please in their business relationships; but we have asked this in exchange for the protection which the state can give against exploitation by their fellow men or by combinations of their fellow men.

I congratulate this Congress upon the courage, the earnestness, and the efficiency with which you met the crisis at the special session. It was your fine understanding of the national problem that furnished the example which the country has so splendidly followed. I venture to say that the task confronting the First Congress of 1789 was no greater than your own.

I shall not attempt to set forth either the many phases of the crisis which we experienced last March, or the many measures which you and I undertook during the special session that we might initiate recovery and reform.

It is sufficient that I should speak in broad terms of the results of our common counsel.

The credit of the government has been fortified by drastic reduction in the cost of its permanent agencies through the Economy Act.

With the twofold purpose of strengthening the whole financial structure and of arriving eventually at a medium of exchange which over the years will have less variable purchasing and debt-paying power for our people than that of the past, I have used the authority granted me to purchase all American-produced gold and silver and to buy additional gold in the world markets. Careful investigation and constant study prove that in the matter of foreign exchange rates certain of our sister nations find themselves so handicapped by internal and other conditions that they feel unable at this time to enter into stabilization discussion based on permanent and worldwide objectives.

The overwhelming majority of the banks, both national and state, which reopened last spring, are in sound condition and have been brought within the protection of federal insurance. In the case of those banks which were not permitted to reopen, nearly $600 million of frozen deposits are being restored to the depositors through the assistance of the national government.

We have made great strides toward the objectives of the National Industrial Recovery Act, for not only have several millions of our unemployed been restored to work, but industry is organizing itself with a greater understanding that reasonable profits can be earned while at the same time protection can be assured to guarantee to labor adequate pay and proper conditions of work. Child labor is abolished. Uniform standards of hours and wages apply today to 95 percent of industrial employment within the field of the National Industrial Recovery Act. We seek the definite end of preventing combinations in furtherance of monopoly and in restraint of trade, while at the same time we seek to prevent ruinous rivalries within industrial groups which in many cases resemble the gang wars of the underworld and in which the real victim in every case is the public itself. . . .

You recognized last spring that the most serious part of the debt burden affected those who stood in danger of losing their farms and their homes. I am glad to tell you that refinancing in both of these cases is proceeding with good success and in all probability within the financial limits set by the Congress.

But agriculture had suffered from more than its debts. Actual experience with the operation of the Agricultural Adjustment Act leads to my belief that thus far the experiment of seeking a balance between production and consumption is succeeding and has made progress entirely in line with reasonable expectations toward the restoration of farm prices to parity. I continue in my conviction that industrial progress and prosperity can only be attained by bringing the purchasing power of that portion of our population which in one form or another is dependent upon agriculture up to a level which will restore a proper balance between every section of the country and between every form of work.

In this field, through carefully planned flood control, power development, and land-use policies in the Tennessee Valley and in other great watersheds, we are seeking the elimination of waste, the removal of poor lands from agriculture, and the encouragement of small local industries, thus furthering this principle of a better balanced national life. . . .

I cannot, unfortunately, present to you a picture of complete optimism regarding world affairs.

The delegation representing the United States has worked in close cooperation with the other American republics assembled at Montevideo to make that conference an outstanding success. We have, I hope, made it clear to our neighbors that we seek with them future avoidance of territorial expansion and of interference by one nation in the internal affairs of another. Furthermore, all of us are seeking the restoration of commerce in ways which will preclude the building up of large favorable trade balances by any one nation at the expense of trade debits on the part of other nations.

In other parts of the world, however, fear of immediate or future aggression and with it the spending of vast sums on armament and the continued building up of defensive trade barriers prevent any great progress in peace or trade agreements. I have made it clear that the United States cannot take part in political arrangements in Europe but that we stand ready to cooperate at any time in practicable measures on a world basis looking to immediate reduction of armaments and the lowering of the barriers against commerce.

I expect to report to you later in regard to debts owed the government and people of this country by the governments and peoples of other countries. Several nations, acknowledging the debt, have paid in small part; other nations have failed to pay.

One nation—Finland—has paid the installments due this country in full.

Returning to home problems, we have been shocked by many notorious examples of injuries done our citizens by persons or groups who have been living off their neighbors by the use of methods either unethical or criminal.

In the first category—a field which does not involve violations of the letter of our laws—practices have been brought to light which have shocked those who believe that we were in the past generation raising the ethical standards of business. They call for stringent preventive or regulatory measures. I am speaking of those individuals who have evaded the spirit and purpose of our tax laws, of those high officials of banks or corporations who have grown rich at the expense of their stockholders or the public, of those reckless speculators with their own or other people's money whose operations have injured the values of the farmers' crops and the savings of the poor.

In the other category, crimes of organized banditry, cold-blooded shooting, lynching, and kidnapping have threatened our security.

These violations of ethics and these violations of law call on the strong arm of government for their immediate suppression; they call also on the country for an aroused public opinion.

The adoption of the Twenty-first Amendment should give material aid to the elimination of those new forms of crime which came from the illegal traffic in liquor.

I shall continue to regard it as my duty to use whatever means may be necessary to supplement state, local, and private agencies for the relief of suffering caused by unemployment. With respect to this question, I have recognized the dangers inherent in the direct giving of relief and have sought the means to provide not mere relief, but the opportunity for useful and remunerative work. We shall, in the process of recovery, seek to move as rapidly as possible from direct relief to publicly supported work and from that to the rapid restoration of private employment.

It is to the eternal credit of the American people that this tremendous readjustment of our national life is being accomplished peacefully, without serious dislocation, with only a minimum of injustice, and with a great, willing spirit of cooperation throughout the country.

Disorder is not an American habit. Self-help and self-control are the essence of the American tradition—not of necessity the form of that tradition, but its spirit. The program itself comes from the American people. . . .

We have plowed the furrow and planted the good seed; the hard beginning is over. If we would reap the full harvest, we must cultivate the soil where this good seed is sprouting and the plant is reaching up to mature growth.

A final personal word. I know that each of you will appreciate that I am speaking no mere politeness when I assure you how much I value the fine relationship that we have shared during these months of hard and incessant work. Out of these friendly contacts we are, fortunately, building a strong and permanent tie between the legislative and executive branches of the government. The letter of the Constitution wisely declared a separation, but the impulse of common purpose declares a union. In this spirit we join once more in serving the American people.

Address to the Conference on the Mobilization for Human Needs

September 28, 1934

I am happy that for the second time the Conference on the Mobilization for Human Needs comes here to the White House. In doing this you are emphasizing with me the national character of our common task. I like to feel that I share the responsibility with all of you who are here representing every part of the country.

Your work in the past has been of such outstanding success that I am confident that this year you will achieve an all-time record.

Last year, when I had the privilege of speaking to you, I emphasized the simple fact that the responsibility of the individual and of the family for the well-being of their neighbors must never cease. If we go back in our own history to those earliest days of the white man in America, with those first winters of suffering in Jamestown and at Plymouth, we know it has been the American habit from that time on continuously to render aid to those who need it. Through the centuries, as the first struggling villages developed into communities and cities and counties and states, destitution and want of every description have been cared for, in the first instance by community help, and in the last instance as well.

With the enormous growth of population we have had, with the complexities of the past generation, community efforts have now been supplemented by the formation of great national organizations. These organizations are designed to coordinate and stimulate local groups which are striving not only to take care of those in need but also to stimulate better conditions of health, of child welfare, of mental hygiene, of recreation, and to attain all those many other splendid objectives which are part and parcel of our national life today.

The mere reading of the names of the organizations that are working solidly behind this great task is enough to make this country realize the unity of purpose, the solidarity, behind what we are doing. It is right, I think, for us to emphasize that the American family must be the unit which engages our greatest interest and concern. With this we must stress once more the task of each community to assist in maintaining and building up that family unit.

No thinking or experienced person insists today that the responsibility of the community shall be eliminated by passing this great and humane task on to any central body at the seat of federal government. You and I know that it has been with reluctance and only because we have realized the imperative need for additional help that the federal government has been compelled to undertake the task of supplementing the more normal methods which have been in use during all the preceding generations.

I repeat what I told you last year because it is something that is a fundamental of our present-day civilization: that the primary responsibility for community needs rests upon the community itself. That if every effort has been used by any given community and has proven insufficient, then it is the duty of the state to supplement, with the resources of the state, the additional needs up to the limit of the power of the state. And that, finally, and only finally, it is only when both of these efforts, taken together, have proven insufficient that the federal government has any duty to add its resources to the common cause.

It is inevitable, of course, that in carrying on relief—whether in the form of work relief or home relief—in an area that includes every state, every county, and every city in the Union, local inefficiency is bound to exist in some instances. It is very definitely your task, and mine, to see to it that during the coming winter there shall be increased vigilance in every locality, vigilance against the giving of relief or of aid of any kind except to those who definitely and clearly need it and are entitled to it.

In this great emergency system we are establishing, with each passing month, a greater degree of efficiency, and we are eliminating many of the evils which of necessity attended our first efforts of over a year ago. The trained workers who belong to the many organizations represented in this conference have an opportunity and a duty to see to it, first of all, that destitution is relieved and, secondly, that no family and no individual shall receive public assistance if that individual or that family does not deserve it.

Your work and the work of local, state, and federal agencies are so closely associated that your success is very vital to the success of government itself. I am confident that the people of this country, in each and every community, will understand the true importance of cooperating in this great Mobilization for Human Needs.

I always like to emphasize the word *privilege* rather than the word *duty;* for it is clearly the privilege of the individual American to bear his personal share in a work which must be kept personal insofar as it is possible to make it so. It is that personal appeal, that personal service, which has carried us through all these trying years. A unity of effort for a little while longer will, I am confident, bring national success to our nationally unified efforts to bring Old Man Depression to the point where we can finally master and destroy him.

The church groups and the social groups organized on private lines, whether they act separately or jointly through Community Chests, or in any other way, are an essential part of the structure of our life. The American people believe in you, believe in the work you are doing. The American people support your fine objectives. That support will attend again this year the excellent enterprise you are launching today.

SECOND ANNUAL
MESSAGE TO CONGRESS

January 4, 1935

Mr. President, Mr. Speaker, Members of the Senate and of the House of Representatives: The Constitution wisely provides that the chief executive shall report to the Congress on the state of the Union, for through you, the chosen legislative representatives, our citizens everywhere may fairly judge the progress of our governing. I am confident that today, in the light of the events of the past two years, you do not consider it merely a trite phrase when I tell you that I am truly glad to greet you and that I look forward to common counsel, to useful cooperation, and to genuine friendships between us.

We have undertaken a new order of things; yet we progress to it under the framework and in the spirit and intent of the American Constitution. We have proceeded throughout the nation a measurable distance on the road toward this new order. Materially, I can report to you substantial benefits to our agricultural population, increased industrial activity, and profits to our merchants. Of equal moment, there is evident a restoration of that spirit of confidence and faith which marks the American character. Let him who for speculative profit or partisan purpose, without just warrant, would seek to disturb or dispel this assurance take heed before he assumes responsibility for any act which slows our onward steps.

Throughout the world, change is the order of the day. In every nation economic problems, long in the making, have brought crises of many kinds for which the masters of old practice and theory were unprepared. In most nations social justice, no longer a distant ideal, has become a definite goal, and ancient governments are beginning to heed the call.

Thus, the American people do not stand alone in the world

in their desire for change. We seek it through tested liberal traditions, through processes which retain all of the deep essentials of that republican form of representative government first given to a troubled world by the United States. . . .

We find our population suffering from old inequalities, little changed by past sporadic remedies. In spite of our efforts and in spite of our talk, we have not weeded out the overprivileged and we have not effectively lifted up the underprivileged. Both of these manifestations of injustice have retarded happiness. No wise man has any intention of destroying what is known as the profit motive; because by the profit motive we mean the right by work to earn a decent livelihood for ourselves and for our families.

We have, however, a clear mandate from the people, that Americans must forswear that conception of the acquisition of wealth which, through excessive profits, creates undue private power over private affairs and, to our misfortune, over public affairs as well. In building toward this end we do not destroy ambition, nor do we seek to divide our wealth into equal shares on stated occasions. We continue to recognize the greater ability of some to earn more than others. But we do assert that the ambition of the individual to obtain for him and his a proper security, a reasonable leisure, and a decent living throughout life is an ambition to be preferred to the appetite for great wealth and great power.

I recall to your attention my message to the Congress last June in which I said: "Among our objectives I place the security of the men, women, and children of the nation first." That remains our first and continuing task; and in a very real sense every major legislative enactment of this Congress should be a component part of it.

In defining immediate factors which enter into our quest, I have spoken to the Congress and the people of three great divisions:

1. The security of a livelihood through the better use of the national resources of the land in which we live.

2. The security against the major hazards and vicissitudes of life.

3. The security of decent homes.

I am now ready to submit to the Congress a broad program designed ultimately to establish all three of these factors of security—a program which because of many lost years will take many future years to fulfill.

A study of our national resources, more comprehensive than any previously made, shows the vast amount of necessary and practicable work which needs to be done for the development and preservation of our natural wealth for the enjoyment and advantage of our people in generations to come. The sound use of land and water is far more comprehensive than the mere planting of trees, building of dams, distributing of electricity, or retirement of submarginal land. It recognizes that stranded populations, either in the country or the city, cannot have security under the conditions that now surround them.

To this end we are ready to begin to meet this problem— the intelligent care of population throughout our nation, in accordance with an intelligent distribution of the means of livelihood for that population. A definite program for putting people to work, of which I shall speak in a moment, is a component part of this greater program of security of livelihood through the better use of our national resources.

Closely related to the broad problem of livelihood is that of security against the major hazards of life. Here also, a comprehensive survey of what has been attempted or accomplished in many nations and in many states proves to me that the time has come for action by the national government. I shall send to you, in a few days, definite recommendations based on these studies. These recommendations will cover the broad subjects of unemployment insurance and old-age insurance, of benefits for children, for mothers, for the handicapped, for maternity care, and for other aspects of dependency and illness where a beginning can now be made.

The third factor—better homes for our people—has also

been the subject of experimentation and study. Here, too, the first practical steps can be made through the proposals which I shall suggest in relation to giving work to the unemployed. . . .

The first objectives of emergency legislation of 1933 were to relieve destitution, to make it possible for industry to operate in a more rational and orderly fashion, and to put behind industrial recovery the impulse of large expenditures in government undertakings. The purpose of the National Industrial Recovery Act to provide work for more people succeeded in a substantial manner within the first few months of its life, and the act has continued to maintain employment gains and greatly improved working conditions in industry. . . .

More than two billions of dollars have also been expended in direct relief to the destitute. Local agencies of necessity determined the recipients of this form of relief. With inevitable exceptions the funds were spent by them with reasonable efficiency and as a result actual want of food and clothing in the great majority of cases has been overcome.

But the stark fact before us is that great numbers still remain unemployed.

A large proportion of these unemployed and their dependents have been forced on the relief rolls. The burden on the federal government has grown with great rapidity. We have here a human as well as an economic problem. When humane considerations are concerned, Americans give them precedence. The lessons of history, confirmed by the evidence immediately before me, show conclusively that continued dependence upon relief induces a spiritual and moral disintegration fundamentally destructive to the national fiber. To dole out relief in this way is to administer a narcotic, a subtle destroyer of the human spirit. It is inimical to the dictates of sound policy. It is in violation of the traditions of America. Work must be found for able-bodied but destitute workers.

The federal government must and shall quit this business of relief.

I am not willing that the vitality of our people be further sapped by the giving of cash, of market baskets, of a few hours of weekly work cutting grass, raking leaves, or picking up papers in the public parks. We must preserve not only the bodies of the unemployed from destitution but also their self-respect, their self-reliance and courage and determination. This decision brings me to the problem of what the government should do with approximately five million unemployed now on the relief rolls.

About one million and a half of these belong to the group which in the past was dependent upon local welfare efforts. Most of them are unable for one reason or another to maintain themselves independently—for the most part, through no fault of their own. Such people, in the days before the Great Depression, were cared for by local efforts—by states, by counties, by towns, by cities, by churches, and by private welfare agencies. It is my thought that in the future they must be cared for as they were before. . . .

The security legislation which I shall propose to the Congress will, I am confident, be of assistance to local effort in the care of this type of cases. Local responsibility can and will be resumed, for, after all, common sense tells us that the wealth necessary for this task existed and still exists in the local community, and the dictates of sound administration require that this responsibility be in the first instance a local one.

There are, however, an additional three and one-half million employable people who are on relief. With them the problem is different and the responsibility is different. This group was the victim of a nationwide depression caused by conditions which were not local but national. The federal government is the only governmental agency with sufficient power and credit to meet this situation. We have assumed this task and we shall not shrink from it in the future. It is a duty dictated by every intelligent consideration of national policy to ask you to make it possible for the United States to give employment to all of these three and one-half million employable people now on relief, pending their absorption in a rising tide of private employment.

It is my thought that with the exception of certain of the normal public building operations of the government, all emergency public works shall be united in a single new and greatly enlarged plan.

With the establishment of this new system we can supersede the Federal Emergency Relief Administration with a coordinated authority which will be charged with the orderly liquidation of our present relief activities and the substitution of a national chart for the giving of work.

This new program of emergency public employment should be governed by a number of practical principles.

1. All work undertaken should be useful—not just for a day, or a year, but useful in the sense that it affords permanent improvement in living conditions or that it creates future new wealth for the nation.

2. Compensation on emergency public projects should be in the form of security payments which should be larger than the amount now received as a relief dole, but at the same time not so large as to encourage the rejection of opportunities for private employment or the leaving of private employment to engage in government work.

3. Projects should be undertaken on which a large percentage of direct labor can be used.

4. Preference should be given to those projects which will be self-liquidating in the sense that there is a reasonable expectation that the government will get its money back at some future time.

5. The projects undertaken should be selected and planned so as to compete as little as possible with private enterprises. This suggests that if it were not for the necessity of giving useful work to the unemployed now on relief, these projects in most instances would not now be undertaken.

6. The planning of projects would seek to assure work during the coming fiscal year to the individuals now on relief, or

until such time as private employment is available. In order to make adjustment to increasing private employment, work should be planned with a view to tapering it off in proportion to the speed with which the emergency workers are offered positions with private employers.

7. Effort should be made to locate projects where they will serve the greatest unemployment needs as shown by present relief rolls, and the broad program of the National Resources Board should be freely used for guidance in selection. Our ultimate objective being the enrichment of human lives, the government has the primary duty to use its emergency expenditures as much as possible to serve those who cannot secure the advantages of private capital. . . .

The work itself will cover a wide field including clearance of slums, which for adequate reasons cannot be undertaken by private capital; in rural housing of several kinds, where, again, private capital is unable to function; in rural electrification; in the reforestation of the great watersheds of the nation; in an intensified program to prevent soil erosion and to reclaim blighted areas; in improving existing road systems and in constructing national highways designed to handle modern traffic; in the elimination of grade crossings; in the extension and enlargement of the successful work of the Civilian Conservation Corps; in nonfederal works, mostly self-liquidating and highly useful to local divisions of government; and on many other projects which the nation needs and cannot afford to neglect. . . .

We have already begun to feel the bracing effect upon our economic system of a restored agriculture. The hundreds of millions of additional income that farmers are receiving are finding their way into the channels of trade. The farmers' share of the national income is slowly rising. The economic facts justify the widespread opinion of those engaged in agriculture that our provisions for maintaining a balanced production give at this time the most adequate remedy for an old and vexing problem. For the present, and especially in view of abnormal world conditions, agricultural adjustment with certain necessary improvements in methods should continue. . . .

I cannot with candor tell you that general international relationships outside the borders of the United States are improved. On the surface of things many old jealousies are resurrected, old passions aroused; new strivings for armament and power, in more than one land, rear their ugly heads. I hope that calm counsel and constructive leadership will provide the steadying influence and the time necessary for the coming of new and more practical forms of representative government throughout the world wherein privilege and power will occupy a lesser place and world welfare a greater.

I believe, however, that our own peaceful and neighborly attitude toward other nations is coming to be understood and appreciated. The maintenance of international peace is a matter in which we are deeply and unselfishly concerned. Evidence of our persistent and undeniable desire to prevent armed conflict has recently been more than once afforded. . . .

The ledger of the past year shows many more gains than losses. Let us not forget that, in addition to saving millions from utter destitution, child labor has been for the moment outlawed, thousands of homes saved to their owners, and most important of all, the morale of the nation has been restored. Viewing the year 1934 as a whole, you and I can agree that we have a generous measure of reasons for giving thanks.

It is not empty optimism that moves me to a strong hope in the coming year. We can, if we will, make 1935 a genuine period of good feeling, sustained by a sense of purposeful progress. Beyond the material recovery, I sense a spiritual recovery as well. The people of America are turning as never before to those permanent values that are not limited to the physical objectives of life. There are growing signs of this on every hand. In the face of these spiritual impulses we are sensible of the Divine Providence to which nations turn now, as always, for guidance and fostering care.

MESSAGE TO CONGRESS ON SOCIAL SECURITY

January 17, 1935

In addressing you on June 8, 1934, I summarized the main objectives of our American program. Among these was, and is, the security of the men, women, and children of the nation against certain hazards and vicissitudes of life. This purpose is an essential part of our task. In my Annual Message to you I promised to submit a definite program of action. This I do in the form of a report to me by a Committee on Economic Security, appointed by me for the purpose of surveying the field and of recommending the basis of legislation.

I am gratified with the work of this committee and of those who have helped it: the Technical Board on Economic Security drawn from various departments of the government, the Advisory Council on Economic Security, consisting of informed and public-spirited private citizens, and a number of other advisory groups, including a committee on actuarial consultants, a medical advisory board, a dental advisory committee, a hospital advisory committee, a public-health advisory committee, a child-welfare committee, and an advisory committee on employment relief. All of those who participated in this notable task of planning this major legislative proposal are ready and willing, at any time, to consult with and assist in any way the appropriate congressional committees and members, with respect to detailed aspects.

It is my best judgment that this legislation should be brought forward with a minimum of delay. Federal action is necessary to, and conditioned upon, the action of states. Forty-four legislatures are meeting or will meet soon. In order that the necessary state action may be taken promptly it is important that the federal government proceed speedily.

The detailed report of the committee sets forth a series of proposals that will appeal to the sound sense of the American people. It has not attempted the impossible, nor has it failed to exercise sound caution and consideration of all of the factors concerned: the national credit, the rights and responsibilities of states, the capacity of industry to assume financial responsibilities, and the fundamental necessity of proceeding in a manner that will merit the enthusiastic support of citizens of all sorts.

It is overwhelmingly important to avoid any danger of permanently discrediting the sound and necessary policy of federal legislation for economic security by attempting to apply it on too ambitious a scale before actual experience has provided guidance for the permanently safe direction of such efforts. The place of such a fundamental in our future civilization is too precious to be jeopardized now by extravagant action. It is a sound idea—a sound ideal. Most of the other advanced countries of the world have already adopted it and their experience affords the knowledge that social insurance can be made a sound and workable project.

Three principles should be observed in legislation on this subject. First, the system adopted, except for the money necessary to initiate it, should be self-sustaining in the sense that funds for the payment of insurance benefits should not come from the proceeds of general taxation. Second, excepting in old-age insurance, actual management should be left to the states subject to standards established by the federal government. Third, sound financial management of the funds and the reserves, and protection of the credit structure of the nation should be assured by retaining federal control over all funds through trustees in the Treasury of the United States.

At this time, I recommend the following types of legislation looking to economic security:

1. Unemployment compensation.

2. Old-age benefits, including compulsory and voluntary annuities.

3. Federal aid to dependent children through grants to states for the support of existing mothers' pension systems and for services for the protection and care of homeless, neglected, dependent, and crippled children.

4. Additional federal aid to state and local public-health agencies and the strengthening of the Federal Public Health Service. I am not at this time recommending the adoption of so-called health insurance, although groups representing the medical profession are cooperating with the federal government in the further study of the subject and definite progress is being made.

With respect to unemployment compensation, I have concluded that the most practical proposal is the levy of a uniform federal payroll tax, 90 percent of which should be allowed as an offset to employers contributing under a compulsory state unemployment compensation act. The purpose of this is to afford a requirement of a reasonably uniform character for all states cooperating with the federal government and to promote and encourage the passage of unemployment compensation laws in the states. The 10 percent not thus offset should be used to cover the costs of federal and state administration of this broad system. Thus, states will largely administer unemployment compensation, assisted and guided by the federal government. An unemployment compensation system should be constructed in such a way as to afford every practicable aid and incentive toward the larger purpose of employment stabilization. This can be helped by the intelligent planning of both public and private employment. It also can be helped by correlating the system with public employment so that a person who has exhausted his benefits may be eligible for some form of public work as is recommended in this report. Moreover, in order to encourage the stabilization of private employment, federal legislation should not foreclose the states from establishing means for inducing industries to afford an even greater stabilization of employment.

In the important field of security for our old people, it seems necessary to adopt three principles. First, noncontributory old-age pensions for those who are now too old to build up their own insurance. It is, of course, clear that for perhaps thirty years to come funds will have to be provided by the states and the federal government to meet these pensions. Second, compulsory contributory annuities which in time will establish a self-supporting system for those now young and for future generations. Third, voluntary contributory annuities by which individual initiative can increase the annual amounts received in old age. It is proposed that the federal government assume one-half of the cost of the old-age pension plan, which ought ultimately to be supplanted by self-supporting annuity plans.

The amount necessary at this time for the initiation of unemployment compensation, old-age security, children's aid, and the promotion of public health, as outlined in the report of the Committee on Economic Security, is approximately $100 million.

The establishment of sound means toward a greater future economic security of the American people is dictated by a prudent consideration of the hazards involved in our national life. No one can guarantee this country against the dangers of future depressions but we can reduce these dangers. We can eliminate many of the factors that cause economic depressions, and we can provide the means of mitigating their results. This plan for economic security is at once a measure of prevention and a method of alleviation.

We pay now for the dreadful consequence of economic insecurity—and dearly. This plan presents a more equitable and infinitely less expensive means of meeting these costs. We cannot afford to neglect the plain duty before us. I strongly recommend action to attain the objectives sought in this report.

FIRESIDE CHAT ON THE WORKS RELIEF PROGRAM

April 28, 1935

Since my Annual Message to the Congress on January 4 last, I have not addressed the general public over the air. In the many weeks since that time the Congress has devoted itself to the arduous task of formulating legislation necessary to the country's welfare. It has made and is making distinct progress.

Before I come to any of the specific measures, however, I want to leave in your minds one clear fact. The administration and the Congress are not proceeding in any haphazard fashion in this task of government. Each of our steps has a definite relationship to every other step. The job of creating a program for the nation's welfare is, in some respects, like the building of a ship. At different points on the coast where I often visit they build great seagoing ships. When one of these ships is under construction and the steel frames have been set in the keel, it is difficult for a person who does not know ships to tell how it will finally look when it is sailing the high seas.

It may seem confused to some, but out of the multitude of detailed parts that go into the making of the structure, the creation of a useful instrument for man ultimately comes. It is that way with the making of a national policy. The objective of the nation has greatly changed in three years. Before that time individual self-interest and group selfishness were paramount in public thinking. The general good was at a discount.

Three years of hard thinking have changed the picture. More and more people, because of clearer thinking and a better understanding, are considering the whole rather than a mere part relating to one section, or to one crop, or to one industry, or to an individual private occupation. That is a tremendous gain for the principles of democracy. The overwhelming majority of people in this country know how to sift the wheat from the chaff in what they hear and what they read. They know that the process of the constructive rebuilding of America cannot be done in a day or a year, but that it is being done in spite of the few who seek to confuse them and to profit by their confusion. Americans as a whole are feeling a lot better—a lot more cheerful than for many, many years.

The most difficult place in the world to get a clear and open perspective of the country as a whole is Washington. I am reminded sometimes of what President Wilson once said: "So many people come to Washington who know things that are not so, and so few people who know what the people of the United States are thinking about." That is why I occasionally leave this scene of action for a few days to go fishing or back home to Hyde Park so that I can have a chance to think quietly about the country as a whole. "To get away from the trees," as they say, "and to look at the whole forest." This duty of seeing the country in a long-range perspective is one which, in a very special manner, attaches to this office to which you have chosen me. Did you ever stop to think that there are, after all, only two positions in the nation that are filled by the vote of all of the voters—the president and the vice president? That makes it particularly necessary for the vice president and for me to conceive of our duty toward the entire country. Tonight, therefore, I speak to and of the American people as a whole.

My most immediate concern is in carrying out the purposes of the great work program just enacted by the Congress. Its first objective is to put men and women now on the relief rolls to work and, incidentally, to assist materially in our already unmistakable march toward recovery. I shall not confuse my discussion by a multitude of figures. So many figures are quoted to prove so many things. Sometimes it depends upon what paper you read and what broadcast you hear. Therefore, let us keep our minds on two or three simple, essential facts in connection with this problem of unemployment. It is true that while business and industry are definitely better, our relief rolls are still too large. However, for the first time in five years the relief rolls have declined instead of increased during the winter months. They are still declining. The simple fact is that many millions more people have private work today than two years ago today or one year ago today and every day that passes offers more chances to work for those who want to work. In spite of the fact that unemployment remains a serious problem here as in every other nation, we have come to recognize the possibility and the necessity of certain helpful remedial measures. These measures are of two kinds. The first is to make provisions intended to relieve, to minimize, and to prevent future unemployment; the second is to establish the practical means to help those who are unemployed in this present emergency. Our Social Security legislation is an attempt to answer the first of these questions; our Works Relief program, the second.

The program for Social Security now pending before the Congress is a necessary part of the future unemployment policy of the government. While our present and projected expenditures for work relief are wholly within the reasonable limits of our national credit resources, it is obvious that we cannot continue to create governmental deficits for that purpose year after year. We must begin now to make provision for the future. That is why our Social Security program is an important part of the complete picture. It proposes, by means of old-age pensions, to help those who have reached the age of retirement to give up their jobs and thus give to the younger generation greater opportunities for work and to give to all a feeling of security as they look toward old age.

The unemployment-insurance part of the legislation will not only help to guard the individual in future periods of layoff against dependence upon relief, but it will, by sustaining purchasing power, cushion the shock of economic distress. Another helpful feature of unemployment insurance is the incentive it will give to employers to plan more carefully in order that unemployment may be prevented by the stabilizing of employment itself.

Provisions for Social Security, however, are protections for the future. Our responsibility for the immediate necessities of the unemployed has been met by the Congress through the most comprehensive work plan in the history of the nation. Our problem is to put to work three and one-half million employable persons now on the relief rolls. It is a problem quite as much for private industry as for the government.

We are losing no time getting the government's vast Works Relief program under way and we have every reason to believe that it should be in full swing by autumn. In directing it, I shall recognize six fundamental principles:

1. The projects should be useful.

2. Projects shall be of a nature that a considerable proportion of the money spent will go into wages for labor.

3. Projects will be sought which promise ultimate return to the federal Treasury of a considerable proportion of the costs.

4. Funds allotted for each project should be actually and promptly spent and not held over until later years.

5. In all cases projects must be of a character to give employment to those on the relief rolls.

6. Projects will be allocated to localities or relief areas in relation to the number of workers on relief rolls in those areas.

I next want to make it clear exactly how we shall direct the work.

1. I have set up a Division of Applications and Information to which all proposals for the expenditure of money must go for preliminary study and consideration.

2. After the Division of Applications and Information has sifted these projects, they will be sent to an Allotment Division composed of representatives of the more important governmental agencies charged with carrying on work relief projects. The group will also include representatives of cities, and of labor, farming, banking, and industry. This Allotment Division will

consider all of the recommendations submitted to it and such projects as they approve will be next submitted to the president who under the act is required to make final allocations.

3. The next step will be to notify the proper government agency in whose field the project falls, and also to notify another agency which I am creating—a Progress Division. This division will have the duty of coordinating the purchase of materials and supplies and of making certain that people who are employed will be taken from the relief rolls. It will also have the responsibility of determining work payments in various localities, of making full use of existing employment services, and of assisting people engaged in relief work to move as rapidly as possible back into private employment when such employment is available. Moreover, this division will be charged with keeping projects moving on schedule.

4. I have felt it to be essentially wise and prudent to avoid, so far as possible, the creation of new governmental machinery for supervising this work. The national government now has at least sixty different agencies with the staff and the experience and the competence necessary to carry on the 250 or 300 kinds of work that will be undertaken. These agencies, therefore, will simply be doing on a somewhat enlarged scale the same sort of things that they have been doing. This will make certain that the largest possible portion of the funds allotted will be spent for actually creating new work and not for building up expensive overhead organizations here in Washington.

For many months preparations have been under way. The allotment of funds for desirable projects has already begun. The key men for the major responsibilities of this great task already have been selected. I well realize that the country is expecting before this year is out to see the "dirt fly," as they say, in carrying on the work, and I assure my fellow citizens that no energy will be spared in using these funds effectively to make a major attack upon the problem of unemployment.

Our responsibility is to all of the people in this country. This is a great national crusade to destroy enforced idleness which is an enemy of the human spirit generated by this depression. Our attack upon these enemies must be without stint and without discrimination. No sectional, no political distinctions can be permitted.

It must, however, be recognized that when an enterprise of this character is extended over more than three thousand counties throughout the nation, there may be occasional instances of inefficiency, bad management, or misuse of funds. When cases of this kind occur, there will be those, of course, who will try to tell you that the exceptional failure is characteristic of the entire endeavor. It should be remembered that in every big job there are some imperfections. There are chiselers in every walk of life, there are those in every industry who are guilty of unfair practices; every profession has its black sheep, but long experience in government has taught me that the exceptional instances of wrongdoing in government are probably less numerous than in almost every other line of endeavor. The most effective means of preventing such evils in this Works Relief program will be the eternal vigilance of the American people themselves. I call upon my fellow citizens everywhere to cooperate with me in making this the most efficient and the cleanest example of public enterprise the world has ever seen.

It is time to provide a smashing answer for those cynical men who say that a democracy cannot be honest and efficient. If you will help, this can be done. I, therefore, hope you will watch the work in every corner of this nation. Feel free to criticize. Tell me of instances where work can be done better, or where improper practices prevail. Neither you nor I want criticism conceived in a purely fault-finding or partisan spirit, but I am jealous of the right of every citizen to call to the attention of his or her government examples of how the public money can be more effectively spent for the benefit of the American people.

I now come, my friends, to a part of the remaining business before the Congress. It has under consideration many measures which provide for the rounding out of the program of economic and social reconstruction with which we have been concerned for two years. I can mention only a few of them tonight, but I do not want my mention of specific measures to be interpreted as lack of interest in or disapproval of many other important proposals that are pending.

The National Industrial Recovery Act expires on the sixteenth of June. After careful consideration, I have asked the Congress to extend the life of this useful agency of government. As we have proceeded with the administration of this act, we have found from time to time more and more useful ways of promoting its purposes. No reasonable person wants to abandon our present gains—we must continue to protect children, to enforce minimum wages, to prevent excessive hours, to safeguard, define, and enforce collective bargaining, and, while retaining fair competition, to eliminate, so far as humanly possible, the kinds of unfair practices by selfish minorities which unfortunately did more than anything else to bring about the recent collapse of industries.

There is likewise pending before the Congress legislation to provide for the elimination of unnecessary holding companies in the public utility field.

I consider this legislation a positive recovery measure. Power production in this country is virtually back to the 1929 peak. The operating companies in the gas and electric utility field are by and large in good condition. But under holding company domination the utility industry has long been hopelessly at war within itself and with public sentiment. By far the greater part of the general decline in utility securities had occurred before I was inaugurated. The absentee management of unnecessary holding company control has lost touch with, and has lost the sympathy of, the communities it pretends to serve. Even more significantly it has given the country as a whole an uneasy apprehension of overconcentrated economic power.

A business that loses the confidence of its customers and the goodwill of the public cannot long continue to be a good risk for the investor. This legislation will serve the investor by ending the conditions which have caused that lack of confidence and goodwill. It will put the public utility operating industry on a sound basis for the future, both in its public relations and in its internal relations.

This legislation will not only in the long run result in providing lower electric and gas rates to the consumer but it will protect the actual value and earning power of properties now owned by thousands of investors who have little protection under the old laws against what used to be called frenzied finance. It will not destroy values.

Not only business recovery, but the general economic recovery of the nation will be greatly stimulated by the enactment of legislation designed to improve the status of our transportation agencies. There is need for legislation for the regulation of interstate transportation by buses and trucks, for the regulation of transportation by water, for the strengthening of our Merchant Marine and Air Transport, for the strengthening of the Interstate Commerce Commission to enable it to carry out a rounded conception of the national transportation system in which the benefits of private ownership are retained while the public stake in these important services is protected by the public's government.

Finally, the reestablishment of public confidence in the banks of the nation is one of the most hopeful results of our efforts as a nation to reestablish public confidence in private banking. We all know that private banking actually exists by virtue of the permission of and regulation by the people as a whole, speaking through their government. Wise public policy, however, requires not only that banking be safe but that its resources be most fully utilized in the economic life of the country. To this end it was decided more than twenty years ago that the government should assume the responsibility of providing a means by which the credit of the nation might be controlled, not by a few private banking institutions, but by a body with public prestige and authority. The answer to this demand was the Federal Reserve System. Twenty years of experience with this system have justified the efforts made to create it, but these twenty years have shown by experience definite possibilities for improvement. Certain proposals made to amend the Federal Reserve Act deserve prompt and favorable action by the Congress. They are a minimum of wise readjustments of our Federal Reserve System in the light of past experience and present needs.

These measures I have mentioned are, in large part, the program which under my constitutional duty I have recommended to the Congress. They are essential factors in a rounded program for national recovery. They contemplate the enrichment of our national life by a sound and rational ordering of its various elements and wise provisions for the protection of the weak against the strong.

Never since my inauguration in March 1933 have I felt so unmistakably the atmosphere of recovery. But it is more than the recovery of the material basis of our individual lives. It is the recovery of confidence in our democratic processes and institutions. We have survived all of the arduous burdens and the threatening dangers of a great economic calamity. We have in the darkest moments of our national trials retained our faith in our own ability to master our destiny. Fear is vanishing and confidence is growing on every side, faith is being renewed in the vast possibilities of human beings to improve their material and spiritual status through the instrumentality of the democratic form of government. That faith is receiving its just reward. For that we can be thankful to the God who watches over America.

STATEMENT ON SIGNING THE NATIONAL LABOR RELATIONS ACT

July 5, 1935

This act defines, as a part of our substantive law, the right of self-organization of employees in industry for the purpose of collective bargaining, and provides methods by which the government can safeguard that legal right. It establishes a National Labor Relations Board to hear and determine cases in which it is charged that this legal right is abridged or denied, and to hold fair elections to ascertain who are the chosen representatives of employees.

A better relationship between labor and management is the high purpose of this act. By assuring the employees the right of collective bargaining it fosters the development of the employment contract on a sound and equitable basis. By providing an orderly procedure for determining who is entitled to represent the employees, it aims to remove one of the chief causes of wasteful economic strife. By preventing practices which tend to destroy the independence of labor, it seeks, for every worker within its scope, that freedom of choice and action which is justly his.

The National Labor Relations Board will be an independent quasi-judicial body. It should be clearly understood that it will not act as mediator or conciliator in labor disputes. The function of mediation remains, under this act, the duty of the secretary of labor and of the Conciliation Service of the Department of Labor. It is important that the judicial function and the mediation function should not be confused. Compromise, the essence of mediation, has no place in the interpretation and enforcement of the law.

This act, defining rights, the enforcement of which is recognized by the Congress to be necessary as an act of both common justice and economic advance, must not be misinterpreted. It may eventually eliminate one major cause of labor disputes, but it will not stop all labor disputes. It does not cover all industry and labor, but is applicable only when violation of the legal right of independent self-organization would burden or obstruct interstate commerce. Accepted by management, labor, and the public with a sense of sober responsibility and of willing cooperation, however, it should serve as an important step toward the achievement of just and peaceful labor relations in industry.

SPEECH AT BOULDER DAM

Colorado River, Arizona/Nevada, September 30, 1935

Senator Pittman, Secretary Ickes, Governors of the Colorado's States, and You Especially Who Have Built Boulder Dam: This morning I came, I saw, and I was conquered, as everyone would be who sees for the first time this great feat of mankind.

Ten years ago the place where we are gathered was an unpeopled, forbidding desert. In the bottom of a gloomy canyon, whose precipitous walls rose to a height of more than a thousand feet, flowed a turbulent, dangerous river. The mountains on either side of the canyon were difficult of access with neither road nor trail, and their rocks were protected by neither trees nor grass from the blazing heat of the sun. The site of Boulder City was a cactus-covered waste. The transformation wrought here in these years is a twentieth-century marvel.

We are here to celebrate the completion of the greatest dam in the world, rising 726 feet above the bedrock of the river and altering the geography of a whole region; we are here to see the creation of the largest artificial lake in the world—115 miles long, holding enough water, for example, to cover the state of Connecticut to a depth of ten feet; and we are here to see nearing completion a powerhouse which will contain the largest generators and turbines yet installed in this country, machinery that can continuously supply nearly two million horsepower of electric energy.

All these dimensions are superlative. They represent and embody the accumulated engineering knowledge and experience of centuries; and when we behold them it is fitting that we pay tribute to the genius of their designers. We recognize also the energy, resourcefulness, and zeal of the builders, who, under the greatest physical obstacles, have pushed this work forward to completion two years in advance of the contract requirements.

But especially, we express our gratitude to the thousands of workers who gave brain and brawn to this great work of construction.

Beautiful and great as this structure is, it must also be considered in its relationship to the agricultural and industrial development and in its contribution to the health and comfort of the people of America who live in the Southwest.

To divert and distribute the waters of an arid region, so that there shall be security of rights and efficiency in service, is one of the greatest problems of law and of administration to be found in any government. The farms, the cities, the people who live along the many thousands of miles of this river and its tributaries—all of them depend upon the conservation, the regulation, and the equitable division of its ever-changing water supply. What has been accomplished on the Colorado in working out such a scheme of distribution is inspiring to the whole country. Through the cooperation of the states whose people depend upon this river, and of the federal government which is concerned in the general welfare, there is being constructed a system of distributive works and of laws and practices which will insure to the millions of people who now dwell in this basin, and the millions of others who will come to dwell here in future generations, a just, safe, and permanent system of water rights. In devising these policies and the means for putting them into practice, the Bureau of Reclamation of the federal government has taken, and is destined to take in the future, a leading and helpful part. The bureau has been the instrument which gave effect to the legislation introduced in Congress by Senator Hiram Johnson and Congressman Phil Swing.

We know that, as an unregulated river, the Colorado added little of value to the region this dam serves. When in flood the river was a threatening torrent. In the dry months of the year it shrank to a trickling stream. For a generation the people of Imperial Valley had lived in the shadow of disaster from this river which provided their livelihood, and which is the foundation of their hopes for themselves and their children. Every spring they awaited with dread the coming of a flood, and at the end of nearly every summer they feared a shortage of water would destroy their crops.

The gates of these great diversion tunnels were closed here at Boulder Dam last February. In June a great flood came down the river. It came roaring down the canyons of the Colorado, through Grand Canyon, Iceberg and Boulder canyons, but it was caught and safely held behind Boulder Dam.

Last year a drought of unprecedented severity was visited upon the West. The watershed of this Colorado River did not escape. In July the canals of the Imperial Valley went dry. Crop losses in that valley alone totaled $10 million that summer. Had Boulder Dam been completed one year earlier, this loss would have been prevented, because the spring flood would have been stored to furnish a steady water supply for the long dry summer and fall.

Across the San Jacinto Mountains southwest of Boulder Dam, the cities of Southern California are constructing an aqueduct to cost $220 million, which they have raised, for the purpose of carrying the regulated waters of the Colorado River to the Pacific Coast, 259 miles away.

Across the desert and mountains to the west and south run great electric transmission lines by which factory motors, street and household lights, and irrigation pumps will be operated in southern Arizona and California. Part of this power will be used in pumping the water through the aqueduct to supplement the domestic supplies of Los Angeles and surrounding cities.

Navigation of the river from Boulder Dam to the Grand Canyon has been made possible, a 115-mile stretch that has been traversed less than half a dozen times in history. An immense new park has been created for the enjoyment of all our people.

At what cost was this done? Boulder Dam and the power houses together cost a total of $108 million, all of which will be repaid with interest in fifty years under the contracts for sale of the power. Under these contracts, already completed, not only will the cost be repaid, but the way is opened for the provision of needed light and power to the consumer at reduced rates. In the expenditure of the price of Boulder Dam during the depression years work was provided for four thousand men, most of them heads of families, and many thousands more were enabled to earn a livelihood through manufacture of materials and machinery.

And this picture is true on different scales in regard to the thousands of projects undertaken by the federal government, by the states, and by the counties and municipalities in recent years. The overwhelming majority of them are of definite and permanent usefulness.

Throughout our national history we have had a great program of public improvements, and in these past two years all that we have done has been to accelerate that program. We know, too, that the reason for this speeding up was the need of giving relief to several million men and women whose earning capacity had been destroyed by the complexities and lack of thought of the economic system of the past generation.

No sensible person is foolish enough to draw hard and fast classifications as to usefulness or need. Obviously, for instance, this great Boulder Dam warrants universal approval because it will prevent floods and flood damage, because it will irrigate thousands of acres of tillable land, and because it will generate electricity to turn the wheels of many factories and illuminate countless homes. But can we say that a five-foot brushwood dam across the head waters of an arroyo, and costing only a millionth part of Boulder Dam, is an undesirable project or a waste of money? Can we say that the great brick high school, costing $2 million, is a useful expenditure but that a little wooden schoolhouse project, costing five or ten thousand dollars, is a wasteful extravagance? Is it fair to approve a huge city boulevard and, at the same time, disapprove the improvement of a muddy farm-to-market road?

While we do all of this, we give actual work to the unemployed and at the same time we add to the wealth and assets of the nation. These efforts meet with the approval of the people of the nation.

In a little over two years this great national work has accomplished much. We have helped mankind by the works themselves and, at the same time, we have created the necessary purchasing power to throw in the clutch to start the wheels of what we call private industry. Such expenditures on all of these works, great and small, flow out to many beneficiaries; they revive other and more remote industries and businesses. Money is put in circulation. Credit is expanded and the financial and industrial mechanism of America is stimulated to more and more activity. Labor makes wealth. The use of materials makes wealth. To employ workers and materials when private employment has failed is to translate into great national possessions the energy that otherwise would be wasted. Boulder Dam is a splendid symbol of that principle. The mighty waters of the Colorado were running unused to the sea. Today we translate them into a great national possession.

I might go further and suggest to you that use begets use. Such works as this serve as a means of making useful other national possessions. Vast deposits of precious metals are scattered within a short distance of where we stand today. They await the development of cheap power.

These great government power projects will affect not only the development of agriculture and industry and mining in the sections that they serve, but they will also prove useful yardsticks to measure the cost of power throughout the United States. It is my belief that the government should proceed to lay down the first yardstick from this great power plant in the form of a state power line, assisted in its financing by the government, and tapping the wonderful natural resources of southern Nevada. Doubtless the same policy of financial assistance to state authorities can be followed in the development of Nevada's sister state, Arizona, on the other side of the river.

With it all, with work proceeding in every one of the more

than three thousand counties in the United States, and of a vastly greater number of local divisions of government, the actual credit of government agencies is on a stronger and safer basis than at any time in the past six years. Many states have actually improved their financial position in the past two years. Municipal tax receipts are being paid when the taxes fall due, and tax arrearages are steadily declining.

It is a simple fact that government spending is already beginning to show definite signs of its effect on consumer spending; that the putting of people to work by the government has put other people to work through private employment, and that in two years and a half we have come to the point today where private industry must bear the principal responsibility of keeping the processes of greater employment moving forward with accelerated speed.

The people of the United States are proud of Boulder Dam. With the exception of the few who are narrow-visioned, people everywhere on the Atlantic Seaboard, people in the Middle West and the Northwest, people in the South must surely recognize that the national benefits which will be derived from the completion of this project will make themselves felt in every one of the forty-eight states. They know that poverty or distress in a community two thousand miles away may affect them, and equally that prosperity and higher standards of living across a whole continent will help them back home.

Today marks the official completion and dedication of Boulder Dam, the first of four great government regional units. This is an engineering victory of the first order—another great achievement of American resourcefulness, American skill and determination.

That is why I have the right once more to congratulate you who have built Boulder Dam and on behalf of the nation to say to you, "Well done."

Radio Address on the Third Anniversary of the Civilian Conservation Corps

April 17, 1936

To the million and a half young men and war veterans who have been or are today enrolled in the Civilian Conservation Corps camps, I extend greetings on this third anniversary of the establishment of the first CCC camp. Idle through no fault of your own, you were enrolled from city and rural homes and offered an opportunity to engage in healthful, outdoor work on forest, park, and soil-conservation projects of definite practical value to all the people of the nation. The promptness with which you seized the opportunity to engage in honest work, the willingness with which you have performed your daily tasks, and the fine spirit you have shown in winning the respect of the communities in which your camps have been located merit the admiration of the entire country. You and the men who have guided and supervised your efforts have cause to be proud of the record the CCC has made in the development of sturdy manhood and in the initiation and prosecution of a conservation program of unprecedented proportions.

I recall that on July 17, 1933, at a time when the corps was just getting into stride, I predicted that through the CCC we would graduate a fine group of strong young men, trained to self-discipline and willing and proud to work. I did not misjudge the loyalty, the spirit, the industry, or the temper of American youth. Although many of you entered the camps undernourished and discouraged through inability to obtain employment as you came of working age, the hard work, regular hours, the plain, wholesome food, and the outdoor life of the CCC camps brought a quick response in improved morale. As muscles hardened and you became accustomed to outdoor work you grasped the opportunity to learn by practical training on the job and through camp educational facilities. Many of you rose to responsible positions in the camps. Since the corps began, some 1,150,000 of you have been graduated, improved in health, self-disciplined, alert, and eager for the opportunity to make good in any kind of honest employment.

Our records show that the results achieved in the protection and improvement of our timbered domain, in the arrest of soil wastage, in the development of needed recreational areas, in wildlife conservation, and in flood control have been as impressive as the results achieved in the rehabilitation of youth. Through your spirit and industry it has been demonstrated that young men can be put to work in our forests, parks, and fields on projects which benefit both the nation's youth and conservation generally.

Speech Before the 1936 Democratic National Convention

Philadelphia, Pennsylvania, June 27, 1936

A Rendezvous with Destiny

Senator Robinson, Members of the Democratic Convention, My Friends: Here, and in every community throughout the land, we are met at a time of great moment to the future of the nation. It is an occasion to be dedicated to the simple and sincere expression of an attitude toward problems, the determination of which will profoundly affect America.

I come not only as a leader of a party, not only as a candidate for high office, but as one upon whom many critical hours have imposed and still impose a grave responsibility.

For the sympathy, help and confidence with which Americans have sustained me in my task I am grateful. For their loyalty I salute the members of our great party, in and out of political life in every part of the Union. I salute those of other parties, especially those in the Congress of the United States who on so many occasions have put partisanship aside. I thank the governors of the several states, their legislatures, their state and local officials who participated unselfishly and regardless of party in our efforts to achieve recovery and destroy abuses. Above all I thank the millions of Americans who have borne disaster bravely and have dared to smile through the storm.

America will not forget these recent years, will not forget that the rescue was not a mere party task. It was the concern of all of us. In our strength we rose together, rallied our energies together, applied the old rules of common sense, and together survived.

In those days we feared fear. That was why we fought fear. And today, my friends, we have won against the most dangerous of our foes. We have conquered fear.

But I cannot, with candor, tell you that all is well with the world. Clouds of suspicion, tides of ill-will and intolerance gather darkly in many places. In our own land we enjoy indeed a fullness of life greater than that of most nations. But the rush of modern civilization itself has raised for us new difficulties, new problems which must be solved if we are to preserve to the United States the political and economic freedom for which Washington and Jefferson planned and fought.

Philadelphia is a good city in which to write American history. This is fitting ground on which to reaffirm the faith of our fathers; to pledge ourselves to restore to the people a wider freedom; to give to 1936 as the founders gave to 1776—an American way of life.

That very word *freedom,* in itself and of necessity, suggests freedom from some restraining power. In 1776 we sought freedom from the tyranny of a political autocracy—from the eighteenth-century royalists who held special privileges from the crown. It was to perpetuate their privilege that they governed without the consent of the governed; that they denied the right of free assembly and free speech; that they restricted the worship of God; that they put the average man's property and the average man's life in pawn to the mercenaries of dynastic power; that they regimented the people.

And so it was to win freedom from the tyranny of political autocracy that the American Revolution was fought. That victory gave the business of governing into the hands of the average man, who won the right with his neighbors to make and order his own destiny through his own government. Political tyranny was wiped out at Philadelphia on July 4, 1776.

Since that struggle, however, man's inventive genius released new forces in our land which reordered the lives of our people. The age of machinery, of railroads; of steam and electricity; the telegraph and the radio; mass production, mass distribution—all of these combined to bring forward a new civilization and with it a new problem for those who sought to remain free.

For out of this modern civilization economic royalists carved new dynasties. New kingdoms were built upon concentration of control over material things. Through new uses of corporations, banks and securities, new machinery of industry and agriculture, of labor and capital—all undreamed of by the Fathers—the whole structure of modern life was impressed into this royal service.

There was no place among this royalty for our many thousands of small-businessmen and merchants who sought to make a worthy use of the American system of initiative and profit. They were no more free than the worker or the farmer. Even honest and progressive-minded men of wealth, aware of their obligation to their generation, could never know just where they fitted into this dynastic scheme of things.

It was natural and perhaps human that the privileged princes of these new economic dynasties, thirsting for power, reached out for control over government itself. They created a new despotism and wrapped it in the robes of legal sanction. In its service new mercenaries sought to regiment the people, their labor, and their property. And as a result the average man once more confronts the problem that faced the Minute Man.

The hours men and women worked, the wages they received, the conditions of their labor—these had passed beyond the control of the people, and were imposed by this new industrial dictatorship. The savings of the average family, the capital of the small-businessman, the investments set aside for old age —other people's money—these were tools which the new economic royalty used to dig itself in.

Those who tilled the soil no longer reaped the rewards which were their right. The small measure of their gains was decreed by men in distant cities.

Throughout the nation, opportunity was limited by monopoly. Individual initiative was crushed in the cogs of a great machine. The field open for free business was more and more restricted. Private enterprise, indeed, became too private. It became privileged enterprise, not free enterprise.

An old English judge once said: "Necessitous men are not free men." Liberty requires opportunity to make a living—a living decent according to the standard of the time, a living which gives man not only enough to live by, but something to live for.

For too many of us the political equality we once had won was meaningless in the face of economic inequality. A small group had concentrated into their own hands an almost complete control over other people's property, other people's money, other people's labor—other people's lives. For too many of us life was no longer free; liberty no longer real; men could no longer follow the pursuit of happiness.

Against economic tyranny such as this, the American citizen could appeal only to the organized power of government. The collapse of 1929 showed up the despotism for what it was. The election of 1932 was the people's mandate to end it. Under that mandate it is being ended.

The royalists of the economic order have conceded that political freedom was the business of the government, but they have maintained that economic slavery was nobody's business. They granted that the government could protect the citizen in his right to vote, but they denied that the government could do anything to protect the citizen in his right to work and his right to live.

Today we stand committed to the proposition that freedom is no half-and-half affair. If the average citizen is guaranteed equal opportunity in the polling place, he must have equal opportunity in the market place.

These economic royalists complain that we seek to overthrow the institutions of America. What they really complain of is that we seek to take away their power. Our allegiance to American institutions requires the overthrow of this kind of power. In vain they seek to hide behind the flag and the Constitution. In their blindness they forget what the flag and the Constitution stand for. Now, as always, they stand for democracy, not tyranny; for freedom, not subjection; and against a dictatorship by mob rule and the overprivileged alike.

The brave and clear platform adopted by this convention, to which I heartily subscribe, sets forth that government in a modern civilization has certain inescapable obligations to its citizens, among which are protection of the family and the home, the establishment of a democracy of opportunity, and aid to those overtaken by disaster.

But the resolute enemy within our gates is ever ready to beat down our words unless in greater courage we will fight for them.

For more than three years we have fought for them. This convention, in every word and deed, has pledged that that fight will go on.

The defeats and victories of these years have given to us as a people a new understanding of our government and of ourselves. Never since the early days of the New England town meeting have the affairs of government been so widely discussed and so clearly appreciated. It has been brought home to us that the only effective guide for the safety of this most worldly of worlds, the greatest guide of all, is moral principle.

We do not see faith, hope, and charity as unattainable ideals, but we use them as stout supports of a nation fighting the fight for freedom in a modern civilization.

Faith—in the soundness of democracy in the midst of dictatorships.

Hope—renewed because we know so well the progress we have made.

Charity—in the true spirit of that grand old word. For charity literally translated from the original means love, the love that understands, that does not merely share the wealth of the giver, but in true sympathy and wisdom helps men to help themselves.

We seek not merely to make government a mechanical implement, but to give it the vibrant personal character that is the very embodiment of human charity.

We are poor indeed if this nation cannot afford to lift from every recess of American life the dread fear of the unemployed that they are not needed in the world. We cannot afford to accumulate a deficit in the books of human fortitude.

In the place of the palace of privilege we seek to build a temple out of faith and hope and charity.

It is a sobering thing, my friends, to be a servant of this great cause. We try in our daily work to remember that the cause belongs not to us, but to the people. The standard is not in the hands of you and me alone. It is carried by America. We seek daily to profit from experience, to learn to do better as our task proceeds.

Governments can err, presidents do make mistakes, but the immortal Dante tells us that Divine justice weighs the sins of the cold-blooded and the sins of the warm-hearted in different scales.

Better the occasional faults of a government that lives in a spirit of charity than the consistent omissions of a government frozen in the ice of its own indifference.

There is a mysterious cycle in human events. To some generations much is given. Of other generations much is expected. This generation of Americans has a rendezvous with destiny.

In this world of ours in other lands, there are some people, who, in times past, have lived and fought for freedom, and seem to have grown too weary to carry on the fight. They have sold their heritage of freedom for the illusion of a living. They have yielded their democracy.

I believe in my heart that only our success can stir their ancient hope. They begin to know that here in America we are waging a great and successful war. It is not alone a war against want and destitution and economic demoralization. It is more than that; it is a war for the survival of democracy. We are fighting to save a great and precious form of government for ourselves and for the world.

I accept the commission you have tendered me. I join with you. I am enlisted for the duration of the war.

FIRESIDE CHAT ON CONSERVATION OF NATURAL RESOURCES

September 6, 1936

I have been on a journey of husbandry. I went primarily to see at first hand conditions in the drought states, to see how effectively federal and local authorities are taking care of pressing problems of relief and also how they are to work together to defend the people of this country against the effects of future droughts.

I saw drought devastation in nine states.

I talked with families who had lost their wheat crop, lost their corn crop, lost their livestock, lost the water in their well, lost their garden, and come through to the end of the summer without one dollar of cash resources, facing a winter without feed or food—facing a planting season without seed to put in the ground.

That was the extreme case, but there are thousands and thousands of families on western farms who share the same difficulties.

I saw cattlemen who because of lack of grass or lack of winter feed have been compelled to sell all but their breeding stock and will need help to carry even these through the coming winter. I saw livestock kept alive only because water had been brought to them long distances in tank cars. I saw other farm families who have not lost everything but who because they have made only partial crops must have some form of help if they are to continue farming next spring.

I shall never forget the fields of wheat so blasted by heat that they cannot be harvested. I shall never forget field after field of corn stunted, earless and stripped of leaves, for what the sun left the grasshoppers took. I saw brown pastures which would not keep a cow on fifty acres.

Yet I would not have you think for a single minute that there is permanent disaster in these drought regions, or that the picture I saw meant depopulating these areas. No cracked earth, no blistering sun, no burning wind, no grasshoppers are a permanent match for the indomitable American farmers and stockmen and their wives and children who have carried on through desperate days, and inspire us with their self-reliance, their tenacity, and their courage. It was their fathers' task to make homes; it is their task to keep those homes; it is our task to help them win their fight.

First, let me talk for a minute about this autumn and the coming winter. We have the option, in the case of families who need actual subsistence, of putting them on the dole or putting them to work. They do not want to go on the dole and they are one thousand percent right. We agree, therefore, that we must put them to work for a decent wage; and when we reach that decision we kill two birds with one stone, because these families will earn enough by working, not only to subsist themselves, but to buy food for their stock, and seed for next year's planting. Into this scheme of things there fit of course the government lending agencies which next year, as in the past, will help with production loans.

Every governor with whom I have talked is in full accord with this program of providing work for these farm families, just as every governor agrees that the individual states will take care of their unemployables, but that the cost of employing those who are entirely able and willing to work must be borne by the federal government.

If then we know, as we do today, the approximate number of farm families who will require some form of work relief from now on through the winter, we face the question of what kind of work they should do. Let me make it clear that this is not a new question because it has already been answered to a greater or less extent in every one of the drought communities. Beginning in 1934, when we also had serious drought conditions, the state and federal governments cooperated in planning a large number of projects, many of them directly aimed at the alleviation of future drought conditions. In accordance with that program literally thousands of ponds or small reservoirs have been built in order to supply water for stock and to lift the level of the underground water to prevent wells from going dry. Thousands of wells have been drilled or deepened; community lakes have been created and irrigation projects are being pushed.

Water conservation by means such as these is being expanded as a result of this new drought all through the Great Plains area, the western Corn Belt, and in the states that lie further south. In the Middle West water conservation is not so pressing a problem. Here the work projects run more to soil erosion control and the building of farm-to-market roads.

Spending like this is not waste. It would spell future waste if we did not spend for such things now. These emergency work projects provide money to buy food and clothing for the winter; they keep the livestock on the farm; they provide seed for a new crop, and, best of all, they will conserve soil and water in the future in those areas most frequently hit by drought.

If, for example, in some local area the water table continues to drop and the topsoil to blow away, the land values will disappear with the water and the soil. People on the farms will drift into the nearby cities; the cities will have no farm trade and the workers in the city factories and stores will have no jobs. Property values in the cities will decline. If, on the other hand, the farms within that area remain as farms with better water supply and no erosion, the farm population will stay on the land and prosper and the nearby cities will prosper too. Property values will increase instead of disappearing. That is why it is worth our while as a nation to spend money in order to save money.

I have used the argument in relation only to a small area. It holds good, however, in its effect on the nation as a whole.

Every state in the drought area is now doing and always will do business with every state outside it. . . .

The Great Plains Drought Area Committee has given me its preliminary recommendations for a longtime program for that region. Using that report as a basis we are cooperating successfully and in entire accord with the governors and state planning boards. As we get this program into operation the people more and more will be able to maintain themselves securely on the land. That will mean a steady decline in the relief burdens which the federal government and states have had to assume in time of drought; but, more important, it will mean a greater contribution to general national prosperity by these regions which have been hit by drought. It will conserve and improve not only property values, but human values. The people in the drought area do not want to be dependent on federal, state, or any other kind of charity. They want for themselves and their families an opportunity to share fairly by their own efforts in the progress of America.

The farmers of America want a sound national agricultural policy in which a permanent land-use program will have an important place. They want assurance against another year like 1932 when they made good crops but had to sell them for prices that meant ruin just as surely as did the drought. Sound policy must maintain farm prices in good crop years as well as in bad crop years. It must function when we have drought; it must also function when we have bumper crops. . . .

In the drought area people are not afraid to use new methods to meet changes in nature, and to correct mistakes of the past. If overgrazing has injured range lands they are willing to reduce the grazing. If certain wheat lands should be returned to pasture they are willing to cooperate. If trees should be planted as wind-breaks or to stop erosion they will work with us. If terracing or summer fallowing or crop rotation is called for they will carry it out. They stand ready to fit, and not to fight, the ways of nature. . . .

With this fine help we are tiding over the present emergency.

We are going to conserve soil, conserve water, and conserve life. We are going to have longtime defenses against both low prices and drought. We are going to have a farm policy that will serve the national welfare. That is our hope for the future.

There are two reasons why I want to end by talking about reemployment. Tomorrow is Labor Day. The brave spirit with which so many millions of working people are winning their way out of depression deserves respect and admiration. It is like the courage of the farmers in the drought areas.

That is my first reason. The second is that healthy employment conditions stand equally with healthy agricultural conditions as a buttress of national prosperity. Dependable employment at fair wages is just as important to the people in the towns and cities as good farm income is to agriculture. Our people must have the ability to buy the goods they manufacture and the crops they produce. Thus city wages and farm buying power are the two strong legs that carry the nation forward.

Reemployment in industry is proceeding rapidly. Government spending was in large part responsible for keeping industry going and putting it in a position to make this reemployment possible. Government orders were the backlog of heavy industry; government wages turned over and over again to make consumer purchasing power and to sustain every merchant in the community. Businessmen with their businesses, small and large, had to be saved. Private enterprise is necessary to any nation which seeks to maintain the democratic form of government. In their case, just as certainly as in the case of drought-stricken farmers, government spending has saved.

Government having spent wisely to save it, private industry begins to take workers off the rolls of the government relief program. Until this administration we had no free employment service, except in a few states and cities. Because there was no unified employment service, the worker, forced to move as industry moved, often traveled over the country, wandering after jobs which seemed always to travel just a little faster than he did. He was often victimized by fraudulent practices of employment clearing houses, and the facts of employment opportunities were at the disposal neither of himself nor of the employer.

In 1933 the United States Employment Service was created —a cooperative state and federal enterprise, through which the federal government matches dollar for dollar the funds provided by the states for registering the occupations and skills of workers and for actually finding jobs for these registered workers in private industry. The federal-state cooperation has been splendid. Already employment services are operating in thirty-two states, and the areas not covered by them are served by the federal government.

We have developed a nationwide service with seven hundred district offices, and one thousand branch offices, thus providing facilities through which labor can learn of jobs available and employers can find workers.

Last spring I expressed the hope that employers would realize their deep responsibility to take men off the relief rolls and give them jobs in private enterprise. Subsequently I was told by many employers that they were not satisfied with the information available concerning the skill and experience of the workers on the relief rolls. On August 25, I allocated a relatively small sum to the employment service for the purpose of getting better and more recent information in regard to those now actively at work on WPA projects—information as to their skills and previous occupations—and to keep the records of such men and women up-to-date for maximum service in making them available to industry. Tonight I am announcing the allocation of two and a half million dollars more to enable the Employment Service to make an even more intensive search than it has yet been equipped to make, to find opportunities in private employment for workers registered with it. . . .

Tomorrow is Labor Day. Labor Day in this country has never been a class holiday. It has always been a national holiday. It has never had more significance as a national holiday than it has now. In other countries the relationship of employer and employee has been more or less accepted as a class relationship not readily to be broken through. In this country we insist, as an essential of the American way of life, that the employer-employee relationship should be one between free men and equals. We refuse to regard those who work with hand or brain as different from or inferior to those who live from their property. We insist that labor is entitled to as much respect as property. But our workers with hand and brain deserve more than respect for their labor. They deserve practical protection in the opportunity to use their labor at a return adequate to support them at a decent and constantly rising standard of living, and to accumulate a margin of security against the inevitable vicissitudes of life. . . .

There is no cleavage between white-collar workers and manual workers, between artists and artisans, musicians and mechanics, lawyers and accountants, and architects and miners.

Tomorrow, Labor Day, belongs to all of us. Tomorrow, Labor Day, symbolizes the hope of all Americans. Anyone who calls it a class holiday challenges the whole concept of American democracy.

The Fourth of July commemorates our political freedom—a freedom which without economic freedom is meaningless indeed. Labor Day symbolizes our determination to achieve an economic freedom for the average man which will give his political freedom reality.

SECOND INAUGURAL ADDRESS

January 20, 1937

ONE-THIRD OF A NATION ILL-HOUSED, ILL-CLAD, ILL-NOURISHED

When four years ago we met to inaugurate a president, the Republic, single-minded in anxiety, stood in spirit here. We dedicated ourselves to the fulfillment of a vision—to speed the time when there would be for all the people that security and peace essential to the pursuit of happiness. We of the Republic pledged ourselves to drive from the temple of our ancient faith those who had profaned it; to end by action, tireless and un-afraid, the stagnation and despair of that day. We did those first things first.

Our covenant with ourselves did not stop there. Instinc-tively we recognized a deeper need—the need to find through government the instrument of our united purpose to solve for the individual the ever-rising problems of a complex civiliza-tion. Repeated attempts at their solution without the aid of government had left us baffled and bewildered. For, without that aid, we had been unable to create those moral controls over the services of science which are necessary to make science a useful servant instead of a ruthless master of mankind. To do this we knew that we must find practical controls over blind economic forces and blindly selfish men.

We of the Republic sensed the truth that democratic govern-ment has innate capacity to protect its people against disasters once considered inevitable, to solve problems once considered unsolvable. We would not admit that we could not find a way to master economic epidemics just as, after centuries of fatalistic suffering, we had found a way to master epidemics of disease. We refused to leave the problems of our common welfare to be solved by the winds of chance and the hurricanes of disaster.

In this we Americans were discovering no wholly new truth; we were writing a new chapter in our book of self-government.

This year marks the 150th anniversary of the Constitutional Convention which made us a nation. At that Convention our forefathers found the way out of the chaos which followed the Revolutionary War; they created a strong government with powers of united action sufficient then and now to solve problems utterly beyond individual or local solution. A century and a half ago they established the federal government in order to promote the general welfare and secure the blessings of liberty to the American people.

Today we invoke those same powers of government to achieve the same objectives.

Four years of new experience have not belied our historic instinct. They hold out the clear hope that government within communities, government within the separate states, and government of the United States can do the things the times require, without yielding its democracy. Our tasks in the last four years did not force democracy to take a holiday.

Nearly all of us recognize that as intricacies of human relationships increase, so power to govern them also must increase —power to stop evil; power to do good. The essential democracy of our nation and the safety of our people depend not upon the absence of power, but upon lodging it with those whom the people can change or continue at stated intervals through an honest and free system of elections. The Constitution of 1787 did not make our democracy impotent.

In fact, in these last four years, we have made the exercise of all power more democratic; for we have begun to bring private autocratic powers into their proper subordination to the public's government. The legend that they were invincible— above and beyond the processes of a democracy—has been shattered. They have been challenged and beaten.

Our progress out of the depression is obvious. But that is not all that you and I mean by the new order of things. Our pledge was not merely to do a patchwork job with secondhand materials. By using the new materials of social justice we have undertaken to erect on the old foundations a more enduring structure for the better use of future generations.

In that purpose we have been helped by achievements of mind and spirit. Old truths have been relearned; untruths have been unlearned. We have always known that heedless self-interest was bad morals; we know now that it is bad economics. Out of the collapse of a prosperity whose builders boasted their practicality has come the conviction that in the long run economic morality pays. We are beginning to wipe out the line that divides the practical from the ideal; and in so doing we are fashioning an instrument of unimagined power for the establishment of a morally better world.

This new understanding undermines the old admiration of worldly success as such. We are beginning to abandon our tolerance of the abuse of power by those who betray for profit the elementary decencies of life.

In this process evil things formerly accepted will not be so easily condoned. Hardheadedness will not so easily excuse hardheartedness. We are moving toward an era of good feeling. But we realize that there can be no era of good feeling save among men of goodwill.

For these reasons I am justified in believing that the greatest change we have witnessed has been the change in the moral climate of America.

Among men of goodwill, science and democracy together offer an ever-richer life and ever-larger satisfaction to the individual. With this change in our moral climate and our rediscovered ability to improve our economic order, we have set our feet upon the road of enduring progress.

Shall we pause now and turn our back upon the road that

lies ahead? Shall we call this the promised land? Or, shall we continue on our way? For "each age is a dream that is dying, or one that is coming to birth."

Many voices are heard as we face a great decision. Comfort says, "Tarry a while." Opportunism says, "This is a good spot." Timidity asks, "How difficult is the road ahead?"

True, we have come far from the days of stagnation and despair. Vitality has been preserved. Courage and confidence have been restored. Mental and moral horizons have been extended.

But our present gains were won under the pressure of more than ordinary circumstance. Advance became imperative under the goad of fear and suffering. The times were on the side of progress.

To hold to progress today, however, is more difficult. Dulled conscience, irresponsibility, and ruthless self-interest already reappear. Such symptoms of prosperity may become portents of disaster! Prosperity already tests the persistence of our progressive purpose.

Let us ask again: Have we reached the goal of our vision of that fourth day of March 1933? Have we found our happy valley?

I see a great nation, upon a great continent, blessed with a great wealth of natural resources. Its 130 million people are at peace among themselves; they are making their country a good neighbor among the nations. I see a United States which can demonstrate that, under democratic methods of government, national wealth can be translated into a spreading volume of human comforts hitherto unknown, and the lowest standard of living can be raised far above the level of mere subsistence.

But here is the challenge to our democracy: in this nation I see tens of millions of its citizens—a substantial part of its whole population—who at this very moment are denied the greater part of what the very lowest standards of today call the necessities of life.

I see millions of families trying to live on incomes so meager that the pall of family disaster hangs over them day by day.

I see millions whose daily lives in city and on farm continue under conditions labeled indecent by a so-called polite society half a century ago.

I see millions denied education, recreation, and the opportunity to better their lot and the lot of their children.

I see millions lacking the means to buy the products of farm and factory and by their poverty denying work and productiveness to many other millions.

I see one-third of a nation ill-housed, ill-clad, ill-nourished.

It is not in despair that I paint you that picture. I paint it for you in hope—because the nation, seeing and understanding the injustice in it, proposes to paint it out. We are determined to make every American citizen the subject of his country's interest and concern; and we will never regard any faithful, law-abiding group within our borders as superfluous. The test of our progress is not whether we add more to the abundance of those who have much; it is whether we provide enough for those who have too little.

If I know aught of the spirit and purpose of our nation, we will not listen to Comfort, Opportunism, and Timidity. We will carry on.

Overwhelmingly, we of the Republic are men and women of goodwill; men and women who have more than warm hearts of dedication; men and women who have cool heads and willing hands of practical purpose as well. They will insist that every agency of popular government use effective instruments to carry out their will.

Government is competent when all who compose it work as trustees for the whole people. It can make constant progress when it keeps abreast of all the facts. It can obtain justified support and legitimate criticism when the people receive true information of all that government does.

If I know aught of the will of our people, they will demand that these conditions of effective government shall be created and maintained. They will demand a nation uncorrupted by cancers of injustice and, therefore, strong among the nations in its example of the will to peace.

Today we reconsecrate our country to long-cherished ideals in a suddenly changed civilization. In every land there are always at work forces that drive men apart and forces that draw men together. In our personal ambitions we are individualists. But in our seeking for economic and political progress as a nation, we all go up, or else we all go down, as one people.

To maintain a democracy of effort requires a vast amount of patience in dealing with differing methods, a vast amount of humility. But out of the confusion of many voices rises an understanding of dominant public need. Then political leadership can voice common ideals, and aid in their realization.

In taking again the oath of office as president of the United States, I assume the solemn obligation of leading the American people forward along the road over which they have chosen to advance.

While this duty rests upon me I shall do my utmost to speak their purpose and to do their will, seeking Divine guidance to help us each and every one to give light to them that sit in darkness and to guide our feet into the way of peace.

Fireside Chat on Reorganization of the Judiciary

March 9, 1937

Last Thursday I described in detail certain economic problems which everyone admits now face the nation. For the many messages which have come to me after that speech, and which it is physically impossible to answer individually, I take this means of saying thank you.

Tonight, sitting at my desk in the White House, I make my first radio report to the people in my second term of office.

I am reminded of that evening in March, four years ago, when I made my first radio report to you. We were then in the midst of the great banking crisis.

Soon after, with the authority of the Congress, we asked the nation to turn over all of its privately held gold, dollar for dollar, to the government of the United States.

Today's recovery proves how right that policy was.

But when, almost two years later, it came before the Supreme Court its constitutionality was upheld only by a five-to-four vote. The change of one vote would have thrown all the affairs of this great nation back into hopeless chaos. In effect, four justices ruled that the right under a private contract to exact a pound of flesh was more sacred than the main objectives of the Constitution to establish an enduring nation.

In 1933 you and I knew that we must never let our economic system get completely out of joint again—that we could not afford to take the risk of another great depression.

We also became convinced that the only way to avoid a repetition of those dark days was to have a government with power to prevent and to cure the abuses and the inequalities which had thrown that system out of joint.

We then began a program of remedying those abuses and inequalities—to give balance and stability to our economic system—to make it bomb-proof against the causes of 1929.

Today we are only part-way through that program—and recovery is speeding up to a point where the dangers of 1929 are again becoming possible, not this week or month perhaps, but within a year or two.

National laws are needed to complete that program. Individual or local or state effort alone cannot protect us in 1937 any better than ten years ago.

It will take time—and plenty of time—to work out our remedies administratively even after legislation is passed. To complete our program of protection in time, therefore, we cannot delay one moment in making certain that our national government has power to carry through.

Four years ago action did not come until the eleventh hour. It was almost too late.

If we learned anything from the depression we will not allow ourselves to run around in new circles of futile discussion and debate, always postponing the day of decision.

The American people have learned from the depression. For in the last three national elections an overwhelming majority of them voted a mandate that the Congress and the president begin the task of providing that protection—not after long years of debate, but now.

The courts, however, have cast doubts on the ability of the elected Congress to protect us against catastrophe by meeting squarely our modern social and economic conditions.

We are at a crisis in our ability to proceed with that protection. It is a quiet crisis. There are no lines of depositors outside closed banks. But to the far-sighted it is far-reaching in its possibilities of injury to America.

I want to talk with you very simply about the need for present action in this crisis—the need to meet the unanswered challenge of one-third of a nation ill-nourished, ill-clad, ill-housed.

Last Thursday I described the American form of government as a three-horse team provided by the Constitution to the American people so that their field might be plowed. The three horses are, of course, the three branches of government—the Congress, the executive, and the courts. Two of the horses are pulling in unison today; the third is not. Those who have intimated that the president of the United States is trying to drive that team, overlook the simple fact that the president, as chief executive, is himself one of the three horses.

It is the American people themselves who are in the driver's seat.

It is the American people themselves who want the furrow plowed.

It is the American people themselves who expect the third horse to pull in unison with the other two.

I hope that you have reread the Constitution of the United States in these past few weeks. Like the Bible, it ought to be read again and again.

It is an easy document to understand when you remember that it was called into being because the Articles of Confederation under which the original thirteen states tried to operate after the Revolution showed the need of a national government with power enough to handle national problems. In its Preamble, the Constitution states that it was intended to form a more perfect Union and promote the general welfare; and the powers given to the Congress to carry out those purposes can be best described by saying that they were all the powers needed to meet each and every problem which then had a national character and which could not be met by merely local action.

But the framers went further. Having in mind that in succeeding generations many other problems then undreamed of would become national problems, they gave to the Congress the ample broad powers "to levy taxes . . . and provide for the common defense and general welfare of the United States."

That, my friends, is what I honestly believe to have been the clear and underlying purpose of the patriots who wrote a federal Constitution to create a national government with national power, intended as they said, "to form a more perfect union . . . for ourselves and our posterity."

For nearly twenty years there was no conflict between the Congress and the Court. Then Congress passed a statute which, in 1803, the Court said violated an express provision of the Constitution. The Court claimed the power to declare it unconstitutional and did so declare it. But a little later the Court itself admitted that it was an extraordinary power to exercise and through Mr. Justice Washington laid down this limitation upon it: "It is but a decent respect due to the wisdom, the integrity, and the patriotism of the legislative body, by which any law is passed, to presume in favor of its validity until its violation of the Constitution is proved beyond all reasonable doubt."

But since the rise of the modern movement for social and economic progress through legislation, the Court has more and more often and more and more boldly asserted a power to veto laws passed by the Congress and state legislatures in complete disregard of this original limitation.

In the last four years the sound rule of giving statutes the benefit of all reasonable doubt has been cast aside. The Court has been acting not as a judicial body, but as a policy-making body.

When the Congress has sought to stabilize national agriculture, to improve the conditions of labor, to safeguard business against unfair competition, to protect our national resources, and in many other ways to serve our clearly national needs, the majority of the Court has been assuming the power to pass on the wisdom of these acts of the Congress—and to approve or disapprove the public policy written into these laws.

That is not only my accusation. It is the accusation of most distinguished justices of the present Supreme Court. I have not the time to quote to you all the language used by dissenting justices in many of these cases. But in the case holding the

Railroad Retirement Act unconstitutional, for instance, Chief Justice Hughes said in a dissenting opinion that the majority opinion was "a departure from sound principles," and placed "an unwarranted limitation upon the commerce clause." And three other justices agreed with him.

In the case holding the AAA unconstitutional, Justice Stone said of the majority opinion that it was a "tortured construction of the Constitution." And two other justices agreed with him.

In the case holding the New York Minimum Wage Law unconstitutional, Justice Stone said that the majority were actually reading into the Constitution their own "personal economic predilections." . . . And two other justices agreed with him. . . .

The Court in addition to the proper use of its judicial functions has improperly set itself up as a third house of the Congress—a superlegislature, as one of the justices has called it—reading into the Constitution words and implications which are not there, and which were never intended to be there.

We have, therefore, reached the point as a nation where we must take action to save the Constitution from the Court and the Court from itself. We must find a way to take an appeal from the Supreme Court to the Constitution itself. We want a Supreme Court which will do justice under the Constitution—not over it. In our courts we want a government of laws and not of men.

I want—as all Americans want—an independent judiciary as proposed by the framers of the Constitution. That means a Supreme Court that will enforce the Constitution as written—that will refuse to amend the Constitution by the arbitrary exercise of judicial power—amendment by judicial say-so. It does not mean a judiciary so independent that it can deny the existence of facts universally recognized. . . .

When I commenced to review the situation with the problem squarely before me, I came by a process of elimination to the conclusion that, short of amendments, the only method which was clearly constitutional, and would at the same time carry out other much needed reforms, was to infuse new blood into all our courts. We must have men worthy and equipped to carry out impartial justice. But, at the same time, we must have judges who will bring to the courts a present-day sense of the Constitution—judges who will retain in the courts the judicial functions of a court, and reject the legislative powers which the courts have today assumed.

In forty-five out of the forty-eight states of the Union, judges are chosen not for life but for a period of years. In many states judges must retire at the age of seventy. Congress has provided financial security by offering life pensions at full pay for federal judges on all courts who are willing to retire at seventy. In the case of Supreme Court justices, that pension is twenty thousand dollars a year. But all federal judges, once appointed, can, if they choose, hold office for life, no matter how old they may get to be.

What is my proposal? It is simply this: whenever a judge or justice of any federal court has reached the age of seventy and does not avail himself of the opportunity to retire on a pension, a new member shall be appointed by the president then in office, with the approval, as required by the Constitution, of the Senate of the United States.

That plan has two chief purposes. By bringing into the judicial system a steady and continuing stream of new and younger blood, I hope, first, to make the administration of all federal justice speedier and, therefore, less costly; secondly, to bring to the decision of social and economic problems younger men who have had personal experience and contact with modern facts and circumstances under which average men have to live and work. This plan will save our national Constitution from hardening of the judicial arteries.

The number of judges to be appointed would depend wholly on the decision of present judges now over seventy, or those who would subsequently reach the age of seventy.

If, for instance, any one of the six justices of the Supreme Court now over the age of seventy should retire as provided under the plan, no additional place would be created. Consequently, although there never can be more than fifteen, there may be only fourteen, or thirteen, or twelve. And there may be only nine.

There is nothing novel or radical about this idea. It seeks to maintain the federal bench in full vigor. It has been discussed and approved by many persons of high authority ever since a similar proposal passed the House of Representatives in 1869. . . .

Those opposing this plan have sought to arouse prejudice and fear by crying that I am seeking to "pack" the Supreme Court and that a baneful precedent will be established.

What do they mean by the words "packing the Court"?

Let me answer this question with a bluntness that will end all *honest* misunderstanding of my purposes.

If by that phrase "packing the Court" it is charged that I wish to place on the bench spineless puppets who would disregard the law and would decide specific cases as I wished them to be decided, I make this answer: that no president fit for his office would appoint, and no Senate of honorable men fit for their office would confirm, that kind of appointees to the Supreme Court.

But if by that phrase the charge is made that I would appoint and the Senate would confirm justices worthy to sit beside present members of the Court who understand those modern conditions, that I will appoint justices who will not undertake to override the judgment of the Congress on legislative policy, that I will appoint justices who will act as justices and not as legislators—if the appointment of such justices can be called "packing the Courts," then I say that I and with me the vast majority of the American people favor doing just that thing—now. . . .

It is the clear intention of our public policy to provide for a constant flow of new and younger blood into the judiciary. Normally every president appoints a large number of district and circuit judges and a few members of the Supreme Court. Until my first term practically every president of the United States had appointed at least one member of the Supreme Court.

President Taft appointed five members and named a Chief Justice; President Wilson, three; President Harding, four, including a Chief Justice; President Coolidge, one; President Hoover, three, including a Chief Justice.

Such a succession of appointments should have provided a Court well-balanced as to age. But chance and the disinclination of individuals to leave the Supreme bench have now given us a Court in which five justices will be over seventy-five years of age before next June and one over seventy. Thus a sound public policy has been defeated.

I now propose that we establish by law an assurance against any such ill-balanced Court in the future. I propose that hereafter, when a judge reaches the age of seventy, a new and younger judge shall be added to the Court automatically. In this way I propose to enforce a sound public policy by law instead of leaving the composition of our federal courts, including the highest, to be determined by chance or the personal decision of individuals. . . .

I have thus explained to you the reasons that lie behind our efforts to secure results by legislation within the Constitution. I hope that thereby the difficult process of constitutional amendment may be rendered unnecessary. . . .

This proposal of mine will not infringe in the slightest upon the civil or religious liberties so dear to every American.

My record as governor and as president proves my devotion to those liberties. You who know me can have no fear that I would tolerate the destruction by any branch of government of any part of our heritage of freedom. . . .

During the past half century the balance of power between the three great branches of the federal government has been tipped out of balance by the courts in direct contradiction of the high purposes of the framers of the Constitution. It is my purpose to restore that balance. You who know me will accept my solemn assurance that in a world in which democracy is under attack, I seek to make American democracy succeed. You and I will do our part.

Speech at
Chicago, Illinois

October 5, 1937

A Quarantine of Aggressor Nations

I am glad to come once again to Chicago and especially to have the opportunity of taking part in the dedication of this important project of civic betterment.

On my trip across the continent and back I have been shown many evidences of the result of common-sense cooperation between municipalities and the federal government, and I have been greeted by tens of thousands of Americans who have told me in every look and word that their material and spiritual well-being has made great strides forward in the past few years.

And yet, as I have seen with my own eyes the prosperous farms, the thriving factories, and the busy railroads, as I have seen the happiness and security and peace which covers our wide land, almost inevitably I have been compelled to contrast our peace with very different scenes being enacted in other parts of the world.

It is because the people of the United States under modern conditions must, for the sake of their own future, give thought to the rest of the world, that I, as the responsible executive head of the nation, have chosen this great inland city and this gala occasion to speak to you on a subject of definite national importance.

The political situation in the world, which of late has been growing progressively worse, is such as to cause grave concern and anxiety to all the peoples and nations who wish to live in peace and amity with their neighbors.

Some fifteen years ago the hopes of mankind for a continuing era of international peace were raised to great heights when more than sixty nations solemnly pledged themselves not to

141

resort to arms in furtherance of their national aims and policies. The high aspirations expressed in the Briand-Kellogg peace pact and the hopes for peace thus raised have of late given way to a haunting fear of calamity. The present reign of terror and international lawlessness began a few years ago.

It began through unjustified interference in the internal affairs of other nations or the invasion of alien territory in violation of treaties, and has now reached a stage where the very foundations of civilization are seriously threatened. The landmarks and traditions which have marked the progress of civilization toward a condition of law, order, and justice are being wiped away.

Without a declaration of war and without warning or justification of any kind, civilians, including vast numbers of women and children, are being ruthlessly murdered with bombs from the air. In times of so-called peace, ships are being attacked and sunk by submarines without cause or notice. Nations are fomenting and taking sides in civil warfare in nations that have never done them any harm. Nations claiming freedom for themselves deny it to others.

Innocent peoples, innocent nations, are being cruelly sacrificed to a greed for power and supremacy which is devoid of all sense of justice and humane considerations. . . .

The peace-loving nations must make a concerted effort in opposition to those violations of treaties and those ignorings of humane instincts which today are creating a state of international anarchy and instability from which there is no escape through mere isolation or neutrality.

Those who cherish their freedom, and recognize and respect the equal right of their neighbors to be free and live in peace, must work together for the triumph of law and moral principles in order that peace, justice, and confidence may prevail in the world. There must be a return to a belief in the pledged word, in the value of a signed treaty. There must be recognition of the fact that national morality is as vital as private morality. . . .

There is a solidarity and interdependence about the modern

world, both technically and morally, which makes it impossible for any nation completely to isolate itself from economic and political upheavals in the rest of the world, especially when such upheavals appear to be spreading and not declining. There can be no stability or peace either within nations or between nations except under laws and moral standards adhered to by all. International anarchy destroys every foundation for peace. It jeopardizes either the immediate or the future security of every nation, large or small. It is, therefore, a matter of vital interest and concern to the people of the United States that the sanctity of international treaties and the maintenance of international morality be restored. . . .

In those nations of the world which seem to be piling armament on armament for purposes of aggression, and those other nations which fear acts of aggression against them and their security, a very high proportion of their national income is being spent directly for armaments. It runs from 30 to as high as 50 percent. We are fortunate. The proportion that we in the United States spend is far less—11 or 12 percent.

How happy we are that the circumstances of the moment permit us to put our money into bridges and boulevards, dams and reforestation, the conservation of our soil, and many other kinds of useful works rather than into huge standing armies and vast supplies of implements of war.

I am compelled and you are compelled, nevertheless, to look ahead. The peace, the freedom, and the security of 90 percent of the population of the world is being jeopardized by the remaining 10 percent who are threatening a breakdown of all international order and law. Surely the 90 percent who want to live in peace under law and in accordance with moral standards that have received almost universal acceptance through the centuries can and must find some way to make their will prevail. . . .

It seems to be unfortunately true that the epidemic of world lawlessness is spreading.

When an epidemic of physical disease starts to spread, the community approves and joins in a quarantine of the patients in order to protect the health of the community against the spread of the disease.

It is my determination to pursue a policy of peace. It is my determination to adopt every practicable measure to avoid involvement in war. It ought to be inconceivable that in this modern era, and in the face of experience, any nation could be so foolish and ruthless as to run the risk of plunging the whole world into war by invading and violating, in contravention of solemn treaties, the territory of other nations that have done them no real harm and are too weak to protect themselves adequately. Yet the peace of the world and the welfare and security of every nation, including our own, is today being threatened by that very thing.

No nation which refuses to exercise forbearance and to respect the freedom and rights of others can long remain strong and retain the confidence and respect of other nations. No nation ever loses its dignity or its good standing by conciliating its differences, and by exercising great patience with, and consideration for, the rights of other nations.

War is a contagion, whether it be declared or undeclared. It can engulf states and peoples remote from the original scene of hostilities. We are determined to keep out of war, yet we cannot insure ourselves against the disastrous effects of war and the dangers of involvement. We are adopting such measures as will minimize our risk of involvement, but we cannot have complete protection in a world of disorder in which confidence and security have broken down.

If civilization is to survive, the principles of the Prince of Peace must be restored. Trust between nations must be revived.

Most important of all, the will for peace on the part of peace-loving nations must express itself to the end that nations that may be tempted to violate their agreements and the rights of others will desist from such a course. There must be positive endeavors to preserve peace.

America hates war. America hopes for peace. Therefore, America actively engages in the search for peace.

Sixth Annual Message
to Congress

January 4, 1939

Mr. Vice President, Mr. Speaker, Members of the Senate and the Congress: In reporting on the state of the nation, I have felt it necessary on previous occasions to advise the Congress of disturbance abroad and of the need of putting our own house in order in the face of storm signals from across the seas. As this Seventy-sixth Congress opens there is need for further warning.

A war which threatened to envelop the world in flames has been averted; but it has become increasingly clear that world peace is not assured.

All about us rage undeclared wars—military and economic. All about us grow more deadly armaments—military and economic. All about us are threats of new aggression—military and economic.

Storms from abroad directly challenge three institutions indispensable to Americans, now as always. The first is religion. It is the source of the other two—democracy and international good faith.

Religion, by teaching man his relationship to God, gives the individual a sense of his own dignity and teaches him to respect himself by respecting his neighbors.

Democracy, the practice of self-government, is a covenant among free men to respect the rights and liberties of their fellows.

International good faith, a sister of democracy, springs from the will of civilized nations of men to respect the rights and liberties of other nations of men.

In a modern civilization, all three—religion, democracy, and international good faith—complement and support each other.

Where freedom of religion has been attacked, the attack has come from sources opposed to democracy. Where democracy has been overthrown, the spirit of free worship has disappeared. And where religion and democracy have vanished, good faith and reason in international affairs have given way to strident ambition and brute force. . . .

We know what might happen to us of the United States if the new philosophies of force were to encompass the other continents and invade our own. We, no more than other nations, can afford to be surrounded by the enemies of our faith and our humanity. Fortunate it is, therefore, that in this Western Hemisphere we have, under a common ideal of democratic government, a rich diversity of resources and of peoples functioning together in mutual respect and peace.

That hemisphere, that peace, and that ideal we propose to do our share in protecting against storms from any quarter. Our people and our resources are pledged to secure that protection. From that determination no American flinches. . . .

In our foreign relations we have learned from the past what not to do. From new wars we have learned what we must do.

We have learned that effective timing of defense, and the distant points from which attacks may be launched are completely different from what they were twenty years ago.

We have learned that survival cannot be guaranteed by arming after the attack begins—for there is new range and speed to offense.

We have learned that long before any overt military act, aggression begins with preliminaries of propaganda, subsidized penetration, the loosening of ties of goodwill, the stirring of prejudice, and the incitement to disunion.

We have learned that God-fearing democracies of the world which observe the sanctity of treaties and good faith in their dealings with other nations cannot safely be indifferent to international lawlessness anywhere. They cannot forever let pass, without effective protest, acts of aggression against sister nations—acts which automatically undermine all of us.

Obviously they must proceed along practical, peaceful lines. But the mere fact that we rightly decline to intervene with arms to prevent acts of aggression does not mean that we must act as if there were no aggression at all. Words may be futile, but war is not the only means of commanding a decent respect for the opinions of mankind. There are many methods short of war, but stronger and more effective than mere words, of bringing home to aggressor governments the aggregate sentiments of our own people.

At the very least, we can and should avoid any action, or any lack of action, which will encourage, assist, or build up an aggressor. We have learned that when we deliberately try to legislate neutrality, our neutrality laws may operate unevenly and unfairly—may actually give aid to an aggressor and deny it to the victim. The instinct of self-preservation should warn us that we ought not to let that happen anymore.

And we have learned something else—the old, old lesson that probability of attack is mightily decreased by the assurance of an ever-ready defense. Since 1931, nearly eight years ago, world events of thunderous import have moved with lightning speed. During these eight years many of our people clung to the hope that the innate decency of mankind would protect the unprepared who showed their innate trust in mankind. Today we are all wiser—and sadder.

Under modern conditions what we mean by "adequate defense"—a policy subscribed to by all of us—must be divided into three elements. First, we must have armed forces and defenses strong enough to ward off sudden attack against strategic positions and key facilities essential to ensure sustained resistance and ultimate victory. Secondly, we must have the organization and location of those key facilities so that they may be immediately utilized and rapidly expanded to meet all needs without danger of serious interruption by enemy attack. . . .

In meeting the troubles of the world we must meet them as one people—with a unity born of the fact that for generations those who have come to our shores, representing many kindreds and tongues, have been welded by common opportunity into a united patriotism. If another form of government can present a united front in its attack on a democracy, the attack must and will be met by a united democracy. Such a democracy can and must exist in the United States.

A dictatorship may command the full strength of a regimented nation. But the united strength of a democratic nation can be mustered only when its people, educated by modern standards to know what is going on and where they are going, have conviction that they are receiving as large a share of opportunity for development, as large a share of material success and of human dignity, as they have a right to receive.

Our nation's program of social and economic reform is therefore a part of defense, as basic as armaments themselves.

Against the background of events in Europe, in Africa, and in Asia during these recent years, the pattern of what we have accomplished since 1933 appears in even clearer focus.

For the first time we have moved upon deep-seated problems affecting our national strength and have forged national instruments adequate to meet them.

Consider what the seemingly piecemeal struggles of these six years add up to in terms of realistic national preparedness.

We are conserving and developing natural resources—land, water power, forests.

We are trying to provide necessary food, shelter, and medical care for the health of our population.

We are putting agriculture—our system of food and fiber supply—on a sounder basis.

We are strengthening the weakest spot in our system of industrial supply—its long-smouldering labor difficulties.

We have cleaned up our credit system so that depositor and investor alike may more readily and willingly make their capital available for peace or war.

We are giving to our youth new opportunities for work and education.

We have sustained the morale of all the population by the

dignified recognition of our obligations to the aged, the helpless, and the needy.

Above all, we have made the American people conscious of their interrelationship and their interdependence. They sense a common destiny and a common need of each other. Differences of occupation, geography, race, and religion no longer obscure the nation's fundamental unity in thought and in action.

We have our difficulties, true—but we are a wiser and a tougher nation than we were in 1929, or in 1932.

Never have there been six years of such far-flung internal preparedness in our history. And this has been done without any dictator's power to command, without conscription of labor or confiscation of capital, without concentration camps and without a scratch on freedom of speech, freedom of the press, or the rest of the Bill of Rights. . . .

We have now passed the period of internal conflict in the launching of our program of social reform. Our full energies may now be released to invigorate the processes of recovery in order to preserve our reforms, and to give every man and woman who wants to work a real job at a living wage.

But time is of paramount importance. The deadline of danger from within and from without is not within our control. The hourglass may be in the hands of other nations. Our own hourglass tells us that we are off on a race to make democracy work, so that we may be efficient in peace and therefore secure in national defense.

This time element forces us to still greater efforts to attain the full employment of our labor and our capital.

The first duty of our statesmanship is to bring capital and manpower together. . . .

We want to get enough capital and labor at work to give us a total turnover of business, a total national income, of at least $80 billion a year. At that figure we shall have a substantial reduction of unemployment; and the federal revenues will be sufficient to balance the current level of cash expenditures on the basis of the existing tax structure. That figure can be attained, working within the framework of our traditional profit system. The factors in attaining and maintaining that amount of national income are many and complicated.

They include more widespread understanding among businessmen of many changes which world conditions and technological improvements have brought to our economy over the last twenty years—changes in the interrelationship of price and volume and employment, for example—changes of the kind in which businessmen are now educating themselves through excellent opportunities like the so-called "monopoly investigation."

They include a perfecting of our farm program to protect farmers' income and consumers' purchasing power from alternate risks of crop gluts and crop shortages.

They include wholehearted acceptance of new standards of honesty in our financial markets.

They include reconcilement of enormous, antagonistic interests—some of them long in litigation—in the railroad and general transportation field.

They include the working out of new techniques—private, state, and federal—to protect the public interest in and to develop wider markets for electric power.

They include a revamping of the tax relationships between federal, state, and local units of government, and consideration of relatively small tax increases to adjust inequalities without interfering with the aggregate income of the American people.

They include the perfecting of labor organization and a universal ungrudging attitude by employers toward the labor movement, until there is a minimum of interruption of production and employment because of disputes, and acceptance by labor of the truth that the welfare of labor itself depends on increased balanced output of goods.

To be immediately practical, while proceeding with a steady evolution in the solving of these and like problems, we must wisely use instrumentalities, like federal investment, which are immediately available to us.

Here, as elsewhere, time is the deciding factor in our choice of remedies.

Therefore, it does not seem logical to me, at the moment we seek to increase production and consumption, for the federal government to consider a drastic curtailment of its own investments. . . .

Investing soundly must preclude spending wastefully. To guard against opportunist appropriations, I have on several occasions addressed the Congress on the importance of permanent long-range planning. I hope, therefore, that following my recommendation of last year, a permanent agency will be set up and authorized to report on the urgency and desirability of the various types of government investment.

Investment for prosperity can be made in a democracy. . . .

Events abroad have made it increasingly clear to the American people that dangers within are less to be feared than dangers from without. If, therefore, a solution of this problem of idle men and idle capital is the price of preserving our liberty, no formless, selfish fears can stand in the way.

Once I prophesied that this generation of Americans had a rendezvous with destiny. That prophecy comes true. To us much is given; more is expected.

This generation will "nobly save or meanly lose the last best hope of earth. . . . The way is plain, peaceful, generous, just— a way which if followed the world will forever applaud and God must forever bless."

MESSAGE TO CHANCELLOR ADOLF HITLER AND PREMIER BENITO MUSSOLINI

April 14, 1939

You realize, I am sure, that throughout the world hundreds of millions of human beings are living today in constant fear of a new war or even a series of wars.

The existence of this fear—and the possibility of such a conflict—are of definite concern to the people of the United States for whom I speak, as they must also be to the peoples of the other nations of the entire Western Hemisphere. All of them know that any major war, even if it were to be confined to other continents, must bear heavily on them during its continuance and also for generations to come.

Because of the fact that after the acute tension in which the world has been living during the past few weeks there would seem to be at least a momentary relaxation—because no troops are at this moment on the march—this may be an opportune moment for me to send you this message.

On a previous occasion I have addressed you in behalf of the settlement of political, economic, and social problems by peaceful methods and without resort to arms.

But the tide of events seems to have reverted to the threat of arms. If such threats continue, it seems inevitable that much of the world must become involved in common ruin. All the world —victor nations, vanquished nations, and neutral nations—

will suffer. I refuse to believe that the world is, of necessity, such a prisoner of destiny. On the contrary, it is clear that the leaders of great nations have it in their power to liberate their peoples from the disaster that impends. It is equally clear that in their own minds and in their own hearts the peoples themselves desire that their fears be ended.

It is, however, unfortunately necessary to take cognizance of recent facts.

Three nations in Europe and one in Africa have seen their independent existence terminated. A vast territory in another independent nation of the Far East has been occupied by a neighboring state. Reports, which we trust are not true, insist that further acts of aggression are contemplated against still other independent nations. Plainly the world is moving toward the moment when this situation must end in catastrophe unless a more rational way of guiding events is found.

You have repeatedly asserted that you and the German people have no desire for war. If this is true there need be no war.

Nothing can persuade the peoples of the earth that any governing power has any right or need to inflict the consequences of war on its own or any other people save in the cause of self-evident home defense.

In making this statement we as Americans speak not through selfishness or fear or weakness. If we speak now it is with the voice of strength and with friendship for mankind. It is still clear to me that international problems can be solved at the council table.

It is therefore no answer to the plea for peaceful discussion for one side to plead that unless they receive assurances beforehand that the verdict will be theirs, they will not lay aside their arms. In conference rooms, as in courts, it is necessary that both sides enter upon the discussion in good faith, assuming that substantial justice will accrue to both; and it is customary and necessary that they leave their arms outside the room where they confer.

I am convinced that the cause of world peace would be greatly advanced if the nations of the world were to obtain a frank statement relating to the present and future policy of governments.

Because the United States, as one of the nations of the Western Hemisphere, is not involved in the immediate controversies which have arisen in Europe, I trust that you may be willing to make such a statement of policy to me as head of a nation far removed from Europe in order that I, acting only with the responsibility and obligation of a friendly intermediary, may communicate such declaration to other nations now apprehensive as to the course which the policy of your government may take.

Are you willing to give assurance that your armed forces will not attack or invade the territory or possessions of the following independent nations: Finland, Estonia, Latvia, Lithuania, Sweden, Norway, Denmark, the Netherlands, Belgium, Great Britain and Ireland, France, Portugal, Spain, Switzerland, Liechtenstein, Luxembourg, Poland, Hungary, Rumania, Yugoslavia, Russia, Bulgaria, Greece, Turkey, Iraq, the Arabias, Syria, Palestine, Egypt, and Iran?

Such an assurance clearly must apply not only to the present day but also to a future sufficiently long to give every opportunity to work by peaceful methods for a more permanent peace. I therefore suggest that you construe the word *future* to apply to a minimum period of assured nonaggression—ten years at the least—a quarter of a century, if we dare look that far ahead.

If such assurance is given by your government, I shall immediately transmit it to the governments of the nations I have named and I shall simultaneously inquire whether, as I am reasonably sure, each of the nations enumerated will in turn give like assurance for transmission to you.

Reciprocal assurances such as I have outlined will bring to the world an immediate measure of relief.

I propose that if it is given, two essential problems shall promptly be discussed in the resulting peaceful surroundings, and in those discussions the government of the United States will gladly take part.

The discussions which I have in mind relate to the most effective and immediate manner through which the peoples of the world can obtain progressive relief from the crushing burden of armament which is each day bringing them more closely to the brink of economic disaster. Simultaneously the government of the United States would be prepared to take part in discussions looking toward the most practical manner of opening up avenues of international trade to the end that every nation of the earth may be enabled to buy and sell on equal terms in the world market as well as to possess assurance of obtaining the materials and products of peaceful economic life.

At the same time, those governments other than the United States which are directly interested could undertake such political discussions as they may consider necessary or desirable.

We recognize complex world problems which affect all humanity but we know that study and discussion of them must be held in an atmosphere of peace. Such an atmosphere of peace cannot exist if negotiations are overshadowed by the threat of force or by the fear of war.

I think you will not misunderstand the spirit of frankness in which I send you this message. Heads of great governments in this hour are literally responsible for the fate of humanity in the coming years. They cannot fail to hear the prayers of their peoples to be protected from the foreseeable chaos of war. History will hold them accountable for the lives and the happiness of all—even unto the least.

I hope that your answer will make it possible for humanity to lose fear and regain security for many years to come.

A similar message is being addressed to the chief of the Italian government.

SPEECH AT THE
NEW YORK
WORLD'S FAIR

Flushing, New York, April 30, 1939

Governor Lehman, Mayor LaGuardia, President Grover Whalen, Ladies and Gentlemen: I have seen only a small fraction of the Fair; but even from the little I have seen, I am able to congratulate all of you who conceived and planned the Fair and all you men and women who built it.

From henceforth in our history the thirtieth day of April will have a dual significance: the inauguration of the first president of the United States, which began the executive branch of the federal government, and the opening of the New York World's Fair of 1939.

Today, also, the cycle of sesquicentennial commemorations is complete. Two years ago, in Philadelphia and other communities, was celebrated the Constitutional Convention of 1787, which gave to us the form of government under which we have lived ever since. Last year was celebrated in many states the ratification of the Constitution by the original thirteen states. On March 4 of this year the first meeting of the First Congress was commemorated at a distinguished gathering in the House of Representatives in the national capitol. And two weeks ago, on April 14, I went to Mount Vernon with the Cabinet in memory of that day, exactly 150 years before, when General Washington was formally notified of his election as president.

As you remember, two days later he left that home he loved so well and proceeded by easy stages to New York, greeted with triumphal arches and flower-strewn streets in the large communities through which he passed on his way to this city. Fortunately, there have been preserved for us many generations later accounts of his taking of the oath of office on April 30 on the balcony of the old Federal Hall. In a scene of republican simplicity and surrounded by the great men of the time, most of whom had served with him in the cause of independence through the Revolution, the oath was administered to him by the chancellor of the state of New York, Robert R. Livingston. And so we, in New York, have a very personal connection with that thirtieth of April, 150 years ago.

The permanent government of the United States had become a fact. The period of Revolution and the critical days that followed were over. The long future lay ahead.

In the framework of government which had been devised, and in the early years of its administration, it is of enormous significance to us today that those early leaders successfully planned for such use of the Constitution as would fit it to a constantly expanding nation. That the original framework was capable of expansion from its application to thirteen states with less than 4 million people, to its newer application to forty-eight states with more than 130 million people, is the best tribute to the vision of the Fathers. In this it stands unique in the whole history of the world, for no other form of government has remained unchanged so long and seen, at the same time, any comparable expansion of population or of area.

It is significant that the astounding changes and advances in almost every phase of human life have made necessary so relatively few changes in the Constitution itself. All of the earlier amendments may be accepted by us as a part of the original Constitution because that sacred Bill of Rights, which guaranteed and has maintained personal liberty through freedom of speech, freedom of the press, freedom of religion, and freedom of assembly, was already popularly accepted by the inhabitants of thirteen states while the Constitution itself was in the process of ratification.

There followed the amendments which put an end to the practice of human slavery, and a number of later amendments which made our practice of government more direct, including the extension of the franchise to the women of the nation. And we remember also that the only restrictive amendment which deliberately took away one form of wholly personal liberty was, after a trial, an unhappy trial, of a few years, overwhelmingly repealed.

Once only has the permanence of the Constitution been threatened. It was threatened by an internal war brought about principally by the very fact of the expansion of American civilization across the continent—a threat which resulted eventually and happily in a closer union than ever before.

And of these later years—these very recent years—the history books of the next generation will set it forth that sectionalism and regional jealousies diminished, and that the people of every part of our land acquired a national solidarity of economic and social thought such as had never been seen before.

That this has been accomplished, that it has been done, has been due first to our form of government itself, and, secondly, to a spirit of wise tolerance which, with few exceptions, has been our American rule. We in the United States, and, indeed, in all the Americas, North America, Central America, and South America, remember that our population stems from many races and kindreds and tongues. Often, I think, we Americans offer up a silent prayer that on the continent of Europe, from which the American hemisphere was principally colonized, the years to come will break down many barriers to intercourse between nations—barriers which may be historic, but which so greatly, through the centuries, have led to strife and have hindered friendship and normal intercourse.

The United States stands today as a completely homogeneous nation, similar in its civilization from coast to coast and from North to South, united in a common purpose to work for the greatest good of the greatest number, united in the desire to move forward to better things in the use of its great resources of nature and its even greater resources of intelligent, educated manhood and womanhood, and united in its desire to encourage peace and goodwill among all the nations of the earth.

Born of that unity of purpose, that knowledge of strength, that singleness of ideal, two great expositions, one at each end of our continent, mark this year in which we live. And it is fitting that they commemorate the 150th anniversary of the birth of our permanent government.

Opened two months ago, the exposition on the magic island in San Francisco Bay presents to visitors from all the world a view of the amazing development of our own Far West and of our neighbors of the American continent and the nations of the Pacific and its isles.

Here at the New York World's Fair of 1939 many nations are also represented—indeed most of the nations of the world —and the theme is "The World of Tomorrow."

This general, and I might almost say spontaneous, participation by other countries is a gesture of friendship and goodwill toward the United States for which I render most grateful thanks. It is not through the physical exhibits alone that this gesture has manifested itself. The magic of modern communications makes possible a continuing participation by word of mouth itself. Already, on Sunday afternoon radio programs, no fewer than seventeen foreign nations have shown their goodwill to this country since the first of January this year.

In many instances the chiefs of state in the countries taking part in the programs have spoken, and in every case the principal speaker has extended greetings to the president of the United States. And so in this place and at this time, as we open the New York World's Fair, I desire to thank all of them and to assure them that we, as a nation, heartily reciprocate all of their cordial sentiments.

All who come to this World's Fair in New York and to the Exposition in San Francisco will, I need not tell them, receive the heartiest of welcomes. They will find that the eyes of the United States are fixed on the future. Yes, our wagon is still hitched to a star.

But it is a star of friendship, a star of progress for mankind, a star of greater happiness and less hardship, a star of international goodwill, and, above all, a star of peace.

May the months to come carry us forward in the rays of that eternal hope.

And so, my friends, the time has come for me to announce with solemnity, perhaps, but with great happiness, a fact: I hereby dedicate the New York World's Fair of 1939, and I declare it open to all mankind.

STATEMENT ON SIGNING THE HATCH ACT

August 2, 1939

Because there have been so many misrepresentations, some unpremeditated, some deliberate, in regard to the attitude of the executive branch of the government in relation to Senate Bill 1871, "An Act to Prevent Pernicious Political Activities," and because a number of questions have been raised as to the meaning and application of some of its provisions, I deem it advisable at the time of executive approval to make certain observations to the Congress of the United States.

The genesis of this legislation lies in the message of the president of January 5, 1939, respecting an additional appropriation for the Works Progress Administration. I said in that message: "It is my belief that improper political practices can be eliminated only by the imposition of rigid statutory regulations and penalties by the Congress, and that this should be done. Such penalties should be imposed not only upon persons within the administrative organization of the Works Progress Administration, but also upon outsiders who have in fact in many instances been the principal offenders in this regard. My only reservation in this matter is that no legislation should be enacted which will in any way deprive workers on the Works Progress Administration program of the civil rights to which they are entitled in common with other citizens."

Furthermore, in applying to all employees of the federal government (with a few exceptions) the rules to which the Civil Service employees have been subject for many years, this measure is in harmony with the policy that I have consistently advocated during all my public life, namely, the wider extension of Civil Service as opposed to its curtailment.

It is worth noting that nearly all exemptions from the Civil Service, which have been made during the past six years and a half, have originated in the Congress itself and not in the executive.

Furthermore, it is well known that I have consistently advocated the objectives of the present bill. It has been currently suggested that partisan political reasons have entered largely into the passage of the bill: but with this I am not concerned, because it is my hope that if properly administered the measure can be made an effective instrument of good government.

As is usual with all bills passed by the Congress, this bill has been examined, on its receipt at the executive offices, by the appropriate departments or agencies, in this case the attorney general of the United States and the Civil Service Commission.

The attorney general has advised me that it seems clear that the federal government has the power to describe as qualifications for its employees that they refrain from taking part in other endeavors which, in the light of common experience, may well consume time and attention required by their duties as public officials. He points out, however, that such qualifications cannot properly preclude government employees from the exercise of the right of free speech or from their right to exercise the franchise.

The question of constitutionality being resolved in favor of the bill, our next inquiry relates to the exercise and preservation of these rights. It is obvious that the intent of the bill is to follow broadly the provisions of Civil Service regulations that have existed for many years in regard to political activities of federal employees.

It is because I have received and will continue to receive so many queries asking what a government employee may or may not do that it seems appropriate at the outset to postulate the broad principle that if the bill is administered in accord with its spirit, and if it is in the future administered without abuse, oppression, or groundless fear, it will serve the purpose intended by the Congress.

For example, I have been asked by employees of the government whether under this law they would lose their positions if they merely attend political meetings. The answer is, of course, no.

I have been asked whether they would lose their positions if they contributed voluntarily to party or individual campaign funds without being solicited. The answer is, of course, no.

I have been asked whether they would lose their positions if they should merely express their opinion or preference publicly —orally, by radio, or in writing—without doing so as part of an organized political campaign. The answer is no.

I have been asked if citizens who have received loans from the Home Owners' Loan Corporation, from the Farm Credit Administration or its subsidiaries, from the Farm Security Administration, from the Reconstruction Finance Corporation, and other government lending agencies would be subject to the terms of this bill. The answer is no.

I have been asked whether farmers receiving farm benefits would be bound by the terms of the bill. Again, the answer is no.

I have been asked if government employees who belong to Young Republican clubs, Young Democratic clubs, Civil Service Reform associations, the League of Women Voters, the American Federation of Labor, the Congress of Industrial Organizations, and similar bodies are subject to the penalties of the measure because of mere membership in these organizations. The answer is no.

There will be hundreds of similar questions raised in the actual administration and enforcement of this bill. Such questions will be asked in most cases by individuals in good faith. And it is only fair that they should receive an answer. I am, therefore, asking the attorney general to take the necessary steps through the new Civil Liberties unit of the Department of Justice in order that the civil rights of every government employee may be duly protected and that the element of fear may be removed.

I have been asked if the bill applies to veterans—Civil War, Indian Wars, the War with Spain, the World War—retired officers and men of the army, navy, and Marine Corps who, though not government employees, are receiving benefits or pensions of one kind or another. The answer is, of course, no.

I have been asked if the act applies to those who get government benefits under the Social Security Act in the form of old age pensions or in the form of unemployment compensation. The answer is no.

Finally, I have been asked various questions relating to the right of a government employee publicly to answer unwarranted attacks made on him or on his work or on the work of his superiors or on the work of his subordinates, notwithstanding the fact that such attacks or misrepresentations were made for political purposes by newspapers or by individuals as a part of a political campaign.

This raises the interesting question as to whether all government officials except the president and vice president, persons in the office of the president, heads and assistant heads of executive departments and policy-determining officers appointed by, and with the advice and consent of, the Senate must remain mute if and when they or the work with which they are concerned are attacked and misrepresented in a political campaign or preliminary thereto.

It will be noted that the language of the bill wholly excludes members or employees of the legislative branch of the government from its operation.

It can hardly be maintained that it is an American way of doing things to allow newspapers, magazines, radio broadcasters, members and employees of the Senate and House of Representatives, and all kinds of candidates for public office and their friends to make any form of charge, misrepresentation, falsification, or vituperation against the acts of any individual or group of individuals employed in the executive branch of the federal government with complete immunity against reply except by a handful of high executive officials. That, I repeat, would be un-American because it would be unfair, and the great mass of

Americans like fair play and insist on it. They do not stand for any gag act.

It is, therefore, my considered opinion, in which the attorney general of the United States joins me, that all federal employees, from the highest to the lowest, have the right publicly to answer any attack or misrepresentation, provided, of course, they do not make such reply as part of active participation in political campaigns.

The same definition of fair and proper administration of the bill applies to the right of any government employee, from the highest to the lowest, to give to the public factual information relating to the conduct of governmental affairs. To rule otherwise would make it impossible for the people of the United States to learn from those who serve the government vital, necessary, and interesting facts relating to the manifold activities of the federal government. To rule otherwise would give a monopoly to originate and disseminate information to those who, primarily for political purposes, unfortunately have been given to the spreading of false information. That again is unfair and, therefore, un-American.

It is, I am confident, the purpose of the proponents of this legislation that the new law be thus administered so that the right of free speech will remain, even to those who serve their government; and that the government itself shall have full right to place all facts in its possession before the public. If some future administration should undertake to administer this legislation to the detriment of these rights, such action would be contrary to the purpose of the act itself, and might well infringe upon the constitutional rights of citizens. I trust that public vigilance will for all time prevent this.

The attorney general calls my attention to a practical difficulty which should be corrected by additional legislation as soon as possible. For many years there has been an exception to the Civil Service regulation whereby employees permanently residing in the District of Columbia or in municipalities adjacent thereto may become candidates for or hold municipal office in their municipalities. This and a few similar exceptions should, I believe, be maintained.

The other question relates to the fact that the bill does not in any way cover the multitude of state and local employees who greatly outnumber federal employees and who may continue to take part in elections in which there are candidates for federal office on the same ballot with candidates for state and local office. It is held by many who have examined the constitutional question that because the Congress, under the Constitution, may maintain the integrity of federal elections, it has the power to extend the objectives of this bill so as to cover state and local government employees who participate actively in federal elections. This is at least worth the study of the Congress at its next session and therefore before the next federal election.

It is because for so many years I have striven in public life and in private life for decency in political campaigns, both on the part of government servants, of candidates, of newspapers, of corporations, and of individuals, that I regard this new legislation as at least a step in the right direction.

MESSAGE TO CHANCELLOR ADOLF HITLER DURING THE POLISH CRISIS

August 24, 1939

In the message which I sent to you on April 14 last I stated that it appeared to me that the leaders of great nations had it in their power to liberate their peoples from the disaster that impended, but that unless the effort were immediately made with goodwill on all sides to find a peaceful and constructive solution of existing controversies, the crisis which the world was confronting must end in catastrophe. Today that catastrophe appears to be very near at hand indeed.

To the message which I sent to you last April I have received no reply, but because of my confident belief that the cause of world peace—which is the cause of humanity itself—rises above all other considerations, I am again addressing myself to you with the hope that the war which impends and the consequent disaster to all peoples everywhere may yet be averted.

I therefore urge with all earnestness—and I am likewise urging the president of the Republic of Poland—that the governments of Germany and of Poland agree by common accord to refrain from any positive act of hostility for a reasonable and stipulated period, and that they agree likewise by common accord to solve the controversies which have arisen between them by one of the three following methods: first, by direct negotiation; second, by submission of these controversies to an impartial arbitration in which they can both have confidence; or, third, that they agree to the solution of these controversies through the procedure of conciliation, selecting as conciliator or moderator a national of one of the traditionally neutral states of

Europe, or a national of one of the American republics which are all of them free from any connection with or participation in European political affairs.

Both Poland and Germany being sovereign governments, it is understood, of course, that upon resort to any one of the alternatives I suggest, each nation will agree to accord complete respect to the independence and territorial integrity of the other.

The people of the United States are as one in their opposition to policies of military conquest and domination. They are as one in rejecting the thesis that any ruler, or any people, possess the right to achieve their ends or objectives through the taking of action which will plunge countless millions of people into war and which will bring distress and suffering to every nation of the world, belligerent and neutral, when such ends and objectives, so far as they are just and reasonable, can be satisfied through processes of peaceful negotiation or by resort to judicial arbitration.

I appeal to you in the name of the people of the United States, and I believe in the name of peace-loving men and women everywhere, to agree to the solution of the controversies existing between your government and that of Poland through the adoption of one of the alternative methods I have proposed. I need hardly reiterate that should the governments of Germany and of Poland be willing to solve their differences in the peaceful manner suggested, the government of the United States still stands prepared to contribute its share to the solution of the problems which are endangering world peace in the form set forth in my message of April 14.

FIRESIDE CHAT ON THE WAR IN EUROPE

September 3, 1939

Tonight my single duty is to speak to the whole of America.

Until 4:30 this morning I had hoped against hope that some miracle would prevent a devastating war in Europe and bring to an end the invasion of Poland by Germany.

For four long years a succession of actual wars and constant crises have shaken the entire world and have threatened in each case to bring on the gigantic conflict which is today unhappily a fact.

It is right that I should recall to your minds the consistent and at times successful efforts of your government in these crises to throw the full weight of the United States into the cause of peace. In spite of spreading wars, I think that we have every right and every reason to maintain as a national policy the fundamental moralities, the teachings of religion, and the continuation of efforts to restore peace—for some day, though the time may be distant, we can be of even greater help to a crippled humanity.

It is right, too, to point out that the unfortunate events of these recent years have, without question, been based on the use of force and the threat of force. And it seems to me clear, even at the outbreak of this great war, that the influence of America should be consistent in seeking for humanity a final peace which will eliminate, as far as it is possible to do so, the continued use of force between nations.

It is, of course, impossible to predict the future. I have my constant stream of information from American representatives and other sources throughout the world. You, the people of this country, are receiving news through your radios and your newspapers at every hour of the day.

You are, I believe, the most enlightened and the best informed people in all the world at this moment. You are subjected to no censorship of news, and I want to add that your government has no information which it withholds or which it has any thought of withholding from you.

At the same time, as I told my press conference on Friday, it is of the highest importance that the press and the radio use the utmost caution to discriminate between actual verified fact on the one hand, and mere rumor on the other.

I can add to that by saying that I hope the people of this country will also discriminate most carefully between news and rumor. Do not believe of necessity everything you hear or read. Check up on it first.

You must master at the outset a simple but unalterable fact in modern foreign relations between nations. When peace has been broken anywhere, the peace of all countries everywhere is in danger.

It is easy for you and for me to shrug our shoulders and to say that conflicts taking place thousands of miles from the continental United States, and, indeed, thousands of miles from the whole American Hemisphere, do not seriously affect the Americas—and that all the United States has to do is to ignore them and go about its own business. Passionately though we may desire detachment, we are forced to realize that every word that comes through the air, every ship that sails the sea, every battle that is fought does affect the American future.

Let no man or woman thoughtlessly or falsely talk of America sending its armies to European fields. At this moment there is being prepared a proclamation of American neutrality. This would have been done even if there had been no neutrality statute on the books, for this proclamation is in accordance with international law and in accordance with American policy.

This will be followed by a proclamation required by the

existing Neutrality Act. And I trust that in the days to come our neutrality can be made a true neutrality.

It is of the utmost importance that the people of this country, with the best information in the world, think things through. The most dangerous enemies of American peace are those who, without well-rounded information on the whole broad subject of the past, the present, and the future, undertake to speak with assumed authority, to talk in terms of glittering generalities, to give to the nation assurances or prophesies which are of little present or future value.

I myself cannot and do not prophesy the course of events abroad—and the reason is that, because I have of necessity such a complete picture of what is going on in every part of the world, I do not dare to do so. And the other reason is that I think it is honest for me to be honest with the people of the United States.

I cannot prophesy the immediate economic effect of this new war on our nation, but I do say that no American has the moral right to profiteer at the expense either of his fellow citizens or of the men, the women, and the children who are living and dying in the midst of war in Europe.

Some things we do know. Most of us in the United States believe in spiritual values. Most of us, regardless of what church we belong to, believe in the spirit of the New Testament—a great teaching which opposes itself to the use of force, of armed force, of marching armies and falling bombs. The overwhelming masses of our people seek peace—peace at home, and the kind of peace in other lands which will not jeopardize our peace at home.

We have certain ideas and certain ideals of national safety, and we must act to preserve that safety today, and to preserve the safety of our children in future years.

That safety is and will be bound up with the safety of the Western Hemisphere and of the seas adjacent thereto. We seek to keep war from our own firesides by keeping war from coming to the Americas. For that we have historic precedent that goes back to the days of the administration of President George Washington. It is serious enough and tragic enough to every American family in every state in the Union to live in a world that is torn by wars on other continents. Those wars today affect every American home. It is our national duty to use every effort to keep them out of the Americas.

And at this time let me make the simple plea that partisanship and selfishness be adjourned; and that national unity be the thought that underlies all others.

This nation will remain a neutral nation, but I cannot ask that every American remain neutral in thought as well. Even a neutral has a right to take account of facts. Even a neutral cannot be asked to close his mind or his conscience.

I have said not once, but many times, that I have seen war and that I hate war. I say that again and again.

I hope the United States will keep out of this war. I believe that it will. And I give you assurance and reassurance that every effort of your government will be directed toward that end.

As long as it remains within my power to prevent, there will be no blackout of peace in the United States.

MESSAGE TO CONGRESS URGING REPEAL OF THE EMBARGO PROVISIONS OF THE NEUTRALITY ACT

September 21, 1939

Mr. President, Mr. Speaker, Members of the Senate and House of Representatives: I have asked the Congress to reassemble in extraordinary session in order that it may consider and act on the amendment of certain legislation, which, in my best judgment, so alters the historic foreign policy of the United States that it impairs the peaceful relations of the United States with foreign nations.

At the outset I proceed on the assumption that every member of the Senate and of the House of Representatives, and every member of the executive branch of the government, including the president and his associates, personally and officially, are equally and without reservation in favor of such measures as will protect the neutrality, the safety, and the integrity of our country and at the same time keep us out of war.

Because I am wholly willing to ascribe an honorable desire for peace to those who hold different views from my own as to what those measures should be, I trust that these gentlemen will be sufficiently generous to ascribe equally lofty purposes to those with whom they disagree. Let no man or group in any walk of life assume exclusive protectorate over the future well-being of America, because I conceive that regardless of party or section the mantle of peace and of patriotism is wide enough to cover us all. Let no group assume the exclusive label of the "peace bloc." We all belong to it.

I have at all times kept the Congress and the American people informed of events and trends in foreign affairs. I now review them in a spirit of understatement.

Since 1931 the use of force instead of the council table has constantly increased in disputes between nations—except in the Western Hemisphere, where in all those years there has been only one war, now happily terminated.

During those years also the building up of vast armies and navies and storehouses of war has proceeded abroad with growing speed and intensity. But, during these years, and extending back even to the days of the Kellogg-Briand Pact, the United States has constantly, consistently, and conscientiously done all in its power to encourage peaceful settlements, to bring about reduction of armaments, and to avert threatened wars. We have done this not only because any war anywhere necessarily hurts American security and American prosperity, but because of the more important fact that any war anywhere retards the progress of morality and religion, and impairs the security of civilization itself.

For many years the primary purpose of our foreign policy has been that this nation and this government should strive to the utmost to aid in avoiding war among nations. But if and when war unhappily comes, the government and the nation must exert every possible effort to avoid being drawn into the war.

The executive branch of the government did its utmost, within our traditional policy of noninvolvement, to aid in averting the present appalling war. Having thus striven and failed, this government must lose no time or effort to keep our nation from being drawn into the war.

In my candid judgment we shall succeed in those efforts.

We are proud of the historical record of the United States and of all the Americans during all these years, because we have thrown every ounce of our influence for peace into the scale of peace. . . .

Last January I told the Congress that "a war which threatened to envelop the world in flames has been averted, but it has become increasingly clear that peace is not assured."

By April new tensions had developed; a new crisis was in the making. Several nations with whom we had had friendly diplomatic and commercial relations had lost, or were in the process of losing, their independent identity and their very sovereignty.

During the spring and summer the trend was definitely toward further acts of military conquest and away from peace. As late as the end of July I spoke to members of the Congress about the definite possibility of war. I should have called it the probability of war.

Last January, also, I spoke to this Congress of the need for further warning of new threats of conquest, military and economic; of challenge to religion, to democracy, and to international good faith. . . .

It was because of what I foresaw last January from watching the trend of foreign affairs and their probable effect upon us that I recommended to the Congress in July of this year that changes be enacted in our neutrality law.

The essentials for American peace in this war-torn world have not changed since last January or since last July. That is why I ask you again to reexamine our own legislation.

Beginning with the foundation of our constitutional government in the year 1789, the American policy in respect to belligerent nations, with one notable exception, has been based on international law. Be it remembered that what we call international law has always had as its primary objectives the avoidance of causes of war and the prevention of the extension of war.

The single exception to which I refer was the policy adopted by this nation during the Napoleonic Wars, when, seeking to avoid involvement, we acted for some years under the so-called

Embargo and Non-Intercourse Acts. That policy turned out to be a disastrous failure—first, because it brought our own nation close to ruin, and, secondly, because it was the major cause of bringing us into active participation in European wars in our own War of 1812. It is merely reciting history to recall to you that one of the results of the policy of embargo and nonintercourse was the burning in 1814 of part of this Capitol in which we are assembled today.

Our next deviation by statute from the sound principles of neutrality and peace through international law did not come for 130 years. It was the so-called Neutrality Act of 1935—only four years ago—an act continued in force by the Joint Resolution of May 1, 1937, despite grave doubts expressed as to its wisdom by many senators and representatives and by officials charged with the conduct of our foreign relations, including myself.

I regret that the Congress passed that act. I regret equally that I signed that act.

On July 14 of this year, I asked the Congress in the cause of peace and in the interest of real American neutrality and security, to take action to change that act.

I now ask again that such action be taken in respect to that part of the act which is wholly inconsistent with ancient precepts of the law of nations—the embargo provisions. I ask it because they are, in my opinion, most vitally dangerous to American neutrality, American security and, above all, American peace.

These embargo provisions, as they exist today, prevent the sale to a belligerent by an American factory of any completed implements of war, but they allow the sale of many types of uncompleted implements of war, as well as all kinds of general material and supplies. They, furthermore, allow such products of industry and agriculture to be taken in American flagships to belligerent nations. There in itself—under the present law—lies definite danger to our neutrality and our peace. . . .

Let me set forth the present paradox of the existing legislation in its simplest terms. If, prior to 1935, a general war had broken out in Europe, the United States would have sold to, and bought from, belligerent nations such goods and products of all kinds as the belligerent nations, with their existing facilities and geographical situations, were able to buy from us or sell to us. This would have been the normal practice under the age-old doctrines of international law.

Our prior position accepted the facts of geography and of conditions of land power and sea power and air power alike, as they existed in all parts of the world.

If a war had broken out in Europe prior to 1935, there would have been no difference, for example, between our exports of sheets of aluminum and airplane wings; today there is an artificial legal difference.

Before 1935 there would have been no difference between the export of cotton and the export of gun cotton. Today there is.

Before 1935 there would have been no difference between the shipment of brass tubing in pipe form and brass tubing in shell form. Today there is.

Before 1935 there would have been no difference between the export of a motor truck and an armored motor truck. Today there is.

Let us be factual, let us recognize that a belligerent nation often needs wheat and lard and cotton for the survival of its population just as much as it needs antiaircraft guns and antisubmarine depth charges. Let those who seek to retain the present embargo position be wholly consistent. Let them seek new legislation to cut off cotton and cloth and copper and meat and wheat and a thousand other articles from all of the nations at war.

I seek a greater consistency through the repeal of the embargo provisions, and a return to international law. I seek reenactment of the historic and traditional American policy which, except for the disastrous interlude of the Embargo and Non-Intercourse Acts, has served us well from the very beginning of our constitutional existence.

It has been erroneously said that return to that policy might bring us nearer to war. I give to you my deep and unalterable conviction, based on years of experience as a worker in the field of international peace, that by the repeal of the embargo the United States will more probably remain at peace than if the law remains as it stands today. I say this because with the repeal of the embargo, this government clearly and definitely will insist that American citizens and American ships keep away from the immediate perils of the actual zones of conflict. . . .

When and if—I do not like even to mention the word "if," I would rather say "when"—repeal of the embargo is accomplished, certain other phases of policy reinforcing American safety should be considered. While nearly all of us are in agreement on their objectives, the only questions relate to method.

I believe that American merchant vessels should, as far as possible, be restricted from entering war zones. But, war zones may change so swiftly and so frequently in the days to come, that it is impossible to fix them permanently by act of Congress; specific legislation may prevent adjustment to constant and quick change. It seems, therefore, more practical to delimit the actual geography of the war zones through action of the State Department and administrative agencies. . . .

The second objective is to prevent American citizens from traveling on belligerent vessels, or in danger areas. This can also be accomplished either by legislation, through continuance in force of certain provisions of existing law, or by proclamation making it clear to all Americans that any such travel is at their own risk.

The third objective, requiring the foreign buyer to take transfer of title in this country to commodities purchased by belligerents, is also a result that can be attained by legislation or substantially achieved through due notice by proclamation.

The fourth objective is the preventing of war credits to belligerents. This can be accomplished by maintaining in force existing provisions of law, or by proclamation making it clear that if credits are granted by American citizens to belligerents, our government will take no steps in the future to relieve them of risk or loss.

The result of these last two objectives will be to require all purchases to be made in cash, and all cargoes to be carried in the purchasers' own ships, at the purchasers' own risk.

Two other objectives have been amply attained by existing law, namely, regulating collection of funds in this country for belligerents, and the maintenance of a license system covering import and export of arms, ammunition, and implements of war. Under present enactments, such arms cannot be carried to belligerent countries on American vessels, and this provision should not be disturbed. . . .

To those who say that this program would involve a step toward war on our part, I reply that it offers far greater safeguards than we now possess or have ever possessed, to protect American lives and property from danger. It is a positive program for giving safety. This means less likelihood of incidents and controversies which tend to draw us into conflict, as they unhappily did in the last World War. There lies the road to peace! . . .

In respect to our own defense, you are aware that I have issued a proclamation setting forth "A National Emergency in Connection with Observance, Safeguarding, and Enforcement of Neutrality and the Strengthening of the National Defense within the Limits of Peacetime Authorization." This was done solely to make wholly constitutional and legal certain obviously necessary measures. I have authorized increases in the personnel of the army, the navy, the Marine Corps, and the Coast Guard, which will bring all four of them to a total still below peacetime strength as authorized by the Congress.

I have authorized the State Department to use, for the repatriation of Americans caught in the war zone, the sum of five hundred thousand dollars already authorized by the Congress.

I have authorized the addition of 150 persons to the Department of Justice to be used in the protection of the United States against subversive foreign activities within our borders.

At this time I ask for no further authority from the Congress. At this time I see no need for further executive action under the proclamation of limited national emergency.

Therefore, I see no impelling reason for the consideration of other legislation at this extraordinary session of the Congress.

It is, of course, possible that in the months to come unforeseen needs for further legislation may develop but they are not imperative today. . . .

I should like to be able to offer the hope that the shadow over the world might swiftly pass. I cannot. The facts compel my stating, with candor, that darker periods may lie ahead. The disaster is not of our making; no act of ours engendered the forces which assault the foundations of civilization. Yet we find ourselves affected to the core; our currents of commerce are changing, our minds are filled with new problems, our position in world affairs has already been altered.

In such circumstances our policy must be to appreciate in the deepest sense the true American interest. Rightly considered, this interest is not selfish. Destiny first made us, with our sister nations on this hemisphere, joint heirs of European culture. Fate seems now to compel us to assume the task of helping to maintain in the Western world a citadel wherein that civilization may be kept alive. The peace, the integrity, and the safety of the Americas—these must be kept firm and serene.

In a period when it is sometimes said that free discussion is no longer compatible with national safety, may you by your deeds show the world that we of the United States are one people, of one mind, one spirit, one clear resolution, walking before God in the light of the living.

Radio Address to the 1940 Democratic National Convention

July 19, 1940

Members of the Convention—My Friends: It is very late; but I have felt that you would rather that I speak to you now than wait until tomorrow.

It is with a very full heart that I speak tonight. I must confess that I do so with mixed feelings—because I find myself, as almost everyone does sooner or later in his lifetime, in a conflict between deep personal desire for retirement on the one hand, and that quiet, invisible thing called "conscience" on the other.

Because there are self-appointed commentators and interpreters who will seek to misinterpret or question motives, I speak in a somewhat personal vein; and I must trust to the good faith and common sense of the American people to accept my own good faith—and to do their own interpreting.

When, in 1936, I was chosen by the voters for a second time as president, it was my firm intention to turn over the responsibilities of government to other hands at the end of my term. That conviction remained with me. Eight years in the presidency, following a period of bleak depression, and covering one world crisis after another, would normally entitle any man to the relaxation that comes from honorable retirement.

During the spring of 1939, world events made it clear to all but the blind or the partisan that a great war in Europe had become not merely a possibility but a probability, and that such a war would of necessity deeply affect the future of this nation.

When the conflict first broke out last September, it was still my intention to announce clearly and simply, at an early date, that under no conditions would I accept reelection. This fact was well known to my friends, and I think was understood by many citizens.

It soon became evident, however, that such a public statement on my part would be unwise from the point of view of sheer public duty. As president of the United States, it was my clear duty, with the aid of the Congress, to preserve our neutrality, to shape our program of defense, to meet rapid changes, to keep our domestic affairs adjusted to shifting world conditions, and to sustain the policy of the Good Neighbor.

It was also my obvious duty to maintain to the utmost the influence of this mighty nation in our effort to prevent the spread of war, and to sustain by all legal means those governments threatened by other governments which had rejected the principles of democracy.

Swiftly moving foreign events made necessary swift action at home and beyond the seas. Plans for national defense had to be expanded and adjusted to meet new forms of warfare. American citizens and their welfare had to be safeguarded in many foreign zones of danger. National unity in the United States became a crying essential in the face of the development of unbelievable types of espionage and international treachery.

Every day that passed called for the postponement of personal plans and partisan debate until the latest possible moment. The normal conditions under which I would have made public declaration of my personal desires were wholly gone.

And so, thinking solely of the national good and of the international scene, I came to the reluctant conclusion that such declaration should not be made before the national convention. It was accordingly made to you within an hour after the permanent organization of this convention.

Like any other man, I am complimented by the honor you have done me. But I know you will understand the spirit in which I say that no call of party alone would prevail upon me to accept reelection to the presidency.

The real decision to be made in these circumstances is not

the acceptance of a nomination, but rather an ultimate willingness to serve if chosen by the electorate of the United States. Many considerations enter into this decision.

During the past few months, with due congressional approval, we in the United States have been taking steps to implement the total defense of America. I cannot forget that in carrying out this program I have drafted into the service of the nation many men and women, taking them away from important private affairs, calling them suddenly from their homes and their businesses. I have asked them to leave their own work, and to contribute their skill and experience to the cause of their nation.

I, as the head of their government, have asked them to do this. Regardless of party, regardless of personal convenience, they came—they answered the call. Every single one of them, with one exception, has come to the nation's capital to serve the nation. . . .

Just as a system of national defense based on manpower alone, without the mechanized equipment of modern warfare, is totally insufficient for adequate national defense, so also planes and guns and tanks are wholly insufficient unless they are implemented by the power of men trained to use them.

Such manpower consists not only of pilots and gunners and infantry and those who operate tanks. For every individual in actual combat service, it is necessary for adequate defense that we have ready at hand at least four or five other trained individuals organized for noncombat services.

Because of the millions of citizens involved in the conduct of defense, most right-thinking persons are agreed that some form of selection by draft is as necessary and fair today as it was in 1917 and 1918.

Nearly every American is willing to do his share or her share to defend the United States. It is neither just nor efficient to permit that task to fall upon any one section or any one group. For every section and every group depend for their existence upon the survival of the nation as a whole.

Lying awake, as I have, on many nights, I have asked myself

whether I have the right, as commander in chief of the army and navy, to call on men and women to serve their country or to train themselves to serve and, at the same time, decline to serve my country in my own personal capacity, if I am called upon to do so by the people of my country.

In times like these—in times of great tension, of great crisis—the compass of the world narrows to a single fact. The fact which dominates our world is the fact of armed aggression, the fact of successful armed aggression, aimed at the form of government, the kind of society that we in the United States have chosen and established for ourselves. It is a fact which no one longer doubts, which no one is longer able to ignore.

It is not an ordinary war. It is a revolution imposed by force of arms, which threatens all men everywhere. It is a revolution which proposes not to set men free but to reduce them to slavery—to reduce them to slavery in the interest of a dictatorship which has already shown the nature and the extent of the advantage which it hopes to obtain.

That is the fact which dominates our world and which dominates the lives of all of us, each and every one of us. In the face of the danger which confronts our time, no individual retains, or can hope to retain, the right of personal choice which free men enjoy in times of peace. He has a first obligation to serve in the defense of our institutions of freedom—a first obligation to serve his country in whatever capacity his country finds him useful.

Like most men of my age, I had made plans for myself, plans for a private life of my own choice and for my own satisfaction, a life of that kind to begin in January 1941. These plans, like so many other plans, had been made in a world which now seems as distant as another planet. Today all private plans, all private lives, have been in a sense repealed by an overriding public danger. In the face of that public danger all those who can be of service to the Republic have no choice but to offer themselves for service in those capacities for which they may be fitted.

Those, my friends, are the reasons why I have had to admit

to myself, and now to state to you, that my conscience will not let me turn my back upon a call to service.

The right to make that call rests with the people through the American method of a free election. Only the people themselves can draft a president. If such a draft should be made upon me, I say to you, in the utmost simplicity, I will, with God's help, continue to serve with the best of my ability and with the fullness of my strength. . . .

In some respects, as I think my good wife suggested an hour or so ago, the next few months will be different from the usual national campaigns of recent years.

Most of you know how important it is that the president of the United States in these days remain close to the seat of government. Since last summer I have been compelled to abandon proposed journeys to inspect many of our great national projects from the Alleghenies to the Pacific Coast.

Events move so fast in other parts of the world that it has become my duty to remain either in the White House itself or at some nearby point where I can reach Washington and even Europe and Asia by direct telephone—where, if need be, I can be back at my desk in the space of a very few hours. And in addition, the splendid work of the new defense machinery will require me to spend vastly more time in conference with the responsible administration heads under me. Finally, the added task which the present crisis has imposed also upon the Congress, compelling them to forego their usual adjournment, calls for constant cooperation between the executive and legislative branches, to the efficiency of which I am glad indeed now to pay tribute.

I do expect, of course, during the coming months to make my usual periodic reports to the country through the medium of press conferences and radio talks. I shall not have the time or the inclination to engage in purely political debate. But I shall never be loath to call the attention of the nation to deliberate or unwitting falsifications of fact, which are sometimes made by political candidates.

I have spoken to you in a very informal and personal way. The exigencies of the day require, however, that I also talk with you about things which transcend any personality and go very deeply to the roots of American civilization.

Our lives have been based on those fundamental freedoms and liberties which we Americans have cherished for a century and a half. The establishment of them and the preservation of them in each succeeding generation have been accomplished through the processes of free elective government—the demo-cratic-republican form, based on the representative system and the coordination of the executive, the legislative, and the judicial branches.

The task of safeguarding our institutions seems to me to be twofold. One must be accomplished, if it becomes necessary, by the armed defense forces of the nation. The other, by the united effort of the men and women of the country to make our federal and state and local governments responsive to the growing re-quirements of modern democracy.

There have been occasions, as we remember, when reactions in the march of democracy have set in, and forward-looking progress has seemed to stop.

But such periods have been followed by liberal and progres-sive times which have enabled the nation to catch up with new developments in fulfilling new human needs. Such a time has been the past seven years. Because we had seemed to lag in previous years, we have had to develop, speedily and efficiently, the answers to aspirations which had come from every state and every family in the land.

We have sometimes called it social legislation; we have sometimes called it legislation to end the abuses of the past; we have sometimes called it legislation for human security; and we have sometimes called it legislation to better the condition of life of the many millions of our fellow citizens who could not have the essentials of life or hope for an American standard of living.

Some of us have labeled it a wider and more equitable distribution of wealth in our land. It has included among its aims to liberalize and broaden the control of vast industries— lodged today in the hands of a relatively small group of individuals of very great financial power.

But all of these definitions and labels are essentially the expression of one consistent thought. They represent a constantly growing sense of human decency, human decency throughout our nation.

This sense of human decency is happily confined to no group or class. You find it in the humblest home. You find it among those who toil, and among the shopkeepers and the farmers of the nation. You find it, to a growing degree, even among those who are listed in that top group which has so much control over the industrial and financial structure of the nation. Therefore, this urge of humanity can by no means be labeled a war of class against class. It is rather a war against poverty and suffering and ill-health and insecurity, a war in which all classes are joining in the interest of a sound and enduring democracy.

I do not believe for a moment, and I know that you do not believe either, that we have fully answered all the needs of human security. But we have covered much of the road. . . .

But we all know that our progress at home and in the other American nations toward this realization of a better human decency—progress along free lines—is gravely endangered by what is happening on other continents. In Europe, many nations, through dictatorships or invasions, have been compelled to abandon normal democratic processes. They have been compelled to adopt forms of government which some call "new and efficient."

They are not new, my friends, they are only a relapse—a relapse into ancient history. The omnipotent rulers of the greater part of modern Europe have guaranteed efficiency, and work, and a type of security.

But the slaves who built the pyramids for the glory of the dictator pharaohs of Egypt had that kind of security, that kind of efficiency, that kind of corporative state.

So did the inhabitants of that world which extended from

Britain to Persia under the undisputed rule of the proconsuls sent out from Rome.

So did the henchmen, the tradesmen, the mercenaries, and the slaves of the feudal system which dominated Europe a thousand years ago.

So did the people of those nations of Europe who received their kings and their government at the whim of the conquering Napoleon.

Whatever its new trappings and new slogans, tyranny is the oldest and most discredited rule known to history. And whenever tyranny has replaced a more human form of government, it has been due more to internal causes than external. Democracy can thrive only when it enlists the devotion of those whom Lincoln called the common people. Democracy can hold that devotion only when it adequately respects their dignity by so ordering society as to assure to the masses of men and women reasonable security and hope for themselves and for their children. . . .

The government of the United States for the past seven years has had the courage openly to oppose by every peaceful means the spread of the dictator form of government. If our government should pass to other hands next January—untried hands, inexperienced hands—we can merely hope and pray that they will not substitute appeasement and compromise with those who seek to destroy all democracies everywhere, including here.

I would not undo, if I could, the efforts I made to prevent war from the moment it was threatened and to restrict the area of carnage, down to the last minute. I do not now soften the condemnation expressed by Secretary Hull and myself from time to time for the acts of aggression that have wiped out ancient liberty-loving, peace-pursuing countries which had scrupulously maintained neutrality. I do not recant the sentiments of sympathy with all free peoples resisting such aggression, or begrudge the material aid that we have given to them. I do not regret my consistent endeavor to awaken this country to the menace for us and for all we hold dear.

I have pursued these efforts in the face of appeaser fifth columnists who charged me with hysteria and war-mongering. But I felt it my duty—my simple, plain, inescapable duty—to arouse my countrymen to the danger of the new forces let loose in the world.

So long as I am president, I will do all I can to insure that that foreign policy remain our foreign policy.

All that I have done to maintain the peace of this country and to prepare it morally, as well as physically, for whatever contingencies may be in store, I submit to the judgment of my countrymen.

We face one of the great choices of history.

It is not alone a choice of government by the people versus dictatorship.

It is not alone a choice of freedom versus slavery.

It is not alone a choice between moving forward or falling back.

It is all of these rolled into one.

It is the continuance of civilization as we know it versus the ultimate destruction of all that we have held dear—religion against godlessness; the ideal of justice against the practice of force; moral decency versus the firing squad; courage to speak out, and to act, versus the false lullaby of appeasement.

But it has been well said that a selfish and greedy people cannot be free.

The American people must decide whether these things are worth making sacrifices of money, of energy, and of self. They will not decide by listening to mere words or by reading mere pledge, interpretations, and claims. They will decide on the record—the record as it has been made, the record of things as they are.

The American people will sustain the progress of a representative democracy, asking the Divine Blessing as they face the future with courage and with faith.

Statement on the Adoption of Peacetime Selective Service

September 16, 1940

America has adopted Selective Service in time of peace, and, in doing so, has broadened and enriched our basic concept of citizenship. Beside the clear democratic ideals of equal rights, equal privileges, and equal opportunities, we have set forth the underlying other duties, obligations, and responsibilities of equal service.

In thus providing for national defense, we have not carved a new and uncharted trail in the history of our democratic institutions. On the contrary, we have merely reasserted an old and accepted principle of democratic government. The militia system, the self-armed citizenry with the obligation of military service incumbent upon every free man, has its roots in the old common law. It was brought to this continent by our forefathers. It was an accepted institution in colonial days. At the time of the adoption of the federal Constitution, nine of the thirteen states explicitly provided for universal service in their basic laws.

In those days, little was required in the way of equipment and training for the man in arms. The average American had his flintlock and knew how to use it. In addition, he was healthy, strong, and accustomed to hardship. When he reported for military duty, he brought with him his musket and his powder horn. His daily life inured him to the rigors of warfare.

Today, the art of war calls for a wide variety of technical weapons. Modern life does not emphasize the qualities demanded of soldiers. Moreover, behind the armed forces, we must have a munitions industry as a part of an economic system capable of providing the fighting man with his full requirements of arms and equipment. Many individuals, therefore, may serve their country best by holding their posts on the production line. The object of Selective Service is to provide men for our army and navy and at the same time disturb as little as possible the normal life of the nation.

Selective Service consists of four steps, which singly and in the group have been developed to operate with the fairness and justice characteristic of free, democratic institutions. These steps are: registration, classification, selection, and induction.

Wednesday, October 16, has been set aside, on which day every male between twenty-one and thirty-five, inclusive, will be expected to report to a neighborhood precinct to fill out a registration card and a registration certificate. The certificate issued to the individual will be carried by him as a testimonial to his acceptance of the fundamental obligation of citizenship. The registration card will be forwarded to the county clerk or similar official and will be delivered by him to the local Selective Service board. These boards, consisting of three men, each appointed by the president, upon recommendations of the state governors, will be set up in more than six thousand communities. When the states notify the national director of Selective Service that all the local boards have completed this work, a national drawing by lot will determine the order of priority of the registrants in each local board area. The national priority list will be furnished to the local boards and the corresponding order of selection will be entered on the registration cards in their custody.

The priority established by the drawing will determine the order in which questionnaires will be mailed to the registrants. Upon receipt of these questionnaires the registrants will enter on these forms pertinent facts on the basis of which their final classification will be determined.

There will be organized in every community in our nation advisory boards for registrants, composed of patriotic citizens, civilian volunteers, to assist registrants in presenting fairly the facts to be used in determining the place of each individual in the scheme of national defense.

After the return of these questionnaires, the local board, after due consideration, will place the registrants in one of four classes. In Class I will be those who are available for immediate service; in Class II, those who are deferred because of the essential character of the service they are rendering in their present occupations; in Class III, those individuals who should be deferred because of individuals dependent upon them for support; in Class IV, those specifically deferred by the terms of the act.

The total number of individuals needed by the armed forces will be prorated among the several states. In this allocation due consideration will be given to the number of men already furnished by that state for our military forces. Within each state a quota, in a similar manner, will be divided among the local boards. Thus, each locality will be asked to furnish its fair share of individuals for induction into our armed forces.

In each of these local board areas individuals between the ages of eighteen and thirty-five will be offered an opportunity to volunteer for a one-year period of service and training. Such applicants will be accepted before any other individuals are selected, provided they are suitable for military service. It will be the duty of the local board to select as many additional individuals as are necessary to fill the quota for that particular area.

Following the tentative selection of these individuals, a local medical examiner will examine them physically. If they are accepted, they will be sent forward for final physical examination by medical officers of the army, navy, or Marine Corps. Those who pass will be inducted into the service.

In the military service they will be intelligently led, comfortably clothed, well fed, and adequately armed and equipped for basic training. By the time they get physically hardened, mentally disciplined, and properly trained in fundamentals, the flow of critical munitions from factory to combat units will meet the full requirements for their advanced training.

In the military service, Americans from all walks of life—rich and poor, country-bred and city raised, farmer, student, manual laborer, and white-collar worker—will learn to live side by side, to depend upon each other in military drills and maneuvers, and to appreciate each other's dignity as American citizens.

Universal service will bring not only greater preparedness to meet the threat of war, but a wider distribution of tolerance and understanding to enjoy the blessings of peace.

EIGHTH ANNUAL MESSAGE TO CONGRESS

January 6, 1941

THE FOUR FREEDOMS

Mr. President, Mr. Speaker, Members of the Seventy-seventh Congress: I address you, the members of the Seventy-seventh Congress, at a moment unprecedented in the history of the Union. I use the word *unprecedented* because at no previous time has American security been as seriously threatened from without as it is today.

Since the permanent formation of our government under the Constitution, in 1789, most of the periods of crisis in our history have related to our domestic affairs. Fortunately, only one of these—the four-year War Between the States—ever threatened our national unity. Today, thank God, 130 million Americans, in forty-eight states, have forgotten points of the compass in our national unity.

It is true that prior to 1914 the United States often had been disturbed by events in other continents. We had even engaged in two wars with European nations and in a number of undeclared wars in the West Indies, in the Mediterranean, and in the Pacific for the maintenance of American rights and for the principles of peaceful commerce. But in no case had a serious threat been raised against our national safety or our continued independence.

What I seek to convey is the historic truth that the United States as a nation has at all times maintained clear, definite opposition to any attempt to lock us in behind an ancient Chinese wall while the procession of civilization went past. Today, thinking of our children and of their children, we oppose enforced isolation for ourselves or for any other part of the Americas.

That determination of ours, extending over all these years, was proved, for example, during the quarter century of wars following the French Revolution.

While the Napoleonic struggles did threaten interests of the United States because of the French foothold in the West Indies and in Louisiana, and while we engaged in the War of 1812 to vindicate our right to peaceful trade, it is nevertheless clear that neither France nor Great Britain, nor any other nation, was aiming at domination of the whole world.

In like fashion, from 1815 to 1914—ninety-nine years—no single war in Europe or in Asia constituted a real threat against our future or against the future of any other American nation.

Except in the Maximilian interlude in Mexico, no foreign power sought to establish itself in this hemisphere; and the strength of the British fleet in the Atlantic has been a friendly strength. It is still a friendly strength.

Even when the World War broke out in 1914, it seemed to contain only small threat of danger to our own American future. But, as time went on, the American people began to visualize what the downfall of democratic nations might mean to our own democracy.

We need not overemphasize imperfections in the Peace of Versailles. We need not harp on failure of the democracies to deal with problems of world reconstruction. We should remember that the Peace of 1919 was far less unjust than the kind of "pacification" which began even before Munich, and which is being carried on under the new order of tyranny that seeks to spread over every continent today. The American people have unalterably set their faces against that tyranny.

Every realist knows that the democratic way of life is at this moment being directly assailed in every part of the world— assailed either by arms, or by secret spreading of poisonous propaganda by those who seek to destroy unity and promote discord in nations that are still at peace.

During sixteen long months this assault has blotted out the whole pattern of democratic life in an appalling number of independent nations, great and small. The assailants are still on the march, threatening other nations, great and small.

Therefore, as your president, performing my constitutional duty to "give to the Congress information of the state of the Union," I find it, unhappily, necessary to report that the future and the safety of our country and of our democracy are overwhelmingly involved in events far beyond our borders.

Armed defense of democratic existence is now being gallantly waged in four continents. If that defense fails, all the population and all the resources of Europe, Asia, Africa, and Australasia will be dominated by the conquerors. Let us remember that the total of those populations and their resources in those four continents greatly exceeds the sum total of the population and the resources of the whole of the Western Hemisphere—many times over.

In times like these it is immature—and incidentally, untrue—for anybody to brag that an unprepared America, single-handed, and with one hand tied behind its back, can hold off the whole world.

No realistic American can expect from a dictator's peace international generosity, or return of true independence, or world disarmament, or freedom of expression, or freedom of religion—or even good business. . . .

I have recently pointed out how quickly the tempo of modern warfare could bring into our very midst the physical attack which we must eventually expect if the dictator nations win this war.

There is much loose talk of our immunity from immediate and direct invasion from across the seas. Obviously, as long as the British navy retains its power, no such danger exists. Even if there were no British navy, it is not probable that any enemy would be stupid enough to attack us by landing troops in the United States from across thousands of miles of ocean, until it had acquired strategic bases from which to operate.

But we learn much from the lessons of the past years in Europe—particularly the lesson of Norway, whose essential seaports were captured by treachery and surprise built up over a series of years.

The first phase of the invasion of this hemisphere would not be the landing of regular troops. The necessary strategic points would be occupied by secret agents and their dupes—and great numbers of them are already here, and in Latin America.

As long as the aggressor nations maintain the offensive, they —not we—will choose the time and the place and the method of their attack.

That is why the future of all the American republics is today in serious danger. . . .

Our national policy is this:

First, by an impressive expression of the public will and without regard to partisanship, we are committed to all-inclusive national defense.

Second, by an impressive expression of the public will and without regard to partisanship, we are committed to full support of all those resolute peoples, everywhere, who are resisting aggression and are thereby keeping war away from our hemisphere. By this support, we express our determination that the democratic cause shall prevail; and we strengthen the defense and the security of our own nation.

Third, by an impressive expression of the public will and without regard to partisanship, we are committed to the proposition that principles of morality and considerations for our own security will never permit us to acquiesce in a peace dictated by aggressors and sponsored by appeasers. We know that enduring peace cannot be bought at the cost of other people's freedom. . . .

Therefore, the immediate need is a swift and driving increase in our armament production.

Leaders of industry and labor have responded to our summons. Goals of speed have been set. In some cases these goals are being reached ahead of time; in some cases we are on schedule; in other cases there are slight but not serious delays; and in some cases—and I am sorry to say very important cases—we are all concerned by the slowness of the accomplishment of our plans.

The army and navy, however, have made substantial progress during the past year. Actual experience is improving and speeding up our methods of production with every passing day. And today's best is not good enough for tomorrow.

I am not satisfied with the progress thus far made. The men in charge of the program represent the best in training, in ability, and in patriotism. They are not satisfied with the progress thus far made. None of us will be satisfied until the job is done. . . .

To change a whole nation from a basis of peacetime production of implements of peace to a basis of wartime production of implements of war is no small task. And the greatest difficulty comes at the beginning of the program, when new tools, new plant facilities, new assembly lines, and new ship ways must first be constructed before the actual matériel begins to flow steadily and speedily from them. . . .

New circumstances are constantly begetting new needs for our safety. I shall ask this Congress for greatly increased new appropriations and authorizations to carry on what we have begun.

I also ask this Congress for authority and for funds sufficient to manufacture additional munitions and war supplies of many kinds, to be turned over to those nations which are now in actual war with aggressor nations.

Our most useful and immediate role is to act as an arsenal for them as well as for ourselves. They do not need manpower, but they do need billions of dollars worth of the weapons of defense.

The time is near when they will not be able to pay for them all in ready cash. We cannot, and we will not, tell them that they must surrender, merely because of present inability to pay for the weapons which we know they must have.

I do not recommend that we make them a loan of dollars with which to pay for these weapons—a loan to be repaid in dollars.

I recommend that we make it possible for those nations to continue to obtain war materials in the United States, fitting their orders into our own program. Nearly all their matériel would, if the time ever came, be useful for our own defense. . . .

For what we send abroad, we shall be repaid within a reasonable time following the close of hostilities, in similar materials, or, at our option, in other goods of many kinds, which they can produce and which we need.

Let us say to the democracies: "We Americans are vitally concerned in your defense of freedom. We are putting forth our energies, our resources, and our organizing powers to give you the strength to regain and maintain a free world. We shall send you, in ever-increasing numbers, ships, planes, tanks, guns. This is our purpose and our pledge."

In fulfillment of this purpose we will not be intimidated by the threats of dictators that they will regard as a breach of international law or as an act of war our aid to the democracies which dare to resist their aggression. Such aid is not an act of war, even if a dictator should unilaterally proclaim it so to be.

When the dictators—if the dictators—are ready to make war upon us, they will not wait for an act of war on our part. They did not wait for Norway or Belgium or the Netherlands to commit an act of war. . . .

The nation takes great satisfaction and much strength from the things which have been done to make its people conscious of their individual stake in the preservation of democratic life in America. Those things have toughened the fiber of our people, have renewed their faith and strengthened their devotion to the institutions we make ready to protect.

Certainly this is no time for any of us to stop thinking about the social and economic problems which are the root cause of the social revolution which is today a supreme factor in the world.

For there is nothing mysterious about the foundations of a healthy and strong democracy. The basic things expected by our people of their political and economic systems are simple. They are:

Equality of opportunity for youth and for others.

Jobs for those who can work.

Security for those who need it.

The ending of special privilege for the few.

The preservation of civil liberties for all.

The enjoyment of the fruits of scientific progress in a wider and constantly rising standard of living.

These are the simple, basic things that must never be lost sight of in the turmoil and unbelievable complexity of our modern world. The inner and abiding strength of our economic and political systems is dependent upon the degree to which they fulfill these expectations.

Many subjects connected with our social economy call for immediate improvement.

As examples:

We should bring more citizens under the coverage of old-age pensions and unemployment insurance.

We should widen the opportunities for adequate medical care.

We should plan a better system by which persons deserving or needing gainful employment may obtain it.

I have called for personal sacrifice. I am assured of the willingness of almost all Americans to respond to that call. . . .

In the future days, which we seek to make secure, we look forward to a world founded upon four essential human freedoms.

The first is freedom of speech and expression—everywhere in the world.

The second is freedom of every person to worship God in his own way—everywhere in the world.

The third is freedom from want—which, translated into world terms, means economic understandings which will secure to every nation a healthy peacetime life for its inhabitants—everywhere in the world.

The fourth is freedom from fear—which, translated into world terms, means a worldwide reduction of armaments to such a point and in such a thorough fashion that no nation will be in a position to commit an act of physical aggression against any neighbor—anywhere in the world.

That is no vision of a distant millennium. It is a definite basis for a kind of world attainable in our own time and generation. That kind of world is the very antithesis of the so-called new order of tyranny which the dictators seek to create with the crash of a bomb.

To that new order we oppose the greater conception—the moral order. A good society is able to face schemes of world domination and foreign revolutions alike without fear.

Since the beginning of our American history, we have been engaged in change—in a perpetual peaceful revolution, a revolution which goes on steadily, quietly adjusting itself to changing conditions—without the concentration camp or the quick-lime in the ditch. The world order which we seek is the cooperation of free countries, working together in a friendly, civilized society.

This nation has placed its destiny in the hands and heads and hearts of its millions of free men and women; and its faith in freedom under the guidance of God. Freedom means the supremacy of human rights everywhere. Our support goes to those who struggle to gain those rights or keep them. Our strength is our unity of purpose.

To that high concept there can be no end save victory.

Third Inaugural Address

January 20, 1941

On each national day of inauguration since 1789, the people have renewed their sense of dedication to the United States.

In Washington's day the task of the people was to create and weld together a nation.

In Lincoln's day the task of the people was to preserve that nation from disruption from within.

In this day the task of the people is to save that nation and its institutions from disruption from without.

To us there has come a time, in the midst of swift happenings, to pause for a moment and take stock—to recall what our place in history has been, and to rediscover what we are and what we may be. If we do not, we risk the real peril of isolation, the real peril of inaction.

Lives of nations are determined not by the count of years, but by the lifetime of the human spirit. The life of a man is threescore years and ten: a little more, a little less. The life of a nation is the fullness of the measure of its will to live.

There are men who doubt this. There are men who believe that democracy, as a form of government and a frame of life, is limited or measured by a kind of mystical and artificial fate— that, for some unexplained reason, tyranny and slavery have become the surging wave of the future—and that freedom is an ebbing tide.

But we Americans know that this is not true.

Eight years ago, when the life of this Republic seemed frozen by a fatalistic terror, we proved that this is not true. We were in the midst of shock—but we acted. We acted quickly, boldly, decisively.

These later years have been living years—fruitful years for the people of this democracy. For they have brought to us greater security and, I hope, a better understanding that life's ideals are to be measured in other than material things.

Most vital to our present and to our future is this experience of a democracy which successfully survived crisis at home; put away many evil things; built new structures on enduring lines; and, through it all, maintained the fact of its democracy.

For action has been taken within the three-way framework of the Constitution of the United States. The coordinate branches of the government continue freely to function. The Bill of Rights remains inviolate. The freedom of elections is wholly maintained. Prophets of the downfall of American democracy have seen their dire predictions come to naught.

No, democracy is not dying.

We know it because we have seen it revive—and grow.

We know it cannot die—because it is built on the unhampered initiative of individual men and women joined together in a common enterprise, an enterprise undertaken and carried through by the free expression of a free majority.

We know it because democracy alone, of all forms of government, enlists the full force of men's enlightened will.

We know it because democracy alone has constructed an unlimited civilization capable of infinite progress in the improvement of human life.

We know it because, if we look below the surface, we sense it still spreading on every continent—for it is the most humane, the most advanced, and in the end the most unconquerable of all forms of human society.

A nation, like a person, has a body—a body that must be fed and clothed and housed, invigorated and rested, in a manner that measures up to the standards of our time.

A nation, like a person, has a mind—a mind that must be kept informed and alert, that must know itself, that understands the hopes and the needs of its neighbors—all the other nations that live within the narrowing circle of the world.

A nation, like a person, has something deeper, something more permanent, something larger than the sum of all its parts.

It is that something which matters most to its future, which calls forth the most sacred guarding of its present.

It is a thing for which we find it difficult—even impossible—to hit upon a single, simple word.

And yet, we all understand what it is: the spirit, the faith of America. It is the product of centuries. It was born in the multitudes of those who came from many lands, some of high degree, but mostly plain people—who sought here, early and late, to find freedom more freely.

The democratic aspiration is no mere recent phase in human history. It is human history. It permeated the ancient life of early peoples. It blazed anew in the Middle Ages. It was written in Magna Carta.

In the Americas its impact has been irresistible. America has been the New World in all tongues, and to all peoples, not because this continent was a new-found land, but because all those who came here believed they could create upon this continent a new life—a life that should be new in freedom.

Its vitality was written into our own Mayflower Compact, into the Declaration of Independence, into the Constitution of the United States, into the Gettysburg Address.

Those who first came here to carry out the longings of their spirit, and the millions who followed, and the stock that sprang from them—all have moved forward constantly and consistently toward an ideal which in itself has gained stature and clarity with each generation.

The hopes of the Republic cannot forever tolerate either undeserved poverty or self-serving wealth.

We know that we still have far to go; that we must more greatly build the security and the opportunity and the knowledge of every citizen, in the measure justified by the resources and the capacity of the land.

But it is not enough to achieve these purposes alone. It is not enough to clothe and feed the body of this nation, to instruct and inform its mind. For there is also the spirit. And of the three, the greatest is the spirit.

Without the body and the mind, as all men know, the nation could not live.

But if the spirit of America were killed, even though the nation's body and mind, constricted in an alien world, lived on, the America we know would have perished.

That spirit—that faith—speaks to us in our daily lives in ways often unnoticed, because they seem so obvious. It speaks to us here in the capital of the nation. It speaks to us through the processes of governing in the sovereignties of forty-eight states. It speaks to us in our counties, in our cities, in our towns, and in our villages. It speaks to us from the other nations of the hemisphere, and from those across the seas—the enslaved, as well as the free. Sometimes we fail to hear or heed these voices of freedom because to us the privilege of our freedom is such an old, old story.

The destiny of America was proclaimed in words of prophecy spoken by our first president in his first inaugural in 1789—words almost directed, it would seem, to this year of 1941: "The preservation of the sacred fire of liberty and the destiny of the republican model of government are justly considered . . . deeply, . . . finally, staked on the experiment intrusted to the hands of the American people."

If you and I in this later day lose that sacred fire—if we let it be smothered with doubt and fear—then we shall reject the destiny which Washington strove so valiantly and so triumphantly to establish. The preservation of the spirit and faith of the nation does, and will, furnish the highest justification for every sacrifice that we may make in the cause of national defense.

In the face of great perils never before encountered, our strong purpose is to protect and to perpetuate the integrity of democracy.

For this we muster the spirit of America, and the faith of America.

We do not retreat. We are not content to stand still. As Americans, we go forward, in the service of our country, by the will of God.

RADIO ADDRESS ANNOUNCING AN UNLIMITED NATIONAL EMERGENCY

May 27, 1941

I am speaking tonight from the White House in the presence of the Governing Board of the Pan-American Union, the Canadian minister, and their families. The members of this board are the ambassadors and ministers of the American republics in Washington. It is appropriate that I do this, for now, as never before, the unity of the American republics is of supreme importance to each and every one of us and to the cause of freedom throughout the world. Our future independence is bound up with the future independence of all of our sister republics.

The pressing problems that confront us are military and naval problems. We cannot afford to approach them from the point of view of wishful thinkers or sentimentalists. What we face is cold, hard fact.

The first and fundamental fact is that what started as a European war has developed, as the Nazis always intended it should develop, into a world war for world domination.

Adolf Hitler never considered the domination of Europe as an end in itself. European conquest was but a step toward ultimate goals in all the other continents. It is unmistakably apparent to all of us that, unless the advance of Hitlerism is forcibly checked now, the Western Hemisphere will be within range of the Nazi weapons of destruction.

For our own defense we have accordingly undertaken certain obviously necessary measures:

First, we have joined in concluding a series of agreements with all the other American republics. This further solidified our hemisphere against the common danger.

And then, a year ago, we launched, and are successfully carrying out, the largest armament production program we have ever undertaken.

We have added substantially to our splendid navy, and we have mustered our manpower to build up a new army which is already worthy of the highest traditions of our military service.

We instituted a policy of aid for the democracies—the nations which have fought for the continuation of human liberties.

This policy had its origin in the first month of the war, when I urged upon the Congress repeal of the arms-embargo provisions in the old Neutrality Law, and in that message of September 3, 1939, I said, "I should like to be able to offer the hope that the shadow over the world might swiftly pass. I cannot. The facts compel my stating, with candor, that darker periods may lie ahead."

In the subsequent months, the shadows deepened and lengthened. And the night spread over Poland, Denmark, Norway, Holland, Belgium, Luxembourg, and France.

In June 1940, Britain stood alone, faced by the same machine of terror which had overwhelmed her allies. Our government rushed arms to meet her desperate needs.

In September 1940, an agreement was completed with Great Britain for the trade of fifty destroyers for eight important offshore bases.

And in March 1941, the Congress passed the Lend-Lease Bill and an appropriation of $7 billion to implement it. This law realistically provided for material aid "for the government of any country whose defense the president deems vital to the defense of the United States."

Our whole program of aid for the democracies has been based on hard-headed concern for our own security and for the kind of safe and civilized world in which we wish to live. Every dollar of matériel that we send helps to keep the dictators away from our own hemisphere, and every day that they are held off gives us time to build more guns and tanks and planes and ships.

We have made no pretense about our own self-interest in this aid. Great Britain understands it—and so does Nazi Germany.

And now—after a year—Britain still fights gallantly, on a "far-flung battle line." We have doubled and redoubled our vast production, increasing, month by month, our material supply of the tools of war for ourselves and for Britain and for China— and eventually for all the democracies.

The supply of these tools will not fail—it will increase.

With greatly augmented strength, the United States and the other American republics now chart their course in the situation of today.

Your government knows what terms Hitler, if victorious, would impose. They are, indeed, the only terms on which he would accept a so-called "negotiated" peace.

And, under those terms, Germany would literally parcel out the world—hoisting the swastika itself over vast territories and populations, and setting up puppet governments of its own choosing, wholly subject to the will and the policy of a conqueror.

To the people of the Americas, a triumphant Hitler would say, as he said after the seizure of Austria, and as he said after Munich, and as he said after the seizure of Czechoslovakia: "I am now completely satisfied. This is the last territorial readjustment I will seek." And he would of course add: "All we want is peace, friendship, and profitable trade relations with you in the New World." . . .

No, I am not speculating about all this. I merely repeat what is already in the Nazi book of world conquest. They plan to treat the Latin American nations as they are now treating the Balkans. They plan then to strangle the United States of America and the Dominion of Canada.

The American laborer would have to compete with slave

labor in the rest of the world. Minimum wages, maximum hours? Nonsense! Wages and hours would be fixed by Hitler. The dignity and power and standard of living of the American worker and farmer would be gone. Trade unions would become historical relics, and collective bargaining a joke.

Farm income? What happens to all farm surpluses without any foreign trade? The American farmer would get for his products exactly what Hitler wanted to give. The farmer would face obvious disaster and complete regimentation.

Tariff walls—Chinese walls of isolation—would be futile. Freedom to trade is essential to our economic life. We do not eat all the food we can produce; and we do not burn all the oil we can pump; we do not use all the goods we can manufacture. It would not be an American wall to keep Nazi goods out; it would be a Nazi wall to keep us in. . . .

Yes, even our right of worship would be threatened. The Nazi world does not recognize any God except Hitler; for the Nazis are as ruthless as the Communists in the denial of God. What place has religion which preaches the dignity of the human being, the majesty of the human soul, in a world where moral standards are measured by treachery and bribery and fifth columnists? Will our children, too, wander off, goose-stepping in search of new gods?

We do not accept, we will not permit, this Nazi "shape of things to come." It will never be forced upon us, if we act in this present crisis with the wisdom and the courage which have distinguished our country in all the crises of the past.

Today, the Nazis have taken military possession of the greater part of Europe. In Africa they have occupied Tripoli and Libya, and they are threatening Egypt, the Suez Canal, and the Near East. But their plans do not stop there, for the Indian Ocean is the gateway to the farther East.

They also have the armed power at any moment to occupy Spain and Portugal; and that threat extends not only to French North Africa and the western end of the Mediterranean but it extends also to the Atlantic fortress of Dakar, and to the island outposts of the New World—the Azores and Cape Verde Islands.

The Cape Verde Islands are only seven hours' distance from Brazil by bomber or troop-carrying planes. They dominate shipping routes to and from the South Atlantic.

The war is approaching the brink of the Western Hemisphere itself. It is coming very close to home.

Control or occupation by Nazi forces of any of the islands of the Atlantic would jeopardize the immediate safety of portions of North and South America, and of the island possessions of the United States, and, therefore, the ultimate safety of the continental United States itself.

Hitler's plan of world domination would be near its accomplishment today were it not for two factors. One is the epic resistance of Britain, her colonies, and the great dominions, fighting not only to maintain the existence of the island of Britain, but also to hold the Near East and Africa. The other is the magnificent defense of China, which will, I have reason to believe, increase in strength. All of these, together, are preventing the Axis from winning control of the seas by ships and aircraft.

The Axis powers can never achieve their objective of world domination unless they first obtain control of the seas. That is their supreme purpose today; and to achieve it, they must capture Great Britain. . . .

But if the Axis powers fail to gain control of the seas, then they are certainly defeated. Their dreams of world domination will then go by the board; and the criminal leaders who started this war will suffer inevitable disaster. . . .

All freedom—meaning freedom to live, and not freedom to conquer and subjugate other peoples—depends on freedom of the seas. All of American history—North, Central, and South American history—has been inevitably tied up with those words, "freedom of the seas." . . .

The Battle of the Atlantic now extends from the icy waters

of the North Pole to the frozen continent of the Antarctic. Throughout this huge area, there have been sinkings of merchant ships in alarming and increasing numbers by Nazi raiders or submarines. There have been sinkings even of ships carrying neutral flags. There have been sinkings in the South Atlantic, off West Africa and the Cape Verde Islands; between the Azores and the islands off the American coast; and between Greenland and Iceland. Great numbers of these sinkings have been actually within the waters of the Western Hemisphere itself.

The blunt truth is this—and I reveal this with the full knowledge of the British government—the present rate of Nazi sinkings of merchant ships is more than three times as high as the capacity of British shipyards to replace them; it is more than twice the combined British and American output of merchant ships today.

We can answer this peril by two simultaneous measures: first, by speeding up and increasing our own great shipbuilding program; and second, by helping to cut down the losses on the high seas.

Attacks on shipping off the very shores of land which we are determined to protect present an actual military danger to the Americas. And that danger has recently been heavily underlined by the presence in Western Hemisphere waters of a Nazi battleship of great striking power.

You remember that most of the supplies for Britain go by a northerly route, which comes close to Greenland and the nearby island of Iceland. Germany's heaviest attack is on that route. Nazi occupation of Iceland or bases in Greenland would bring the war close to our own continental shores, because those places are stepping-stones to Labrador and Newfoundland, to Nova Scotia, yes, to the northern United States itself, including the great industrial centers of the North, the East, and the Middle West.

Equally, the Azores and the Cape Verde Islands, if occupied or controlled by Germany, would directly endanger the freedom of the Atlantic and our own American physical safety. Under

German domination those islands would become bases for submarines, warships, and airplanes raiding the waters that lie immediately off our own coasts and attacking the shipping in the South Atlantic. They would provide a springboard for actual attack against the integrity and the independence of Brazil and her neighboring republics.

I have said on many occasions that the United States is mustering its men and its resources only for purposes of defense —only to repel attack. I repeat that statement now. But we must be realistic when we use the word *attack;* we have to relate it to the lightning speed of modern warfare.

Some people seem to think that we are not attacked until bombs actually drop in the streets of New York or San Francisco or New Orleans or Chicago. But they are simply shutting their eyes to the lesson that we must learn from the fate of every nation that the Nazis have conquered.

The attack on Czechoslovakia began with the conquest of Austria. The attack on Norway began with the occupation of Denmark. The attack on Greece began with occupation of Albania and Bulgaria. The attack on the Suez Canal began with the invasion of the Balkans and North Africa, and the attack on the United States can begin with the domination of any base which menaces our security—north or south. . . .

Anyone with an atlas, anyone with a reasonable knowledge of the sudden striking force of modern war, knows that it is stupid to wait until a probable enemy has gained a foothold from which to attack. Old-fashioned common sense calls for the use of a strategy that will prevent such an enemy from gaining a foothold in the first place.

We have, accordingly, extended our patrol in North and South Atlantic waters. We are steadily adding more and more ships and planes to that patrol. It is well known that the strength of the Atlantic Fleet has been greatly increased during the past year, and that it is constantly being built up.

These ships and planes warn of the presence of attacking raiders, on the sea, under the sea, and above the sea. The danger from these raiders is, of course, greatly lessened if their location is definitely known. We are thus being forewarned. We shall be on our guard against efforts to establish Nazi bases closer to our hemisphere. . . .

It is time for us to realize that the safety of American homes even in the center of this our own country has a very definite relationship to the continued safety of homes in Nova Scotia or Trinidad or Brazil.

Our national policy today, therefore, is this:

First, we shall actively resist wherever necessary, and with all our resources, every attempt by Hitler to extend his Nazi domination to the Western Hemisphere, or to threaten it. We shall actively resist his every attempt to gain control of the seas. We insist upon the vital importance of keeping Hitlerism away from any point in the world which could be used or would be used as a base of attack against the Americas.

Second, from the point of view of strict naval and military necessity, we shall give every possible assistance to Britain and to all who, with Britain, are resisting Hitlerism or its equivalent with force of arms. Our patrols are helping now to insure delivery of the needed supplies to Britain. All additional measures necessary to deliver the goods will be taken. Any and all further methods or combination of methods, which can or should be utilized, are being devised by our military and naval technicians, who, with me, will work out and put into effect such new and additional safeguards as may be needed.

I say that the delivery of needed supplies to Britain is imperative. I say that this can be done; it must be done; and it will be done.

To the other American nations—twenty republics and the Dominion of Canada—I say this: the United States does not merely propose these purposes, but is actively engaged today in carrying them out.

I say to them further: you may disregard those few citizens of the United States who contend that we are disunited and cannot act.

There are some timid ones among us who say that we must preserve peace at any price—lest we lose our liberties forever. To them I say this: Never in the history of the world has a nation lost its democracy by a successful struggle to defend its democracy. We must not be defeated by the fear of the very danger which we are preparing to resist. Our freedom has shown its ability to survive war, but our freedom would never survive surrender. "The only thing we have to fear is fear itself." . . .

Your government has the right to expect of all citizens that they take part in the common work of our common defense—take loyal part from this moment forward.

I have recently set up the machinery for civilian defense. It will rapidly organize, locality by locality. It will depend on the organized effort of men and women everywhere. All will have opportunities and responsibilities to fulfill.

Defense today means more than merely fighting. It means morale, civilian as well as military; it means using every available resource; it means enlarging every useful plant. It means the use of a greater American common sense in discarding rumor and distorted statement. It means recognizing, for what they are, racketeers and fifth columnists, who are the incendiary bombs in this country of the moment. . . .

No one of us can waver for a moment in his courage or his faith.

We will not accept a Hitler-dominated world. And we will not accept a world, like the postwar world of the 1920s, in which the seeds of Hitlerism can again be planted and allowed to grow.

We will accept only a world consecrated to freedom of speech and expression—freedom of every person to worship God in his own way—freedom from want—and freedom from terror. . . .

As the president of a united and determined people, I say solemnly:

We reassert the ancient American doctrine of freedom of the seas.

We reassert the solidarity of the twenty-one American republics and the Dominion of Canada in the preservation of the independence of the hemisphere.

We have pledged material support to the other democracies of the world—and we will fulfill that pledge.

We in the Americas will decide for ourselves whether, and when, and where, our American interests are attacked or our security is threatened.

We are placing our armed forces in strategic military position.

We will not hesitate to use our armed forces to repel attack.

We reassert our abiding faith in the vitality of our constitutional republic as a perpetual home of freedom, of tolerance, and of devotion to the word of God.

Therefore, with profound consciousness of my responsibilities to my countrymen and to my country's cause, I have tonight issued a proclamation that an unlimited national emergency exists and requires the strengthening of our defense to the extreme limit of our national power and authority.

The nation will expect all individuals and all groups to play their full parts, without stint, and without selfishness, and without doubt that our democracy will triumphantly survive.

I repeat the words of the signers of the Declaration of Independence—that little band of patriots, fighting long ago against overwhelming odds, but certain, as we are now, of ultimate victory: "With a firm reliance on the protection of Divine Providence, we mutually pledge to each other our lives, our fortunes, and our sacred honor."

Message to Congress on the Operations of the Lend-Lease Act

June 10, 1941

Section 5(b) of Public Law 11, Seventy-seventh Congress, approved by me on March 11, 1941, provides in part as follows:

> The president from time to time, but not less frequently than once every ninety days, shall transmit to the Congress a report of operations under this act except such information as he deems incompatible with the public interest to disclose.

In compliance with this provision I am submitting this report.

We have supplied, and we will supply, planes, guns, ammunition, and other defense articles in ever-increasing quantities to Britain, China, and other democracies resisting aggression.

Wars are not won by guns alone, but wars are not won without guns. We all know this full well now. Beginning with the outbreak of the war the American public began to realize that it was in our own national interest and security to help Britain, China, and other democratic nations.

Beginning with the outbreak of the war British and French orders began to be placed. But dollars could not be immediately turned into airplanes and ships and guns and ammunition.

In those dark days when France was falling, it was clear that this government, to carry out the will of the people, had to render aid over and above the matériel coming off the assembly line. This government, therefore, made available all that it possibly could out of its surplus stocks of munitions.

In June of 1940, the British government received from our

surplus stocks rifles, machine guns, field artillery, ammunition, and aircraft in a value of more than $43 million. This was equipment that would have taken months and months to produce and which, with the exception of the aircraft, cost about $300 million to produce during the World War period. Most of this matériel would not have been usable if we had kept it much longer. This equipment arrived in Britain after the retreat from Dunkirk, where the British had lost great quantities of guns and other military supplies. No one can appraise what effect the delivery of these supplies had upon the successful British resistance in the summer and fall of 1940 when they were fighting against such terrific odds.

Since June 1940, this government has continued to supply war matériel from its surplus stocks, in addition to the matériel produced by private manufacturers. The fifty overage destroyers which Britain received in exchange for the defense bases were a part of the aid supplied by the government.

By the turn of the year 1941, the British commitments in this country for defense articles had reached the limit of their future dollar resources. Their striking power required the assurance that their munitions and equipment would steadily and certainly be augmented, not curtailed.

The will of our people, as expressed through the Congress, was to meet this problem, not only by the passage of the Lend-Lease Act but by the appropriation of $7 billion made on March 27 of this year to carry out this task.

In the ninety days since the Lend-Lease Act was passed, and in the seventy-four days since the funds were appropriated, we have started in motion the vast supply program which is essential to the defeat of the Axis powers.

In these seventy-four days, more than $4.25 billion out of the $7 billion have been allocated to the War, Navy, Agriculture, and Treasury departments and to the Maritime Commission to procure the aid authorized. Contracts have been let for long-range bombers, ships, tanks, and the other sinews of war that will be needed for the defense of the democracies. The balance of less than $2.75 billion is being rapidly allocated.

To be effective, the aid rendered by us must be many sided. Ships are necessary to carry the munitions and the food. We are immediately making available to Britain two million gross tons of cargo ships and oil tankers.

But this is not enough. Adequate shipping for every day to come must be reasonably assured. Since the Appropriation Act was passed, $550 million has been allocated for the construction of new ships under the Lend-Lease Act. Contracts have been let and the new ways required to build these ships are now nearing completion. Allied ships are being repaired by us. Allied ships are being equipped by us to protect them from mines, and are being armed by us to protect them as much as possible against raiders. Naval vessels of Britain are being repaired by us so that they can return quickly to their naval tasks.

The training program of seven thousand British pilots in our schools in this country is under way. Valuable information is being communicated, and other material assistance is being rendered in a mounting benefit to the democracies.

Millions of pounds of food are being and will be sent. Iron and steel, machine tools and the other essentials to maintain and increase the production of war materials in Britain are being sent and received in larger quantities day by day.

Since September 1939, the war goods sent to Britain have risen steadily. The overall total exports to the British Empire have greatly increased in 1941 over 1940. What is more important, the increase of those things which are necessary for fighting have increased far beyond our other exports. In the first five months of this year we have sent more than twelve times as many airplanes to Britain as we did in the first five months of 1940. For the first four months of this year the dollar value of explosives sent to the British Empire was about seventeen times as much as for the first four months of 1940. Ninety times as much in dollar value of firearms and ammunition was sent to Britain during the first four months of this year as for the first four months of 1940.

With our national resources, our productive capacity, and the genius of our people for mass production we will help Britain to outstrip the Axis powers in munitions of war, and we will see to it that these munitions get to the places where they can be effectively used to weaken and defeat the aggressors.

In the report that follows facts and figures are given to the extent advisable without disclosing military secrets to benefit the Axis powers. These facts describe the past and portray the present status of our aid to those nations so gallantly fighting the aggressors. They do not present the most important fact of all —the strong will of our people to see to it that these forces of aggression shall not rule the world.

We have before us a constant purpose not of present safety alone but, equally, of future survival.

EXECUTIVE ORDER ESTABLISHING THE COMMITTEE ON FAIR EMPLOYMENT PRACTICE

June 25, 1941

Whereas it is the policy of the United States to encourage full participation in the national defense program by all citizens of the United States, regardless of race, creed, color, or national origin, in the firm belief that the democratic way of life within the nation can be defended successfully only with the help and support of all groups within its borders; and

Whereas there is evidence that available and needed workers have been barred from employment in industries engaged in defense production solely because of consideration of race, creed, color, or national origin, to the detriment of workers' morale and of national unity:

Now, therefore, by virtue of the authority vested in me by the Constitution and the statutes, and as a prerequisite to the successful conduct of our national defense production effort, I do hereby reaffirm the policy of the United States that there shall be no discrimination in the employment of workers in defense industries or government because of race, creed, color, or national origin, and I do hereby declare that it is the duty of employers and of labor organizations, in furtherance of said policy and of this order, to provide for the full and equitable participation of all workers in defense industries, without discrimination because of race, creed, color, or national origin;

And it is hereby ordered as follows:

1. All departments and agencies of the government of the

United States concerned with vocational and training programs for defense production shall take special measures appropriate to assure that such programs are administered without discrimination because of race, creed, color, or national origin;

2. All contracting agencies of the government of the United States shall include in all defense contracts hereafter negotiated by them a provision obligating the contractor not to discriminate against any worker because of race, creed, color, or national origin;

3. There is established in the Office of Production Management a Committee on Fair Employment Practice, which shall consist of a chairman and four other members to be appointed by the president. The chairman and members of the committee shall serve as such without compensation but shall be entitled to actual and necessary transportation, subsistence, and other expenses incidental to performance of their duties. The committee shall receive and investigate complaints of discrimination in violation of the provisions of this order and shall take appropriate steps to redress grievances which it finds to be valid. The committee shall also recommend to the several departments and agencies of the government of the United States and to the president all measures which may be deemed by it necessary or proper to effectuate the provisions of this order.

MESSAGE TO CONGRESS ON THE ATLANTIC CHARTER

August 21, 1941

Over a week ago I held several important conferences at sea with the British prime minister. Because of the factor of safety to British, Canadian, and American ships and their personnel no prior announcement of these meetings could properly be made.

At the close, a public statement by the prime minister and the president was made. I quote it for the information of the Congress and for the record:

> The president of the United States and the prime minister, Mr. Churchill, representing His Majesty's government in the United Kingdom, have met at sea.
>
> They have been accompanied by officials of their two governments, including high ranking officers of their military, naval, and air services.
>
> The whole problem of the supply of munitions of war, as provided by the Lend-Lease Act, for the armed forces of the United States and for those countries actively engaged in resisting aggression has been further examined.
>
> Lord Beaverbrook, the minister of supply of the British government, has joined in these conferences. He is going to proceed to Washington to discuss further details with appropriate officials of the United States government. These conferences will also cover the supply problems of the Soviet Union.
>
> The president and the prime minister have had several conferences. They have considered the dangers to world civilization arising from the policies of military domination by conquest upon which the Hitlerite government of Germany and other governments associated therewith have embarked, and have

made clear the steps which their countries are respectively taking for their safety in the face of these dangers.

They have agreed upon the following joint declaration:

The president of the United States of America and the prime minister, Mr. Churchill, representing His Majesty's government in the United Kingdom, being met together, deem it right to make known certain common principles in the national policies of their respective countries on which they base their hopes for a better future for the world.

First, their countries seek no aggrandizement, territorial or other;

Second, they desire to see no territorial changes that do not accord with the freely expressed wishes of the peoples concerned;

Third, they respect the right of all peoples to choose the form of government under which they will live; and they wish to see sovereign rights and self-government restored to those who have been forcibly deprived of them;

Fourth, they will endeavor, with the respect of their existing obligations, to further the enjoyment by all states, great and small, victor or vanquished, of access, on equal terms, to the trade and to the raw materials of the world which are needed for their economic prosperity;

Fifth, they desire to bring about the fullest collaboration between all nations in the economic field with the object of securing, for all, improved labor standards, economic advancement, and social security;

Sixth, after the final destruction of the Nazi tyranny, they hope to see established a peace which will afford to all nations the means of dwelling in safety within their own boundaries, and which will afford assurance that all the men in all the lands may live out their lives in freedom from fear and want;

Seventh, such a peace should enable all men to traverse the high seas and oceans without hindrance;

Eighth, they believe that all of the nations of the world, for realistic as well as spiritual reasons must come to the abandonment of the use of force. Since no future peace can be maintained if land, sea, or air armaments continue to be employed by nations which threaten, or may threaten, aggression outside of their frontiers, they believe, pending the establishment of a wider and permanent system of general security, that the disarmament of such nations is essential. They will likewise aid and encourage all other practicable measures which will lighten for peace-loving peoples the crushing burden of armaments.

The Congress and the president having heretofore determined through the Lend-Lease Act on the national policy of American aid to the democracies which East and West are waging war against dictatorships, the military and naval conversations at these meetings made clear gains in furthering the effectiveness of this aid.

Furthermore, the prime minister and I are arranging for conferences with the Soviet Union to aid it in its defense against the attack made by the principal aggressor of the modern world —Germany.

Finally, the declaration of principles at this time presents a goal which is worthwhile for our type of civilization to seek. It is so clear-cut that it is difficult to oppose in any major particular without automatically admitting a willingness to accept compromise with Nazism; or to agree to a world peace which would give to Nazism domination over large numbers of conquered nations. Inevitably such a peace would be a gift to Nazism to take breath—armed breath—for a second war to extend the control over Europe and Asia to the American hemisphere itself.

It is perhaps unnecessary for me to call attention once more to the utter lack of validity of the spoken or written word of the Nazi government.

It is also unnecessary for me to point out that the declaration of principles includes of necessity the world need for freedom of religion and freedom of information. No society of the world organized under the announced principles could survive without these freedoms which are a part of the whole freedom for which we strive.

FIRESIDE CHAT ON NATIONAL DEFENSE

September 11, 1941

The Navy Department of the United States has reported to me that on the morning of September 4 the United States destroyer *Greer,* proceeding in full daylight toward Iceland, had reached a point southeast of Greenland. She was carrying American mail to Iceland. She was flying the American flag. Her identity as an American ship was unmistakable.

She was then and there attacked by a submarine. Germany admits that it was a German submarine. The submarine deliberately fired a torpedo at the *Greer,* followed later by another torpedo attack. In spite of what Hitler's propaganda bureau has invented, and in spite of what any American obstructionist organization may prefer to believe, I tell you the blunt fact that the German submarine fired first upon this American destroyer without warning, and with deliberate design to sink her.

Our destroyer, at the time, was in waters which the government of the United States had declared to be waters of self-defense—surrounding outposts of American protection in the Atlantic.

In the north of the Atlantic, outposts have been established by us in Iceland, in Greenland, in Labrador, and in Newfoundland. Through these waters there pass many ships of many flags. They bear food and other supplies to civilians; and they bear matériel of war, for which the people of the United States are spending billions of dollars, and which, by congressional action, they have declared to be essential for the defense of our own land.

The United States destroyer, when attacked, was proceeding on a legitimate mission.

If the destroyer was visible to the submarine when the torpedo was fired, then the attack was a deliberate attempt by the Nazis to sink a clearly identified American warship. On the other hand, if the submarine was beneath the surface of the sea and, with the aid of its listening devices, fired in the direction of the sound of the American destroyer without even taking the trouble to learn its identity—as the official German communiqué would indicate—then the attack was even more outrageous. For it indicates a policy of indiscriminate violence against any vessel sailing the seas—belligerent or nonbelligerent.

This was piracy—piracy legally and morally. It was not the first nor the last act of piracy which the Nazi government has committed against the American flag in this war. For attack has followed attack.

A few months ago an American flag merchant ship, the *Robin Moor,* was sunk by a Nazi submarine in the middle of the South Atlantic, under circumstances violating long-established international law and violating every principle of humanity. The passengers and the crew were forced into open boats hundreds of miles from land, in direct violation of international agreements signed by nearly all nations including the government of Germany. No apology, no allegation of mistake, no offer of reparations has come from the Nazi government.

In July 1941, an American battleship in North American waters was followed by a submarine which for a long time sought to maneuver itself into a position of attack. The periscope of the submarine was clearly seen. No British or American submarines were within hundreds of miles of this spot at the time, so the nationality of the submarine is clear.

Five days ago a United States Navy ship on patrol picked up three survivors of an American-owned ship operating under the flag of our sister republic of Panama—the SS *Sessa.* On August 17, she had been first torpedoed without warning, and then shelled, near Greenland, while carrying civilian supplies to Iceland. It is feared that the other members of her crew have been drowned. In view of the established presence of German submarines in this vicinity, there can be no reasonable doubt as to the identity of the flag of the attacker.

Five days ago, another United States merchant ship, the *Steel Seafarer,* was sunk by a German aircraft in the Red Sea, 220 miles south of Suez. She was bound for an Egyptian port.

So four of the vessels sunk or attacked flew the American flag and were clearly identifiable. Two of these ships were warships of the American navy. In the fifth case, the vessel sunk clearly carried the flag of our sister republic of Panama. . . .

It would be unworthy of a great nation to exaggerate an isolated incident, or to become inflamed by some one act of violence. But it would be inexcusable folly to minimize such incidents in the face of evidence which makes it clear that the incident is not isolated, but is part of a general plan.

The important truth is that these acts of international lawlessness are a manifestation of a design which has been made clear to the American people for a long time. It is the Nazi design to abolish the freedom of the seas, and to acquire absolute control and domination of these seas for themselves.

For with control of the seas in their own hands, the way can obviously become clear for their next step—domination of the United States, domination of the Western Hemisphere by force of arms. Under Nazi control of the seas, no merchant ship of the United States or of any other American republic would be free to carry on any peaceful commerce, except by the condescending grace of this foreign and tyrannical power. The Atlantic Ocean which has been, and which should always be, a free and friendly highway for us would then become a deadly menace to the commerce of the United States, to the coasts of the United States, and even to the inland cities of the United States. . . .

This Nazi attempt to seize control of the oceans is but a counterpart of the Nazi plots now being carried on throughout the Western Hemisphere—all designed toward the same end. For Hitler's advance guards—not only his avowed agents but also his dupes among us—have sought to make ready for him footholds and bridgeheads in the New World, to be used as soon as he has gained control of the oceans.

His intrigues, his plots, his machinations, his sabotage in this New World are all known to the government of the United States. Conspiracy has followed conspiracy.

For example, last year a plot to seize the government of Uruguay was smashed by the prompt action of that country, which was supported in full by her American neighbors. A like plot was then hatching in Argentina, and that government has carefully and wisely blocked it at every point. More recently, an endeavor was made to subvert the government of Bolivia. And within the past few weeks the discovery was made of secret air-landing fields in Colombia, within easy range of the Panama Canal. I could multiply instance upon instance.

To be ultimately successful in world mastery, Hitler knows that he must get control of the seas. He must first destroy the bridge of ships which we are building across the Atlantic and over which we shall continue to roll the implements of war to help destroy him, to destroy all his works in the end. He must wipe out our patrol on sea and in the air if he is to do it. He must silence the British navy.

I think it must be explained over and over again to people who like to think of the United States Navy as an invincible protection, that this can be true only if the British navy survives. And that, my friends, is simple arithmetic. . . .

It is time for all Americans, Americans of all the Americas to stop being deluded by the romantic notion that the Americas can go on living happily and peacefully in a Nazi-dominated world.

Generation after generation, America has battled for the general policy of the freedom of the seas. And that policy is a very simple one—but a basic, a fundamental one. It means that no nation has the right to make the broad oceans of the world at great distances from the actual theater of land war unsafe for the commerce of others.

That has been our policy, proved time and time again, in all our history.

Our policy has applied from the earliest days of the Republic—and still applies—not merely to the Atlantic but to the Pacific and to all other oceans as well.

Unrestricted submarine warfare in 1941 constitutes a defiance—an act of aggression—against that historic American policy.

It is now clear that Hitler has begun his campaign to control the seas by ruthless force and by wiping out every vestige of international law, every vestige of humanity. . . .

The Nazi danger to our Western world has long ceased to be a mere possibility. The danger is here now—not only from a military enemy but from an enemy of all law, all liberty, all morality, all religion.

There has now come a time when you and I must see the cold, inexorable necessity of saying to these inhuman, unrestrained seekers of world conquest and permanent world domination by the sword: "You seek to throw our children and our children's children into your form of terrorism and slavery. You have now attacked our own safety. You shall go no further."

Normal practices of diplomacy—note writing—are of no possible use in dealing with international outlaws who sink our ships and kill our citizens.

One peaceful nation after another has met disaster because each refused to look the Nazi danger squarely in the eye until it actually had them by the throat.

The United States will not make that fatal mistake.

No act of violence, no act of intimidation will keep us from maintaining intact two bulwarks of American defense: first, our line of supply of matériel to the enemies of Hitler; and second, the freedom of our shipping on the high seas.

No matter what it takes, no matter what it costs, we will keep open the line of legitimate commerce in these defensive waters.

We have sought no shooting war with Hitler. We do not seek it now. But neither do we want peace so much that we are willing to pay for it by permitting him to attack our naval and merchant ships while they are on legitimate business.

I assume that the German leaders are not deeply concerned, tonight or any other time, by what we Americans or the American government say or publish about them. We cannot bring about the downfall of Nazism by the use of long-range invective.

But when you see a rattlesnake poised to strike, you do not wait until he has struck before you crush him.

These Nazi submarines and raiders are the rattlesnakes of the Atlantic. They are a menace to the free pathways of the high seas. They are a challenge to our sovereignty. They hammer at our most precious rights when they attack ships of the American flag—symbols of our independence, our freedom, our very life.

It is clear to all Americans that the time has come when the Americas themselves must now be defended. A continuation of attacks in our own waters, or in waters that could be used for further and greater attacks on us, will inevitably weaken our American ability to repel Hitlerism. . . .

In the waters which we deem necessary for our defense, American naval vessels and American planes will no longer wait until Axis submarines lurking under the water, or Axis raiders on the surface of the sea, strike their deadly blow—first.

Upon our naval and air patrol—now operating in large number over a vast expanse of the Atlantic Ocean—falls the duty of maintaining the American policy of freedom of the seas —now. That means, very simply, very clearly, that our patrolling vessels and planes will protect all merchant ships—not only American ships but ships of any flag—engaged in commerce in our defensive waters. They will protect them from submarines; they will protect them from surface raiders.

This situation is not new. The second president of the United States, John Adams, ordered the United States Navy to clean out European privateers and European ships of war which were infesting the Caribbean and South American waters, destroying American commerce.

The third president of the United States, Thomas Jefferson, ordered the United States Navy to end the attacks being made upon American and other ships by the corsairs of the nations of North Africa.

My obligation as president is historic; it is clear. It is inescapable.

It is no act of war on our part when we decide to protect the seas that are vital to American defense. The aggression is not ours. Ours is solely defense.

But let this warning be clear. From now on, if German or Italian vessels of war enter the waters, the protection of which is necessary for American defense, they do so at their own peril.

The orders which I have given as commander in chief of the United States Army and Navy are to carry out that policy—at once.

The sole responsibility rests upon Germany. There will be no shooting unless Germany continues to seek it.

That is my obvious duty in this crisis. That is the clear right of this sovereign nation. This is the only step possible, if we would keep tight the wall of defense which we are pledged to maintain around this Western Hemisphere.

I have no illusions about the gravity of this step. I have not taken it hurriedly or lightly. It is the result of months and months of constant thought and anxiety and prayer. In the protection of your nation and mine it cannot be avoided.

The American people have faced other grave crises in their history—with American courage, and with American resolution. They will do no less today.

They know the actualities of the attacks upon us. They know the necessities of a bold defense against these attacks. They know that the times call for clear heads and fearless hearts.

And with that inner strength that comes to a free people conscious of their duty, and conscious of the righteousness of what they do, they will—with Divine help and guidance—stand their ground against this latest assault upon their democracy, their sovereignty, and their freedom.

MESSAGE TO
EMPEROR HIROHITO

December 6, 1941

Almost a century ago the president of the United States addressed to the emperor of Japan a message extending an offer of friendship of the people of the United States to the people of Japan. That offer was accepted, and in the long period of unbroken peace and friendship which has followed, our respective nations, through the virtues of their peoples and the wisdom of their rulers, have prospered and have substantially helped humanity.

Only in situations of extraordinary importance to our two countries need I address to Your Majesty messages on matters of state. I feel I should now so address you because of the deep and far-reaching emergency which appears to be in formation.

Developments are occurring in the Pacific area which threaten to deprive each of our nations and all humanity of the beneficial influence of the long peace between our two countries. Those developments contain tragic possibilities.

The people of the United States, believing in peace and in the right of nations to live and let live, have eagerly watched the conversations between our two governments during these past months. We have hoped for a termination of the present conflict between Japan and China. We have hoped that a peace of the Pacific could be consummated in such a way that nationalities of many diverse peoples could exist side by side without fear of invasion; that unbearable burdens of armaments could be lifted for them all; and that all peoples would resume commerce without discrimination against or in favor of any nation.

I am certain that it will be clear to Your Majesty, as it is to me, that in seeking these great objectives both Japan and the

United States should agree to eliminate any form of military threat. This seemed essential to the attainment of the high objectives.

More than a year ago Your Majesty's government concluded an agreement with the Vichy government by which five or six thousand Japanese troops were permitted to enter into northern French Indochina for the protection of Japanese troops which were operating against China further north. And this spring and summer the Vichy government permitted further Japanese military forces to enter into southern French Indochina for the common defense of French Indochina. I think I am correct in saying that no attack has been made upon Indochina, nor that any has been contemplated.

During the past few weeks it has become clear to the world that Japanese military, naval, and air forces have been sent to southern Indochina in such large numbers as to create a reasonable doubt on the part of other nations that this continuing concentration in Indochina is not defensive in its character.

Because these continuing concentrations in Indochina have reached such large proportions and because they extend now to the southeast and the southwest corners of that peninsula, it is only reasonable that the people of the Philippines, of the hundreds of islands of the East Indies, of Malaya, and of Thailand itself are asking themselves whether these forces of Japan are preparing or intending to make attack in one or more of these many directions.

I am sure that Your Majesty will understand that the fear of all these peoples is a legitimate fear inasmuch as it involves their peace and their national existence. I am sure that Your Majesty will understand why the people of the United States in such large numbers look askance at the establishment of military, naval, and air bases manned and equipped so greatly as to constitute armed forces capable of measures of offense.

It is clear that a continuance of such a situation is unthinkable.

None of the peoples whom I have spoken of above can sit

234 ★ The Essential Franklin Delano Roosevelt

either indefinitely or permanently on a keg of dynamite.

There is absolutely no thought on the part of the United States of invading Indochina if every Japanese soldier or sailor were to be withdrawn therefrom.

I think that we can obtain the same assurance from the governments of the East Indies, the governments of Malaya, and the government of Thailand. I would even undertake to ask for the same assurance on the part of the government of China. Thus a withdrawal of the Japanese forces from Indochina would result in the assurance of peace throughout the whole of the South Pacific area.

I address myself to Your Majesty at this moment in the fervent hope that Your Majesty may, as I am doing, give thought in this definite emergency to ways of dispelling the dark clouds. I am confident that both of us, for the sake of the peoples not only of our own great countries but for the sake of humanity in neighboring territories, have a sacred duty to restore traditional amity and prevent further death and destruction in the world.

Address Before Congress Requesting a Declaration of War Between Japan and the United States

December 8, 1941

December 7, 1941— A Date Which Will Live in Infamy

Mr. Vice President, and Mr. Speaker, and Members of the Senate and House of Representatives: Yesterday, December 7, 1941—a date which will live in infamy—the United States of America was suddenly and deliberately attacked by naval and air forces of the Empire of Japan.

The United States was at peace with that nation and, at the solicitation of Japan, was still in conversation with its government and its emperor looking toward the maintenance of peace in the Pacific. Indeed, one hour after Japanese air squadrons had commenced bombing in the American island of Oahu, the Japanese ambassador to the United States and his colleague delivered to our secretary of state a formal reply to a recent American message. And while this reply stated that it seemed useless to continue the existing diplomatic negotiations, it contained no threat or hint of war or of armed attack.

It will be recorded that the distance of Hawaii from Japan makes it obvious that the attack was deliberately planned many days or even weeks ago. During the intervening time the Japanese government has deliberately sought to deceive the United States by false statements and expressions of hope for continued peace.

The attack yesterday on the Hawaiian Islands has caused severe damage to American naval and military forces. I regret to tell you that very many American lives have been lost. In addition American ships have been reported torpedoed on the high seas between San Francisco and Honolulu.

Yesterday the Japanese government also launched an attack against Malaya.

Last night Japanese forces attacked Hong Kong.

Last night Japanese forces attacked Guam.

Last night Japanese forces attacked the Philippine Islands.

Last night the Japanese attacked Wake Island.

And this morning the Japanese attacked Midway Island.

Japan has, therefore, undertaken a surprise offensive extending throughout the Pacific area. The facts of yesterday and today speak for themselves. The people of the United States have already formed their opinions and well understand the implications to the very life and safety of our nation.

As commander in chief of the army and navy I have directed that all measures be taken for our defense.

But always will our whole nation remember the character of the onslaught against us.

No matter how long it may take us to overcome this premeditated invasion, the American people in their righteous might will win through to absolute victory.

I believe that I interpret the will of the Congress and of the people when I assert that we will not only defend ourselves to the uttermost but will make it very certain that this form of treachery shall never again endanger us.

Hostilities exist. There is no blinking at the fact that our people, our territory, and our interests are in grave danger.

With confidence in our armed forces, with the unbounding

determination of our people, we will gain the inevitable triumph —so help us God.

I ask that the Congress declare that since the unprovoked and dastardly attack by Japan on Sunday, December 7, 1941, a state of war has existed between the United States and the Japanese Empire.

FIRESIDE CHAT ON WAR WITH JAPAN

December 9, 1941

The sudden criminal attacks perpetrated by the Japanese in the Pacific provide the climax of a decade of international immorality.

Powerful and resourceful gangsters have banded together to make war upon the whole human race. Their challenge has now been flung at the United States of America. The Japanese have treacherously violated the long-standing peace between us. Many American soldiers and sailors have been killed by enemy action. American ships have been sunk; American airplanes have been destroyed.

The Congress and the people of the United States have accepted that challenge.

Together with other free peoples, we are now fighting to maintain our right to live among our world neighbors in freedom and in common decency, without fear of assault.

I have prepared the full record of our past relations with Japan, and it will be submitted to the Congress. It begins with the visit of Commodore Perry to Japan eighty-eight years ago. It ends with the visit of two Japanese emissaries to the secretary of state last Sunday, an hour after Japanese forces had loosed their bombs and machine guns against our flag, our forces, and our citizens.

I can say with utmost confidence that no Americans, today or a thousand years hence, need feel anything but pride in our patience and in our efforts through all the years toward achieving a peace in the Pacific which would be fair and honorable to every nation, large or small. And no honest person, today or a thousand years hence, will be able to suppress a sense of indignation and horror at the treachery committed by the military dictators of Japan, under the very shadow of the flag of peace borne by their special envoys in our midst.

The course that Japan has followed for the past ten years in Asia has paralleled the course of Hitler and Mussolini in Europe and in Africa. Today, it has become far more than a parallel. It is actual collaboration so well calculated that all the continents of the world, and all the oceans, are now considered by the Axis strategists as one gigantic battlefield.

In 1931, ten years ago, Japan invaded Manchukuo—without warning.

In 1935, Italy invaded Ethiopia—without warning.

In 1938, Hitler occupied Austria—without warning.

In 1939, Hitler invaded Czechoslovakia—without warning.

Later in 1939, Hitler invaded Poland—without warning.

In 1940, Hitler invaded Norway, Denmark, the Netherlands, Belgium, and Luxembourg—without warning.

In 1940, Italy attacked France and later Greece—without warning.

And this year, in 1941, the Axis powers attacked Yugoslavia and Greece and they dominated the Balkans—without warning.

In 1941, also, Hitler invaded Russia—without warning.

And now Japan has attacked Malaya and Thailand—and the United States—without warning.

It is all of one pattern.

We are now in this war. We are all in it—all the way. Every single man, woman, and child is a partner in the most tremendous undertaking of our American history. We must share together the bad news and the good news, the defeats and the victories—the changing fortunes of war.

So far, the news has been all bad. We have suffered a serious setback in Hawaii. Our forces in the Philippines, which include the brave people of that commonwealth, are taking punishment, but are defending themselves vigorously. The reports from Guam and Wake and Midway islands are still confused, but we must be prepared for the announcement that all these three outposts have been seized.

The casualty lists of these first few days will undoubtedly be large. I deeply feel the anxiety of all of the families of the men in our armed forces and the relatives of people in cities which have been bombed. I can only give them my solemn promise that they will get news just as quickly as possible.

This government will put its trust in the stamina of the American people, and will give the facts to the public just as soon as two conditions have been fulfilled: first, that the information has been definitely and officially confirmed; and, second, that the release of the information at the time it is received will not prove valuable to the enemy directly or indirectly.

Most earnestly I urge my countrymen to reject all rumors. These ugly little hints of complete disaster fly thick and fast in wartime. They have to be examined and appraised.

As an example, I can tell you frankly that until further surveys are made, I have not sufficient information to state the exact damage which has been done to our naval vessels at Pearl Harbor. Admittedly the damage is serious. But no one can say how serious, until we know how much of this damage can be repaired and how quickly the necessary repairs can be made.

I cite as another example a statement made on Sunday night that a Japanese carrier had been located and sunk off the Canal Zone. And when you hear statements that are attributed to what they call "an authoritative source," you can be reasonably sure from now on that under these war circumstances the "authoritative source" is not any person in authority.

Many rumors and reports which we now hear originate with enemy sources. For instance, today the Japanese are claiming that as a result of their one action against Hawaii they have gained naval supremacy in the Pacific. This is an old trick of propaganda which has been used innumerable times by the Nazis. The purposes of such fantastic claims are, of course, to spread fear and confusion among us, and to goad us into revealing military information which our enemies are desperately anxious to obtain.

Our government will not be caught in this obvious trap—and neither will the people of the United States.

It must be remembered by each and every one of us that our free and rapid communication these days must be greatly restricted in wartime. It is not possible to receive full, speedy, accurate reports from distant areas of combat. This is particularly true where naval operations are concerned. For in these days of the marvels of radio it is often impossible for the commanders of various units to report their activities by radio at all, for the very simple reason that this information would become available to the enemy, and would disclose their position and their plan of defense or attack.

Of necessity there will be delays in officially confirming or denying reports of operations, but we will not hide facts from the country if we know the facts and if the enemy will not be aided by their disclosure.

To all newspapers and radio stations—all those who reach the eyes and ears of the American people—I say this: You have a most grave responsibility to the nation now and for the duration of this war.

If you feel that your government is not disclosing enough of the truth, you have every right to say so. But—in the absence of all the facts, as revealed by official sources—you have no right in the ethics of patriotism to deal out unconfirmed reports in such a way as to make people believe that they are gospel truth.

Every citizen, in every walk of life, shares this same responsibility. The lives of our soldiers and sailors—the whole future of this nation—depend upon the manner in which each and every one of us fulfills his obligation to our country.

Now a word about the recent past—and the future. A year and a half has elapsed since the fall of France, when the whole world first realized the mechanized might which the Axis nations had been building for so many years. America has used that year and a half to great advantage. Knowing that the attack might reach us in all too short a time, we immediately began greatly to increase our industrial strength and our capacity to meet the demands of modern warfare.

Precious months were gained by sending vast quantities of our war material to the nations of the world still able to resist Axis aggression. Our policy rested on the fundamental truth that the defense of any country resisting Hitler or Japan was in the long run the defense of our own country. That policy has been justified. It has given us time, invaluable time, to build our American assembly lines of production.

Assembly lines are now in operation. Others are being rushed to completion. A steady stream of tanks and planes, of guns and ships, and shells and equipment—that is what these eighteen months have given us.

But it is all only a beginning of what still has to be done. We must be set to face a long war against crafty and powerful bandits. The attack at Pearl Harbor can be repeated at any one of many points, points in both oceans and along both our coast lines and against all the rest of the hemisphere.

It will not only be a long war, it will be a hard war. That is the basis on which we now lay all our plans. That is the yardstick by which we measure what we shall need and demand; money, materials, doubled and quadrupled production—ever-increasing. The production must be not only for our own army and navy and air forces. It must reinforce the other armies and navies and air forces fighting the Nazis and the warlords of Japan throughout the Americas and throughout the world.

I have been working today on the subject of production. Your government has decided on two broad policies.

The first is to speed up all existing production by working on a seven-day-week basis in every war industry, including the production of essential raw materials.

The second policy, now being put into form, is to rush additions to the capacity of production by building more new plants, by adding to old plants, and by using the many smaller plants for war needs.

Over the hard road of the past months, we have at times met obstacles and difficulties, divisions and disputes, indifference and callousness. That is now all past—and, I am sure, forgotten.

The fact is that the country now has an organization in Washington built around men and women who are recognized experts in their own fields. I think the country knows that the people who are actually responsible in each and every one of these many fields are pulling together with a teamwork that has never before been excelled.

On the road ahead there lies hard work—grueling work—day and night, every hour and every minute.

I was about to add that ahead there lies sacrifice for all of us.

But it is not correct to use that word. The United States does not consider it a sacrifice to do all one can, to give one's best to our nation, when the nation is fighting for its existence and its future life.

It is not a sacrifice for any man, old or young, to be in the army or the navy of the United States. Rather is it a privilege.

It is not a sacrifice for the industrialist or the wage earner, the farmer or the shopkeeper, the trainman or the doctor, to pay more taxes, to buy more bonds, to forego extra profits, to work longer or harder at the task for which he is best fitted. Rather is it a privilege.

It is not a sacrifice to do without many things to which we are accustomed if the national defense calls for doing without.

A review this morning leads me to the conclusion that at present we shall not have to curtail the normal use of articles of food. There is enough food today for all of us and enough left over to send to those who are fighting on the same side with us.

But there will be a clear and definite shortage of metals of many kinds for civilian use, for the very good reason that in our increased program we shall need for war purposes more than half of that portion of the principal metals which during the past year have gone into articles for civilian use. Yes, we shall have to give up many things entirely.

And I am sure that the people in every part of the nation are prepared in their individual living to win this war. I am sure that they will cheerfully help to pay a large part of its financial cost while it goes on. I am sure they will cheerfully give up those material things that they are asked to give up.

And I am sure that they will retain all those great spiritual things without which we cannot win through.

I repeat that the United States can accept no result save victory, final and complete. Not only must the shame of Japanese treachery be wiped out, but the sources of international brutality, wherever they exist, must be absolutely and finally broken.

In my message to the Congress yesterday I said that we "will make it very certain that this form of treachery shall never again endanger us." In order to achieve that certainty, we must begin the great task that is before us by abandoning once and for all the illusion that we can ever again isolate ourselves from the rest of humanity.

In these past few years—and, most violently, in the past three days—we have learned a terrible lesson.

It is our obligation to our dead—it is our sacred obligation to their children and to our children—that we must never forget what we have learned.

And what we all have learned is this:

There is no such thing as security for any nation—or any individual—in a world ruled by the principles of gangsterism.

There is no such thing as impregnable defense against powerful aggressors who sneak up in the dark and strike without warning.

We have learned that our ocean-girt hemisphere is not immune from severe attack—that we cannot measure our safety in terms of miles on any map any more.

We may acknowledge that our enemies have performed a

brilliant feat of deception, perfectly timed and executed with great skill. It was a thoroughly dishonorable deed, but we must face the fact that modern warfare as conducted in the Nazi manner is a dirty business. We don't like it—we didn't want to get in it—but we are in it and we're going to fight it with everything we've got.

I do not think any American has any doubt of our ability to administer proper punishment to the perpetrators of these crimes.

Your government knows that for weeks Germany has been telling Japan that if Japan did not attack the United States, Japan would not share in dividing the spoils with Germany when peace came. She was promised by Germany that if she came in she would receive the complete and perpetual control of the whole of the Pacific area—and that means not only the Far East, but also all of the islands in the Pacific, and also a stranglehold on the west coast of North, Central, and South America.

We know also that Germany and Japan are conducting their military and naval operations in accordance with a joint plan. That plan considers all peoples and nations which are not helping the Axis powers as common enemies of each and every one of the Axis powers.

That is their simple and obvious grand strategy. And that is why the American people must realize that it can be matched only with similar grand strategy. We must realize for example that Japanese successes against the United States in the Pacific are helpful to German operations in Libya; that any German success against the Caucasus is inevitably an assistance to Japan in her operations against the Dutch East Indies; that a German attack against Algiers or Morocco opens the way to a German attack against South America, and the Canal.

On the other side of the picture, we must learn also to know that guerrilla warfare against the Germans in, let us say, Serbia or Norway helps us; that a successful Russian offensive against the Germans helps us; and that British successes on land or sea in any part of the world strengthen our hands.

Remember always that Germany and Italy, regardless of any formal declaration of war, consider themselves at war with the United States at this moment just as much as they consider themselves at war with Britain or Russia. And Germany puts all the other republics of the Americas into the same category of enemies. The people of our sister republics of this hemisphere can be honored by that fact.

The true goal we seek is far above and beyond the ugly field of battle. When we resort to force, as now we must, we are determined that this force shall be directed toward ultimate good as well as against immediate evil. We Americans are not destroyers—we are builders.

We are now in the midst of a war, not for conquest, not for vengeance, but for a world in which this nation, and all that this nation represents, will be safe for our children. We expect to eliminate the danger from Japan, but it would serve us ill if we accomplished that and found that the rest of the world was dominated by Hitler and Mussolini.

We are going to win the war and we are going to win the peace that follows.

And in the difficult hours of this day—through dark days that may be yet to come—we will know that the vast majority of the members of the human race are on our side. Many of them are fighting with us. All of them are praying for us. For in representing our cause, we represent theirs as well—our hope and their hope for liberty under God.

Message to Congress Requesting a Declaration of War Between Germany and Italy and the United States

December 11, 1941

On the morning of December 11, the government of Germany, pursuing its course of world conquest, declared war against the United States.

The long known and the long expected has thus taken place. The forces endeavoring to enslave the entire world now are moving toward this hemisphere.

Never before has there been a greater challenge to life, liberty, and civilization.

Delay invites greater danger. Rapid and united effort by all of the peoples of the world who are determined to remain free will insure a world victory of the forces of justice and of righteousness over the forces of savagery and of barbarism.

Italy also has declared war against the United States.

I therefore request the Congress to recognize a state of war between the United States and Germany, and between the United States and Italy.

Ninth Annual Message to Congress

January 6, 1942

In fulfilling my duty to report upon the state of the Union, I am proud to say to you that the spirit of the American people was never higher than it is today—the Union was never more closely knit together—this country was never more deeply determined to face the solemn tasks before it.

The response of the American people has been instantaneous, and it will be sustained until our security is assured.

Exactly one year ago today I said to this Congress: "When the dictators . . . are ready to make war upon us, they will not wait for an act of war on our part. . . . They—not we—will choose the time and the place and the method of their attack."

We now know their choice of the time: a peaceful Sunday morning—December 7, 1941.

We know their choice of the place: an American outpost in the Pacific.

We know their choice of the method: the method of Hitler himself.

Japan's scheme of conquest goes back half a century. It was not merely a policy of seeking living room—it was a plan which included the subjugation of all the peoples in the Far East and in the islands of the Pacific, and the domination of that ocean by Japanese military and naval control of the western coasts of North, Central, and South America.

The development of this ambitious conspiracy was marked by the war against China in 1894; the subsequent occupation of Korea; the war against Russia in 1904; the illegal fortification of the mandated Pacific islands following 1920; the seizure of Manchuria in 1931; and the invasion of China in 1937.

A similar policy of criminal conquest was adopted by Italy. The Fascists first revealed their imperial designs in Libya and Tripoli. In 1935 they seized Abyssinia. Their goal was the domination of all North Africa, Egypt, parts of France, and the entire Mediterranean world.

But the dreams of empire of the Japanese and Fascist leaders were modest in comparison with the gargantuan aspirations of Hitler and his Nazis. Even before they came to power in 1933, their plans for that conquest had been drawn. Those plans provided for ultimate domination, not of any one section of the world, but of the whole earth and all the oceans on it.

When Hitler organized his Berlin-Rome-Tokyo alliance, all these plans of conquest became a single plan. Under this, in addition to her own schemes of conquest, Japan's role was obviously to cut off our supply of weapons of war to Britain and Russia and China—weapons which increasingly were speeding the day of Hitler's doom. The act of Japan at Pearl Harbor was intended to stun us—to terrify us to such an extent that we would divert our industrial and military strength to the Pacific area, or even to our own continental defense.

The plan has failed in its purpose. We have not been stunned. We have not been terrified or confused. This very reassembling of the Seventy-seventh Congress today is proof of that; for the mood of quiet, grim resolution which here prevails bodes ill for those who conspired and collaborated to murder world peace.

That mood is stronger than any mere desire for revenge. It expresses the will of the American people to make very certain that the world will never so suffer again.

Admittedly, we have been faced with hard choices. It was bitter, for example, not to be able to relieve the heroic and historic defenders of Wake Island. It was bitter for us not to be able to land a million men in a thousand ships in the Philippine Islands.

But this adds only to our determination to see to it that the Stars and Stripes will fly again over Wake and Guam. Yes, see to it that the brave people of the Philippines will be rid of Japanese imperialism, and will live in freedom, security, and independence.

Powerful and offensive actions must and will be taken in proper time. The consolidation of the United Nations' total war effort against our common enemies is being achieved.

That was and is the purpose of conferences which have been held during the past two weeks in Washington and Moscow and Chungking. That is the primary objective of the declaration of solidarity signed in Washington on January 1, 1942, by twenty-six nations united against the Axis powers. . . .

Plans have been laid here and in the other capitals for coordinated and cooperative action by all the United Nations—military action and economic action. Already we have established, as you know, unified command of land, sea, and air forces in the southwestern Pacific theater of war. There will be a continuation of conferences and consultations among military staffs, so that the plans and operations of each will fit into the general strategy designed to crush the enemy. We shall not fight isolated wars—each nation going its own way. These twenty-six nations are united—not in spirit and determination alone, but in the broad conduct of the war in all its phases.

For the first time since the Japanese and the Fascists and the Nazis started along their blood-stained course of conquest they now face the fact that superior forces are assembling against them. Gone forever are the days when the aggressors could attack and destroy their victims one by one without unity of resistance. We of the United Nations will so dispose our forces that we can strike at the common enemy wherever the greatest damage can be done him.

The militarists of Berlin and Tokyo started this war. But the massed, angered forces of common humanity will finish it.

Destruction of the material and spiritual centers of civilization—this has been and still is the purpose of Hitler and his Italian and Japanese chessmen. They would wreck the power of the British Commonwealth and Russia and China and the Netherlands—and then combine all their forces to achieve their ultimate goal, the conquest of the United States.

They know that victory for us means victory for freedom.

They know that victory for us means victory for the institution of democracy—the ideal of the family, the simple principles of common decency and humanity.

They know that victory for us means victory for religion.

And they could not tolerate that. The world is too small to provide adequate "living room" for both Hitler and God. In proof of that, the Nazis have now announced their plan for enforcing their new German, pagan religion all over the world —a plan by which the Holy Bible and the Cross of Mercy would be displaced by *Mein Kampf* and the swastika and the naked sword.

Our own objectives are clear; the objective of smashing the militarism imposed by warlords upon their enslaved peoples— the objective of liberating the subjugated nations—the objective of establishing and securing freedom of speech, freedom of religion, freedom from want, and freedom from fear everywhere in the world.

We shall not stop short of these objectives, nor shall we be satisfied merely to gain them and then call it a day. I know that I speak for the American people—and I have good reason to believe that I speak also for all the other peoples who fight with us—when I say that this time we are determined not only to win the war, but also to maintain the security of the peace that will follow. . . .

The superiority of the United Nations in munitions and ships must be overwhelming—so overwhelming that the Axis nations can never hope to catch up with it. And so, in order to attain this overwhelming superiority the United States must build planes and tanks and guns and ships to the utmost limit of our national capacity. We have the ability and capacity to produce arms not only for our own forces, but also for the armies, navies, and air forces fighting on our side.

And our overwhelming superiority of armament must be

adequate to put weapons of war at the proper time into the hands of those men in the conquered nations who stand ready to seize the first opportunity to revolt against their German and Japanese oppressors, and against the traitors in their own ranks, known by the already infamous name of Quislings. And I think that it is a fair prophecy to say that, as we get guns to the patriots in those lands, they too will fire shots heard 'round the world.

This production of ours in the United States must be raised far above present levels, even though it will mean the dislocation of the lives and occupations of millions of our own people. We must raise our sights all along the production line. Let no man say it cannot be done. It must be done—and we have undertaken to do it. . . .

Our task is hard—our task is unprecedented—and the time is short. We must strain every existing armament-producing facility to the utmost. We must convert every available plant and tool to war production. That goes all the way from the greatest plants to the smallest—from the huge automobile industry to the village machine shop.

Production for war is based on men and women—the human hands and brains which collectively we call Labor. Our workers stand ready to work long hours; to turn out more in a day's work; to keep the wheels turning and the fires burning twenty-four hours a day, and seven days a week. They realize well that on the speed and efficiency of their work depend the lives of their sons and their brothers on the fighting fronts.

Production for war is based on metals and raw materials— steel, copper, rubber, aluminum, zinc, tin. Greater and greater quantities of them will have to be diverted to war purposes. Civilian use of them will have to be cut further and still further —and, in many cases, completely eliminated.

War costs money. So far, we have hardly even begun to pay for it. We have devoted only 15 percent of our national income to national defense. As will appear in my Budget Message tomorrow, our war program for the coming fiscal year will cost

$56 billion or, in other words, more than half of the estimated annual national income. That means taxes and bonds and bonds and taxes. It means cutting luxuries and other nonessentials. In a word, it means an "all-out" war by individual effort and family effort in a united country.

Only this all-out scale of production will hasten the ultimate all-out victory. Speed will count. Lost ground can always be regained—lost time never. Speed will save lives; speed will save this nation which is in peril; speed will save our freedom and our civilization—and slowness has never been an American characteristic. . . .

We cannot wage this war in a defensive spirit. As our power and our resources are fully mobilized, we shall carry the attack against the enemy—we shall hit him and hit him again wherever and whenever we can reach him.

We must keep him far from our shores, for we intend to bring this battle to him on his own home grounds.

American armed forces must be used at any place in all the world where it seems advisable to engage the forces of the enemy. In some cases these operations will be defensive, in order to protect key positions. In other cases, these operations will be offensive, in order to strike at the common enemy, with a view to his complete encirclement and eventual total defeat.

American armed forces will operate at many points in the Far East.

American armed forces will be on all the oceans—helping to guard the essential communications which are vital to the United Nations.

American land and air and sea forces will take stations in the British Isles—which constitute an essential fortress in this great world struggle.

American armed forces will help to protect this hemisphere —and also help to protect bases outside this hemisphere, which could be used for an attack on the Americas.

If any of our enemies, from Europe or from Asia, attempt long-range raids by "suicide" squadrons of bombing planes, they will do so only in the hope of terrorizing our people and disrupting our morale. Our people are not afraid of that. We know that we may have to pay a heavy price for freedom. We will pay this price with a will. Whatever the price, it is a thousand times worth it. No matter what our enemies, in their desperation, may attempt to do to us—we will say, as the people of London have said, "We can take it." And what's more we can give it back—and we will give it back—with compound interest. . . .

Many people ask, "When will this war end?" There is only one answer to that. It will end just as soon as we make it end, by our combined efforts, our combined strength, our combined determination to fight through and work through until the end —the end of militarism in Germany and Italy and Japan. Most certainly we shall not settle for less.

That is the spirit in which discussions have been conducted during the visit of the British prime minister to Washington. Mr. Churchill and I understand each other, our motives, and our purposes. Together, during the past two weeks, we have faced squarely the major military and economic problems of this greatest world war.

All in our nation have been cheered by Mr. Churchill's visit. We have been deeply stirred by his great message to us. He is welcome in our midst, and we unite in wishing him a safe return to his home.

For we are fighting on the same side with the British people, who fought alone for long, terrible months, and withstood the enemy with fortitude and tenacity and skill.

We are fighting on the same side with the Russian people who have seen the Nazi hordes swarm up to the very gates of Moscow, and who with almost superhuman will and courage have forced the invaders back into retreat.

We are fighting on the same side as the brave people of China—those millions who for four and a half long years have withstood bombs and starvation and have whipped the invaders time and again in spite of the superior Japanese equipment and arms.

Yes, we are fighting on the same side as the indomitable Dutch.

We are fighting on the same side as all the other governments in exile, whom Hitler and all his armies and all his Gestapo have not been able to conquer.

But we of the United Nations are not making all this sacrifice of human effort and human lives to return to the kind of world we had after the last world war.

We are fighting today for security, for progress, and for peace, not only for ourselves but for all men, not only for one generation but for all generations. We are fighting to cleanse the world of ancient evils, ancient ills.

Our enemies are guided by brutal cynicism, by unholy contempt for the human race. We are inspired by a faith that goes back through all the years to the first chapter of the book of Genesis: "God created man in His own image."

We on our side are striving to be true to that divine heritage. We are fighting, as our fathers have fought, to uphold the doctrine that all men are equal in the sight of God. Those on the other side are striving to destroy this deep belief and to create a world in their own image—a world of tyranny and cruelty and serfdom.

That is the conflict that day and night now pervades our lives. No compromise can end that conflict. There never has been—there never can be—successful compromise between good and evil. Only total victory can reward the champions of tolerance, and decency, and freedom, and faith.

Radio Address on the Scrap Rubber Campaign

June 12, 1942

I want to talk to you about rubber—about rubber and the war —about rubber and the American people.

When I say rubber I mean rubber. I don't mean gasoline. Gasoline is a serious problem only in certain sections of the country.

But rubber is a problem everywhere—from one end of the country to the other—in the Mississippi Valley as well as in the East, in the oil country as well as in the corn country or the iron country or the great industrial centers.

Rubber is a problem for this reason: because modern wars cannot be won without rubber and because 92 percent of our normal supply of rubber has been cut off by the Japanese.

That *is* serious. It would be more serious if we had not built up a stockpile of rubber before the war started, if we were not now building up a great new synthetic rubber industry. That takes time, so we have an immediate need.

Neither the stockpile, nor the synthetic plants which are now being built, nor both together will be enough to provide for the needs of our great new army and navy plus our civilian requirements as they now exist.

The armed services have done what they can. They have eliminated rubber wherever possible. The army, for example, has had to replace rubber treads with less efficient steel treads on many of its tanks. Army and navy estimates of use of rubber have had to be curtailed all along the line.

But there is a limit to that.

You and I want the finest and most efficient army and navy the world has ever seen—an army and navy with the greatest and swiftest striking power. That means rubber—huge quantities of rubber—rubber for trucks and tanks and planes and gun mounts, rubber for gas masks and rubber for landing boats.

But it is not the army and navy alone which need rubber. The process of production also needs rubber. We need rubber to get our war workers back and forth to their plants—some of them far from workers' homes. We need rubber to keep our essential goods and supplies moving.

All this adds up to a very serious problem—a problem which is a challenge to the sound judgment of the government and to the ingenuity of the American people. It is a problem we Americans are laboring to solve—a problem we will solve.

But there is one unknown factor in this problem. We know what our stockpile is. We know what our synthetic capacity will be. But we do not know how much used rubber there is in the country—used rubber which, reclaimed and reprocessed, can be combined with our supplies of new rubber to make those supplies go farther in meeting military and civilian needs.

Specifically, we don't know how much used rubber there is in *your* cellar—*your* barn—*your* stockroom—*your* garage—*your* attic.

There are as many opinions as there are experts, and until we *know* we can't make our plans for the best use of the rubber we have.

The only way to find out is to get the used rubber in where it can stand up and be counted.

And that precisely is what we propose to do.

We are setting aside the two-week period from June 15 to June 30—from 12:01 A.M., June 15, to 12:00 midnight, June 30 —to get the old rubber in.

We have asked the filling station operators—the thousands upon thousands of citizens who operate gas stations and garages from one end of the country to the other—to help. And they have generously and patriotically agreed to help—they and the oil companies which serve them.

They have agreed to take the old rubber in and to pay for

it at the standard rate of a penny a pound, an amount which will later be refunded to them by the government.

I know that I don't need to urge you to take part in this collection drive. All you need to know is the place to take your rubber and the time to take it there—*and* the fact that your country needs it.

We do not want you to turn in essential rubber that you need in your daily life—rubber you will have to replace by buying new things in the store. We do want every bit of rubber you can possibly spare, and in any quantity—less than a pound, many pounds. We want it in every form—old tires, old rubber raincoats, old garden hose, rubber shoes, bathing caps, gloves —whatever you have that is made of rubber. If you think it is rubber, take it to your nearest filling station.

Once the rubber is in, we will know what our supplies of used rubber are and we will make our plans accordingly. One thing you can be sure of: we are going to see to it that there is enough rubber to build the planes to bomb Tokyo and Berlin— enough rubber to build the tanks to crush the enemy wherever we may find him—enough rubber to win this war.

Here are two simple rules for this rubber emergency.

1. Turn in all the old rubber—anywhere and everywhere.

2. Cut the use of your car—save its tires by driving slowly and driving less.

I know the nation will respond.

Fireside Chat on the Federal Seizure of the Coal Mines

May 2, 1943

I am speaking tonight to the American people, and in particular to those of our citizens who are coal miners.

Tonight this country faces a serious crisis. We are engaged in a war on the successful outcome of which will depend the whole future of our country.

This war has reached a new critical phase. After the years that we have spent in preparation, we have moved into active and continuing battle with our enemies. We are pouring into the worldwide conflict everything that we have—our young men, and the vast resources of our nation.

I have just returned from a two weeks' tour of inspection on which I saw our men being trained and our war materials made. My trip took me through twenty states. I saw thousands of workers on the production line, making airplanes and guns and ammunition.

Everywhere I found great eagerness to get on with the war. Men and women are working long hours at difficult jobs and living under difficult conditions without complaint.

Along thousands of miles of track I saw countless acres of newly plowed fields. The farmers of this country are planting the crops that are needed to feed our armed forces, our civilian population, and our allies. Those crops will be harvested.

On my trip, I saw hundreds of thousands of soldiers. Young men who were green recruits last autumn have matured into self-assured and hardened fighting men. They are in splendid physical condition. They are mastering the superior weapons that we are pouring out of our factories.

The American people have accomplished a miracle.

However, all of our massed effort is none too great to meet the demands of this war. We shall need everything that we have and everything that our allies have—to defeat the Nazis and the Fascists in the coming battles on the continent of Europe, and the Japanese on the continent of Asia and in the islands of the Pacific.

This tremendous forward movement of the United States and the United Nations cannot be stopped by our enemies.

And equally, it must not be hampered by any one individual or by the leaders of any one group here back home.

I want to make it clear that every American coal miner who has stopped mining coal—no matter how sincere his motives, no matter how legitimate he may believe his grievances to be—every idle miner directly and individually is obstructing our war effort. We have not yet won this war. We will win this war only as we produce and deliver our total American effort on the high seas and on the battlefronts. And that requires unrelenting, uninterrupted effort here on the home front.

A stopping of the coal supply, even for a short time, would involve a gamble with the lives of American soldiers and sailors and the future security of our whole people. It would involve an unwarranted, unnecessary, and terribly dangerous gamble with our chances for victory.

Therefore, I say to all miners—and to all Americans everywhere, at home and abroad—the production of coal will not be stopped.

Tonight, I am speaking to the essential patriotism of the miners, and to the patriotism of their wives and children. And I am going to state the true facts of this case as simply and as plainly as I know how.

After the attack at Pearl Harbor, the three great labor organizations—the American Federation of Labor, the Congress of Industrial Organizations, and the Railroad Brotherhoods—gave the positive assurance that there would be no strikes as long as the war lasted. And the president of the United Mine

Workers of America was a party to that assurance.

That pledge was applauded throughout the country. It was a forcible means of telling the world that we Americans—135 million of us—are united in our determination to fight this total war with our total will and our total power.

At the request of employers and of organized labor—including the United Mine Workers—the War Labor Board was set up for settling any disputes which could not be adjusted through collective bargaining. The War Labor Board is a tribunal on which workers, employers, and the general public are equally represented.

In the present coal crisis, conciliation and mediation were tried unsuccessfully.

In accordance with the law, the case was then certified to the War Labor Board, the agency created for this express purpose with the approval of organized labor. The members of the board followed the usual practice which has proved successful in other disputes. Acting promptly, they undertook to get all the facts of this case from both the miners and the operators.

The national officers of the United Mine Workers, however, declined to have anything to do with the fact finding of the War Labor Board. The only excuse that they offer is that the War Labor Board is prejudiced.

The War Labor Board has been and is ready to give this case a fair and impartial hearing. I have given my assurance that if any adjustment of wages is made by the board, it will be made retroactive to April 1. But the national officers of the United Mine Workers refused to participate in the hearing when asked to do so last Monday.

On Wednesday of this past week, while the board was proceeding with the case, stoppages began to occur in some mines. On Thursday morning I telegraphed to the officers of the United Mine Workers asking that the miners continue mining coal on Saturday morning. However, a general strike throughout the industry became effective on Friday night.

The responsibility for the crisis that we now face rests

squarely on these national officers of the United Mine Workers, and not on the government of the United States. But the consequences of this arbitrary action threaten all of us everywhere.

At ten o'clock yesterday morning the government took over the mines. I called upon the miners to return to work for their government. The government needs their services just as surely as it needs the services of our soldiers, and sailors, and marines —and the services of the millions who are turning out the munitions of war.

You miners have sons in the army and navy and Marine Corps. You have sons who at this very minute—this split second—may be fighting in New Guinea, or in the Aleutian Islands, or Guadalcanal, or Tunisia, or China, or protecting troop ships and supplies against submarines on the high seas. We have already received telegrams from some of our fighting men overseas, and I only wish they could tell you what they think of the stoppage of work in the coal mines.

Some of your own sons have come back from the fighting fronts, wounded. A number of them, for example, are now here in an army hospital in Washington. Several of them have been decorated by their government.

I could tell you of one from Pennsylvania. He was a coal miner before his induction, and his father is a coal miner. He was seriously wounded by Nazi machine-gun bullets while he was on a bombing mission over Europe in a Flying Fortress.

Another boy, from Kentucky, the son of a coal miner, was wounded when our troops first landed in North Africa six months ago.

There is still another, from Illinois. He was a coal miner— his father and two brothers are coal miners. He was seriously wounded in Tunisia while attempting to rescue two comrades whose jeep had been blown up by a Nazi mine.

These men do not consider themselves heroes. They would probably be embarrassed if I mentioned their names over the air. They were wounded in the line of duty. They know how essential it is to the tens of thousands—hundreds of thousands

—and ultimately millions of other young Americans to get the best of arms and equipment into the hands of our fighting forces, and get them there quickly.

The fathers and mothers of our fighting men, their brothers and sisters and friends—and that includes all of us—are also in the line of duty: the production line. Any failure in production may well result in costly defeat on the field of battle.

There can be no one among us—no one faction—powerful enough to interrupt the forward march of our people to victory.

You miners have ample reason to know that there are certain basic rights for which this country stands, and that those rights are worth fighting for and worth dying for. That is why you have sent your sons and brothers from every mining town in the nation to join in the great struggle overseas. That is why you have contributed so generously, so willingly, to the purchase of war bonds and to the many funds for the relief of war victims in foreign lands. That is why, since this war was started in 1939, you have increased the annual production of coal by almost two hundred million tons a year.

The toughness of your sons in our armed forces is not surprising. They come of fine, rugged stock. Men who work in the mines are not unaccustomed to hardship. It has been the objective of this government to reduce that hardship, to obtain for miners and for all who do the nation's work a better standard of living.

I know only too well that the cost of living is troubling the miners' families, and troubling the families of millions of other workers throughout the country as well.

A year ago it became evident to all of us that something had to be done about living costs. Your government determined not to let the cost of living continue to go up as it did in the First World War.

Your government has been determined to maintain stability of both prices and wages, so that a dollar would buy, so far as possible, the same amount of the necessities of life. And by necessities I mean just that—not the luxuries, not the fancy goods that we have learned to do without in wartime.

So far, we have not been able to keep the prices of some necessities as low as we should have liked to keep them. That is true not only in coal towns but in many other places.

Wherever we find that prices of essentials have risen too high, they will be brought down. Wherever we find that price ceilings are being violated, the violators will be punished.

Rents have been fixed in most parts of the country. In many cities they have been cut to below where they were before we entered the war. Clothing prices have generally remained stable.

These two items make up more than a third of the total budget of the worker's family.

As for food, which today accounts for about another third of the family expenditure on the average, I want to repeat again: your government will continue to take all necessary measures to eliminate unjustified and avoidable price increases. And we are today taking measures to "roll back" the prices of meats.

The war is going to go on. Coal will be mined no matter what any individual thinks about it. The operation of our factories, our power plants, our railroads will not be stopped. Our munitions must move to our troops.

And so, under these circumstances, it is inconceivable that any patriotic miner can choose any course other than going back to work and mining coal.

The nation cannot afford violence of any kind at the coal mines or in coal towns. I have placed authority for the resumption of coal mining in the hands of a civilian, the secretary of the interior. If it becomes necessary to protect any miner who seeks patriotically to go back and work, then that miner must have and his family must have—and will have—complete and adequate protection. If it becomes necessary to have troops at the mine mouths or in coal towns for the protection of working miners and their families, those troops will be doing police duty for the sake of the nation as a whole, and particularly for the sake of the fighting men in the army, the navy, and the marines—your sons and mine—who are fighting our common enemies all over the world.

I understand the devotion of the coal miners to their union. I know of the sacrifices they have made to build it up. I believe now, as I have all my life, in the right of workers to join unions and to protect their unions. I want to make it absolutely clear that this government is not going to do anything now to weaken those rights in the coal fields.

Every improvement in the conditions of the coal miners of this country has had my hearty support, and I do not mean to desert them now. But I also do not mean to desert my obligations and responsibilities as president of the United States and commander in chief of the army and navy.

The first necessity is the resumption of coal mining. The terms of the old contract will be followed by the secretary of the interior. If an adjustment in wages results from a decision of the War Labor Board, or from any new agreement between the operators and miners, which is approved by the War Labor Board, that adjustment will be made retroactive to April 1.

In the message that I delivered to the Congress four months ago, I expressed my conviction that the spirit of this nation is good.

Since then, I have seen our troops in the Caribbean area, in bases on the coasts of our ally, Brazil, and in North Africa. Recently I have again seen great numbers of our fellow countrymen—soldiers and civilians—from the Atlantic Seaboard to the Mexican border and to the Rocky Mountains.

Tonight, in the face of a crisis of serious proportions in the coal industry, I say again that the spirit of this nation is good. I know that the American people will not tolerate any threat offered to their government by anyone. I believe the coal miners will not continue the strike against their government. I believe that the coal miners as Americans will not fail to heed the clear call to duty. Like all other good Americans, they will march shoulder to shoulder with their armed forces to victory.

Tomorrow the Stars and Stripes will fly over the coal mines, and I hope that every miner will be at work under that flag.

MESSAGE TO THE SENATE ON THE SEGREGATION PROGRAM OF THE WAR RELOCATION AUTHORITY

September 14, 1943

On July 6, 1943, the Senate considered and agreed to Senate Resolution 166.

The resolution relates to the program for relocating persons of Japanese ancestry evacuated from West Coast military areas, and asks that the president issue an executive order to accomplish two things: (1) to direct the War Relocation Authority to segregate the disloyal persons, and the persons whose loyalty is questionable, from those whose loyalty to the United States has been established, and (2) to direct the appropriate agency of the government to issue a full and complete authoritative statement on conditions in relocation centers and plans for future operations.

I find that the War Relocation Authority has already undertaken a program of segregation. That program is now under way. The first train movements began in early September.

In response to the resolution I asked the director of the Office of War Mobilization to issue a full and complete authoritative public statement on conditions in relocation centers and plans for future operations. A short preliminary statement on this subject was issued on July 17, 1943. A full and complete statement is being made public today. Copies of these statements are transmitted with this message.

Thus, both of the steps called for in Senate Resolution 166 have already been taken, and it appears that issuance of a further executive order is not necessary for accomplishment of these purposes.

The segregation program of the War Relocation Authority provides for transferring to a single center, the Tule Lake Center in northeastern California, those persons of Japanese ancestry residing in relocation centers who have indicated that their loyalties lie with Japan. All persons among the evacuees who have expressed a wish to return to Japan for permanent residence have been included among the segregants, along with those among the citizen evacuees who have answered in the negative, or have refused to answer, a direct question as to their willingness to declare their loyalty to the United States and to renounce any allegiance to any foreign government. In addition, those evacuees who are found, after investigation and hearing, to be ineligible to secure indefinite leave from a relocation center, under the leave regulations of the War Relocation Authority, are to be included among the segregants.

While the precise number of segregants is not established at this time because a number of leave clearance investigations have not yet been completed, it is established that the disloyal persons among the evacuees constitute but a small minority, and that the great majority of evacuees are loyal to the democratic institutions of the United States.

Arrangements are being completed for the adequate guarding and supervision of the segregated evacuees. They will be adequately fed and housed and their treatment will in all respects be fair and humane; they will not, however, be eligible to leave the Tule Lake Center while the war with Japan continues or so long as the military situation requires their residence there. An appeals procedure to allow for the correction of mistakes made in determining who shall be segregated has been established so that the entire procedure may be fair and equitable.

With the segregation of the disloyal evacuees in a separate center, the War Relocation Authority proposes now to redouble its efforts to accomplish the relocation into normal homes and jobs in communities throughout the United States, but outside the evacuated areas, of those Americans of Japanese ancestry whose loyalty to this country has remained unshaken through the hardships of the evacuation which military necessity made unavoidable. We shall restore to the loyal evacuees the right to return to the evacuated areas as soon as the military situation will make such restoration feasible.

Americans of Japanese ancestry, like those of many other ancestries, have shown that they can, and want to, accept our institutions and work loyally with the rest of us, making their own valuable contribution to the national wealth and well-being. In vindication of the very ideals for which we are fighting this war it is important to us to maintain a high standard of fair, considerate, and equal treatment for the people of this minority as of all other minorities.

Message to Congress
on the Progress
of the War

September 17, 1943

During the two months' recess of the Congress, many important events have occurred at the war fronts and at home. You return at a time when major battles in Europe and in Asia are beginning to be joined. In recent months, the main tides of conflict have been running our way—but we could not and cannot be content merely to drift with this favorable tide.

You know from the news of the past few days that every military operation entails a legitimate military risk and that occasionally we have checks to our plans—checks which necessarily involve severe losses of men and materials.

The Allied forces are now engaged in a very hard battle south of Naples. Casualties are heavy. The desperation with which the Germans are fighting reveals that they are well aware of the consequences to them of our occupation of Italy.

The Congress and the American people can rest assured that the landing on Italy is not the only landing we have in mind. That landing was planned at Casablanca. At Quebec, the leaders and the military staffs of Great Britain and the United States made specific and precise plans to bring to bear further blows of equal or greater importance against Germany and Japan—with definite times and places for other landings on the continent of Europe and elsewhere.

On the tenth of July a carefully prepared expedition landed in Sicily. In spite of heavy German opposition it cleared this large and heavily fortified island in thirty-eight days.

British, Canadian, and American losses in killed, wounded,

and missing in the Sicilian campaign were 31,158, of which the American forces lost 7,445. The casualties among the Italians and Germans were approximately 165,000, including 132,000 prisoners.

The unmistakably sincere welcome given to the Allied troops by the Italian people has proved conclusively that even in a country which had lived for a generation under a complete dictatorship—with all of its propaganda, censorship, and suppression of free speech and discussion—the love of liberty was unconquerable.

It has also proved conclusively that this war was not waged by the people of Italy on their own choice. All of Mussolini's propaganda machine could not make them love Hitler or hate us. The less said about the feelings toward Mussolini, the better.

I believe that equal jubilation and enthusiasm will be shown by the people of the other nations now under the German heel when Nazi Gauleiters and native Quislings are removed through force or flight.

How different was this invading army of the Allies from the German forces that had come into Sicily, ostensibly to "protect it." Food, clothing, cattle, medicines, and household goods had been systematically stolen from the people of Sicily, and sent north to the "master race" in Germany. Sicily, like other parts of Italy and like the other satellite and conquered nations, had been bled white by the Nazi and Fascist governments. Growers of crops were permitted to retain only a small fraction of their own produce for themselves and their families.

With the Allied armies, however, went a carefully planned organization, trained and equipped to give physical care to the local population—food, clothing, medicine. This new organization is also now in the process of restoring to the people of Sicily freedoms which, for many years, had been denied to them. I am confident that, within a year, Sicily will be once more self-supporting—and, in addition to that, once more self-respecting.

From Sicily the advance of the Allied armies has continued to the mainland. On the third day of September they landed on the toe of the Italian peninsula. These were the first Allied troops to invade the continent of Europe in order to liberate the conquered and oppressed countries. History will always remember this day as the beginning of the answer to the prayer of the millions of liberty-loving human beings not only in these conquered lands but all over the world.

On July 25—two weeks after our first landings in Sicily—political events in Italy startled the world. Mussolini, the incubus of Italy for a generation, the man who is more responsible for all of the sorrows of Italy than anyone, except possibly Hitler himself, was forced out of office and stripped of his power as a result of his own dismal failures, his wanton brutalities, and the overwhelming demand of the Italian people. This was the first break in Axis leadership—to be followed, we are determined, by other and similar encouraging downfalls. . . .

Early last month, the relentless application of overwhelming Allied power—particularly air and sea power—convinced the leaders of Italy that it could not continue an active part in the war. Conversations were begun by them with us. These conversations were carried on with the utmost secrecy. Therefore, much as I wished to do so, I could not communicate the facts of the case to the Congress, or the press, or to those who repeatedly expressed dismay or indignation at our apparent course in Italy. These negotiations turned out to be a complete surprise to nearly everyone, not only to the Axis but to the Italian people themselves. . . .

The armistice with Italy was signed on September 3 in Sicily, but it could not be put into effect until September 8, when we were ready to make landings in force in the Naples area. We had planned these landings some time before and were determined to go through with them, armistice or no armistice.

Italian leaders appealed to their army and navy to end hostilities against us. Italian soldiers, though disorganized and ill-supplied, have been fighting the Germans in many regions. In conformity with the terms of unconditional surrender, the Italian fleet has come over to our side; and it can be a powerful weapon in striking at the Nazi enemies of the Italian people.

When Hitler was forced to the conclusion that his offensive was broken, and he must go on the defensive, he started boasting that he had converted Europe into an impregnable fortress. But he neglected to provide that fortress with a roof. He also left various other vulnerable spots in the wall of the so-called fortress—which we shall point out to him in due time.

The British and American air forces have been bombing the roofless fortress with ever-increasing effectiveness. It is now our purpose to establish bases within bombing range of southern and eastern Germany, and to bring devastating war home to these places by day and by night as it has already been brought to western Germany.

When Britain was being subjected to mass bombing in 1940 and 1941—when the British people, including their king and prime minister, were proving that Britain "could take it"—the strategists of the Royal Air Force and of our own army air forces were not idle. They were studying the mistakes that Goering and his staff of Nazi terrorists were making. Those were fatal mistakes, as it turned out.

Today, we and the British are not making those mistakes. We are not bombing tenements for the sheer sadistic pleasure of killing, as the Nazis did. We are striking devastating blows at carefully selected, clearly identified strategic objectives—factories, shipyards, munition dumps, transportation facilities, which make it possible for the Nazis to wage war. And we are hitting these military targets and blowing them to bits.

German power can still do us great injury. But that evil power is being destroyed, surely, inexorably, day by day, and if Hitler does not know it by now, then the last trace of sanity has departed from that distorted mind. . . .

In the remarkable raid on the Ploesti oil fields in Rumania we lost fifty-three of our heavy bombers; and more than five hundred of our finest men are missing. This may seem like a disastrously high loss, unless you figure it against the damage done to the enemy's war power. I am certain that the German or the Japanese high commands would cheerfully sacrifice tens of thousands of men to do the same amount of damage to us, if they could. Those gallant and brilliant young Americans who raided Ploesti won a smashing victory which, I believe, will contribute materially to the shortening of the war and thus save countless lives.

We shall continue to make such raids all over the territory of Germany and the satellite countries. With Italy in our hands, the distances we have to travel will be far less and the risks proportionately reduced.

We have reliable information that there is definite unrest and a growing desire for peace among the peoples of these satellite countries—Rumania, Hungary, Finland, and Bulgaria. We hope that in these nations the spirit of revolt against Nazi dominance which commenced in Italy will burst into flame and become a consuming fire.

Every American is thrilled by the sledgehammer blows delivered against the Nazi aggressors by the Russian armies. This summer there has been no successful German advance against the Russians, as in 1941 and 1942. The shoe today is on the other foot—and is pinching very hard. Instead, the Russians have forced the greatest military reversal since Napoleon's retreat in 1812.

The recapture of Kharkov, Stalino, and other strongholds by the Russians, the opening of the Ukraine and the Donets Basin, and the freeing of millions of valuable acres and hundreds of inhabited places hearten the whole world as the Russian campaign moves toward the elimination of every German from Russian soil—toward the invasion of Germany itself. It is certain that the campaign in North Africa, the occupation of Sicily, the fighting in Italy, and the compelling of large numbers of German planes to go into combat in the skies over Holland, Belgium, and France by reason of our air attacks have given important help to the Russian armies along their advancing front from Leningrad to the Black Sea. We know, too, that we are contributing to that advance by making Germany keep many divisions in the Balkans, in southern France, and along the English Channel. I like to think that these words constitute an understatement.

Similarly, the events in the Mediterranean have a direct bearing upon the war against Japan.

When the American and British expeditionary forces first landed in North Africa last November, some people believed that we were neglecting our obligations to prosecute the war vigorously in the Pacific. Such people continually make the mistake of trying to divide the war into several watertight compartments—the western European front, the Russian front, the Burma front, the New Guinea and Solomons front, and so forth —as though all of these fronts were separate and unrelated to each other. You even hear talk of the "air war" as opposed to the "land war" or the "sea war."

Actually, we cannot think of this as several wars. It is all one war, and it must be governed by one basic strategy.

The freeing of the Mediterranean, which we started last fall, will lead directly to the resumption of our complete control of the waters of the eastern Indian Ocean and the Bay of Bengal. Thus, we shall be enabled to strike the Japanese on another of their highly vulnerable flanks.

As long as Italy remained in the war as our enemy—as long as the Italian fleet remained in being as a threat—a substantial part of British naval strength had to be kept locked up in the Mediterranean. Now that formidable strength is freed to proceed eastward to join in the ever-increasing attack upon the Japanese. It has not been sufficiently emphasized that the freeing of the Mediterranean is a great asset to the war in the Far East. . . .

We face, in the Orient, a long and difficult fight. We must be prepared for heavy losses in winning that fight. The power of Japan will not collapse until it has been literally pounded into the dust. It would be the utmost folly for us to try to pretend otherwise.

Even so, if the future is tough for us, think what it is for

General Tojo and his murderous gang. They may look to the north, to the south, to the east, or to the west. They can see closing in on them, from all directions, the forces of retribution under the Generalissimo Chiang Kai-shek, General MacArthur, Admiral Nimitz, and Admiral Lord Mountbatten.

The forces operating against Japan in the various Pacific theaters are just as much interrelated and dependent on each other as are the forces pounding against Germany in Europe.

With the new threats that we offer from the Aleutians, Japan cannot afford to devote as large a proportion of her forces to hold the lines in other areas. . . .

Japan has been hard put to it to maintain her extended lines. She had to withdraw her garrison from Kiska in the face of the oncoming American-Canadian forces because she could not maintain a steady stream of adequate reinforcements and supplies to the Aleutians.

In the Solomon Islands, with heavy fighting, we have gained so many island air bases that the threat to Australia and New Zealand across the Coral Sea has been practically dissipated. In fact, it is safe to say that our position in that area has become a threat on our part against the Japanese in the seas that lie north of the Solomons and north of New Guinea.

American, Australian, New Zealand, and Dutch forces in a magnificent campaign in New Guinea and the Solomons have destroyed much Japanese strength and have gained for us new bases from which to launch new offensive operations.

After a long period of defensive strategy in Burma, we are determined to take the offensive there. I am also glad to report to you that we are getting more supplies and military help to China. Almost every day word comes that a new air battle has destroyed two and three times more Japanese planes in China and Burma than we ourselves have lost. That process will continue until we are ready to strike right at the heart of Japan itself.

It goes almost without saying that when Japan surrenders, the United Nations will never again let her have authority over the islands which were mandated to her by the League of Nations. Japan obviously is not to be trusted. And the same thing holds good in the case of the vast territories which Japan has stolen from China starting long before this war began. . . .

We have come a great way since this Congress first met in January of this year. But I state only a blunt fact when I tell the Congress that we are still a long, long way from ultimate victory in any major theater of the war.

First, despite our substantial victories in the Mediterranean, we face a hard and costly fight up through Italy—and a major job of organizing our positions before we can take advantage of them.

Second, from bases in the British Isles we must be sure that we have assembled the strength to strike not just in one direction but in many directions—by land and sea and in the air—with overwhelming forces and equipment.

Third, although our Russian allies have made a magnificent counteroffensive, and are driving our common enemies back day by day, the Russian armies still have far to go before they get into Germany itself.

Fourth, the Japanese hold firmly established positions on an enormous front from the Kuriles through the mandated islands to the Solomons and through the Netherlands East Indies to Malaya and Burma and China. To break through this defensive ring we must hit them and hit them hard not merely at one point but at many points, and we must keep on hitting them.

In all of history, there has never been a task so tremendous as that which we now face. We can do it—and we will do it—but we must plan and work and fight with every ounce of intelligence and energy and courage that we possess.

The Congress has reconvened at a time when we are in the midst of the Third War Loan Drive seeking to raise a sum unparalleled in history—$15 billion. This is a dramatic example of the scale on which this war still has to be fought, and presents some idea of how difficult and costly the responsible leaders of this government believe the war will be. . . .

A few facts will show how vast an enterprise this war has been—and how we are constantly increasing the tempo of our production. . . .

In the two and a half years between January 1, 1941, and July 1, 1943, the power plants built for installation in navy vessels had a horsepower equal to all the horsepower of all hydroelectric plants in the United States in January 1941.

The completions of navy ships during the last six months were equal to completions in the entire year of 1942.

We have cut down the time required to build submarines by almost 50 percent.

The antiaircraft and double-purpose guns produced by the navy since the defense program started in May 1940, if fired all together, would throw 4,600 tons of projectiles per minute against the enemy.

The output of underwater ordnance (torpedoes, mines, and depth charges) during the first half of 1943 was equal to the total production of 1942.

During the month of August 1943, we produced almost as many torpedoes as during all of World War I.

Anyone who has had to build a single factory, tool it up, get the necessary help, set up an assembly line, produce and ship the product will have some idea of what that amount of production has meant.

We have had to raise and equip armed forces approaching ten million men. Simultaneously, in spite of this drain on our manpower, we have had to find millions more men and millions of women to operate our war factories, arsenals, shipyards, essential civilian industries—and the farms and mines of America.

There have been the problems of increasing greatly the output of our natural resources—not only for our own army and navy and for our civilians at home, but also for our allies and our own forces all over the world.

Since the outbreak of war in Europe, we have increased our output of petroleum by 66 percent. We have stepped up our bituminous coal production by 40 percent; chemicals by 300 percent; iron ore by 125 percent; hydroelectric power by 79 percent; and steel by 106 percent.

There were the problems of raising and distributing more food than ever before in our history—for our armed services, for our own people, and to help feed our allies.

There was the formidable problem of establishing a rationing system of the necessities of life which would be fair to all of our people.

There was the difficulty of keeping prices from skyrocketing and fighting off the serious specter of inflation.

There was the problem of transporting millions of men and hundreds of millions of tons of weapons and supplies all over our own country and also to all corners of the world. This necessitated the largest railroad and shipping operations in all history.

There were the problems involved in our vast purchases in foreign countries; in our control of foreign funds, located in this country; in our custody of alien property; in our occupation of liberated areas. There were new problems of communications, of censorship, of war information.

There was the problem of maintaining proper management-labor relations; of fair treatment and just compensation to our millions of war workers; of avoiding strikes; of preventing the exploitation of workers or natural resources by those who would seek to become war profiteers and war millionaires.

There were the problems of civilian defense, of lend-lease, of subcontracting war contracts to smaller businesses, of building up stockpiles of strategic material whose normal sources have been seized by the enemy, such as rubber and tin.

There was the problem of providing housing for millions of new war workers all over the country.

And touching all of these, there was the great problem of raising the money to pay for all of them.

No sincere, sensible person doubts that in such an unprecedented, breathtaking enterprise errors of honest judgment were bound to creep in, and that occasional disputes among conscientious officials were bound to occur. And if anyone thinks that we, working under our democratic system, have made major mistakes in this war, he should take a look at some of the blunders made by our enemies in the so-called "efficient" dictatorships. . . .

As the war grows tougher and as new problems constantly arise in our domestic economy, changes in methods and changes in legislation may become necessary.

We should move for the greater economic protection of our returning men and women in the armed forces—and for greater educational opportunities for them. And for all our citizens we should provide a further measure of social security in order to protect them against certain continuing hazards of life.

All these things, as well as eventual demobilization, should be studied now and much of the necessary legislation should be enacted. I do not mean that this statement should be regarded in any way as an intimation that we are approaching the end of the war. Such an intimation could not be based either on fact or on reason. But when the war ends, we do not want to be caught again without planning or legislation, such as occurred at the end of the last war. . . .

Finally, as the war progresses, we seek a national cooperation with other nations toward the end that world aggression be ended and that fair international relationships be established on a permanent basis. The policy of the Good Neighbor has shown such success in the hemisphere of the Americas that its extension to the whole world seems to be the logical next step. In that way we can begin to keep faith with our sons and daughters who are fighting for freedom and justice and security at home and abroad.

FIRESIDE CHAT ON THE TEHERAN AND CAIRO CONFERENCES

December 24, 1943

I have recently returned from extensive journeyings in the region of the Mediterranean and as far as the borders of Russia. I have conferred with the leaders of Britain and Russia and China on military matters of the present—especially on plans for stepping up our successful attack on our enemies as quickly as possible and from many different points of the compass.

On this Christmas Eve there are over 10 million men in the armed forces of the United States alone. One year ago 1.7 million were serving overseas. Today, this figure has been more than doubled to 3.8 million on duty overseas. By next July 1 that number overseas will rise to over 5 million men and women.

That this is truly a world war was demonstrated to me when arrangements were being made with our overseas broadcasting agencies for the time to speak today to our soldiers, sailors, marines, and merchant seamen in every part of the world. In fixing the time for this broadcast, we took into consideration that at this moment here in the United States, and in the Caribbean and on the northeast coast of South America, it is afternoon. In Alaska and in Hawaii and the mid-Pacific, it is still morning. In Iceland, in Great Britain, in North Africa, in Italy and the Middle East, it is now evening.

In the Southwest Pacific, in Australia, in China and Burma and India, it is already Christmas Day. So we can correctly say that at this moment, in those Far Eastern parts where Americans are fighting, today is tomorrow.

But everywhere throughout the world—throughout this

war that covers the world—there is a special spirit that has warmed our hearts since our earliest childhood, a spirit that brings us close to our homes, our families, our friends and neighbors—the Christmas spirit of "peace on earth, goodwill toward men." It is an unquenchable spirit.

During the past years of international gangsterism and brutal aggression in Europe and in Asia, our Christmas celebrations have been darkened with apprehension for the future. We have said, "Merry Christmas—Happy New Year," but we have known in our hearts that the clouds which have hung over our world have prevented us from saying it with full sincerity and conviction.

And even this year, we still have much to face in the way of further suffering, and sacrifice, and personal tragedy. Our men, who have been through the fierce battles in the Solomons, the Gilberts, Tunisia, and Italy, know from their own experience and knowledge of modern war that many bigger and costlier battles are still to be fought.

But—on Christmas Eve this year—I can say to you that at last we may look forward into the future with real, substantial confidence that, however great the cost, "peace on earth, goodwill toward men" can be and will be realized and insured. This year I *can* say that. Last year I could *not* do more than express a hope. Today I express a certainty—though the cost may be high and the time may be long.

Within the past year—within the past few weeks—history has been made, and it is far better history for the whole human race than any that we have known, or even dared to hope for, in these tragic times through which we pass.

A great beginning was made in the Moscow Conference last October by Mr. Molotov, Mr. Eden, and our own Mr. Hull. There and then the way was paved for the later meetings.

At Cairo and Teheran we devoted ourselves not only to military matters; we devoted ourselves also to consideration of the future—to plans for the kind of world which alone can justify all the sacrifices of this war.

Of course, as you all know, Mr. Churchill and I have happily met many times before, and we know and understand each other very well. Indeed, Mr. Churchill has become known and beloved by many millions of Americans, and the heartfelt prayers of all of us have been with this great citizen of the world in his recent serious illness.

The Cairo and Teheran conferences, however, gave me my first opportunity to meet the Generalissimo, Chiang Kai-shek, and Marshal Stalin—and to sit down at the table with these unconquerable men and talk with them face to face. We had planned to talk to each other across the table at Cairo and Teheran; but we soon found that we were all on the same side of the table. We came to the conferences with faith in each other. But we needed the personal contact. And now we have supplemented faith with definite knowledge.

It was well worth traveling thousands of miles over land and sea to bring about this personal meeting, and to gain the heartening assurance that we are absolutely agreed with one another on all the major objectives—and on the military means of attaining them.

At Cairo, Prime Minister Churchill and I spent four days with the Generalissimo, Chiang Kai-shek. It was the first time that we had an opportunity to go over the complex situation in the Far East with him personally. We were able not only to settle upon definite military strategy, but also to discuss certain long-range principles which we believe can assure peace in the Far East for many generations to come.

Those principles are as simple as they are fundamental. They involve the restoration of stolen property to its rightful owners, and the recognition of the rights of millions of people in the Far East to build up their own forms of self-government without molestation. Essential to all peace and security in the Pacific and in the rest of the world is the permanent elimination of the Empire of Japan as a potential force of aggression. Never again must our soldiers and sailors and marines—and other soldiers, sailors, and marines—be compelled to fight from island to island as they are fighting so gallantly and so successfully today.

Increasingly powerful forces are now hammering at the Japanese at many points over an enormous arc which curves down through the Pacific from the Aleutians to the jungles of Burma. Our own army and navy, our air forces, the Australians and New Zealanders, the Dutch, and the British land, air, and sea forces are all forming a band of steel which is slowly but surely closing in on Japan.

On the mainland of Asia, under the Generalissimo's leadership, the Chinese ground and air forces augmented by American air forces are playing a vital part in starting the drive which will push the invaders into the sea.

Following out the military decisions at Cairo, General Marshall has just flown around the world and has had conferences with General MacArthur and Admiral Nimitz—conferences which will spell plenty of bad news for the Japs in the not too far distant future.

I met in the Generalissimo a man of great vision, great courage, and a remarkably keen understanding of the problems of today and tomorrow. We discussed all the manifold military plans for striking at Japan with decisive force from many directions, and I believe I can say that he returned to Chungking with the positive assurance of total victory over our common enemy. Today we and the Republic of China are closer together than ever before in deep friendship and in unity of purpose.

After the Cairo Conference, Mr. Churchill and I went by airplane to Teheran. There we met with Marshal Stalin. We talked with complete frankness on every conceivable subject connected with the winning of the war and the establishment of a durable peace after the war.

Within three days of intense and consistently amicable discussions, we agreed on every point concerned with the launching of a gigantic attack upon Germany.

The Russian army will continue its stern offensives on Germany's eastern front, the Allied armies in Italy and Africa will bring relentless pressure on Germany from the south, and now the encirclement will be complete as great American and British forces attack from other points of the compass.

The commander selected to lead the combined attack from these other points is General Dwight D. Eisenhower. His performances in Africa, in Sicily, and in Italy have been brilliant. He knows by practical and successful experience the way to coordinate air, sea, and land power. All of these will be under his control. Lieutenant General Carl D. Spaatz will command the entire American strategic bombing force operating against Germany.

General Eisenhower gives up his command in the Mediterranean to a British officer whose name is being announced by Mr. Churchill. We now pledge that new commander that our powerful ground, sea, and air forces in the vital Mediterranean area will stand by his side until every objective in that bitter theater is attained.

Both of these new commanders will have American and British subordinate commanders whose names will be announced in a few days.

During the last two days at Teheran, Marshal Stalin, Mr. Churchill, and I looked ahead to the days and months and years that will follow Germany's defeat. We were united in determination that Germany must be stripped of her military might and be given no opportunity within the foreseeable future to regain that might.

The United Nations have no intention to enslave the German people. We wish them to have a normal chance to develop, in peace, as useful and respectable members of the European family. But we most certainly emphasize that word "respectable"—for we intend to rid them once and for all of Nazism and Prussian militarism and the fantastic and disastrous notion that they constitute the "master race."

We did discuss international relationships from the point of view of big, broad objectives, rather than details. But on the basis of what we did discuss, I can say even today that I do not think any insoluble differences will arise among Russia, Great Britain, and the United States.

In these conferences we were concerned with basic principles—principles which involve the security and the welfare and the standard of living of human beings in countries large and small.

To use an American and somewhat ungrammatical colloquialism, I may say that I "got along fine" with Marshal Stalin. He is a man who combines a tremendous, relentless determination with a stalwart good humor. I believe he is truly representative of the heart and soul of Russia; and I believe that we are going to get along very well with him and the Russian people—very well indeed.

Britain, Russia, China, and the United States and their allies represent more than three-quarters of the total population of the earth. As long as these four nations with great military power stick together in determination to keep the peace there will be no possibility of an aggressor nation arising to start another world war.

But those four powers must be united with and cooperate with all the freedom-loving peoples of Europe, and Asia, and Africa, and the Americas. The rights of every nation, large or small, must be respected and guarded as jealously as are the rights of every individual within our own Republic.

The doctrine that the strong shall dominate the weak is the doctrine of our enemies—and we reject it.

But, at the same time, we are agreed that if force is necessary to keep international peace, international force will be applied—for as long as it may be necessary.

It has been our steady policy—and it is certainly a common-sense policy—that the right of each nation to freedom must be measured by the willingness of that nation to fight for freedom. And today we salute our unseen allies in occupied countries—the underground resistance groups and the armies of liberation. They will provide potent forces against our enemies, when the day of the counterinvasion comes.

Through the development of science the world has become so much smaller that we have had to discard the geographical yardsticks of the past. For instance, through our early history the Atlantic and Pacific oceans were believed to be walls of safety for the United States. Time and distance made it physically possible, for example, for us and for the other American republics to obtain and maintain our independence against infinitely stronger powers. Until recently very few people, even military experts, thought that the day would ever come when we might have to defend our Pacific coast against Japanese threats of invasion.

At the outbreak of the First World War relatively few people thought that our ships and shipping would be menaced by German submarines on the high seas or that the German militarists would ever attempt to dominate any nation outside of central Europe.

After the Armistice in 1918, we thought and hoped that the militaristic philosophy of Germany had been crushed; and being full of the milk of human kindness we spent the next twenty years disarming, while the Germans whined so pathetically that the other nations permitted them—and even helped them—to rearm.

For too many years we lived on pious hopes that aggressor and warlike nations would learn and understand and carry out the doctrine of purely voluntary peace.

The well-intentioned but ill-fated experiments of former years did not work. It is my hope that we will not try them again. No, that is putting it too weakly; it is my intention to do all that I humanly can as president and commander in chief to see to it that these tragic mistakes shall not be made again.

There have always been cheerful idiots in this country who believed that there would be no more war for us if everybody in America would only return into their homes and lock their front doors behind them. Assuming that their motives were of the highest, events have shown how unwilling they were to face the facts.

The overwhelming majority of all the people in the world want peace. Most of them are fighting for the attainment of peace—not just a truce, not just an armistice, but peace that is as strongly enforced and as durable as mortal man can make it. If we are willing to fight for peace now, is it not good logic that we should use force if necessary, in the future, to keep the peace?

I believe, and I think I can say, that the other three great nations who are fighting so magnificently to gain peace are in complete agreement that we must be prepared to keep the peace by force. If the people of Germany and Japan are made to realize thoroughly that the world is not going to let them break out again, it is possible, and, I hope, probable, that they will abandon the philosophy of aggression—the belief that they can gain the whole world even at the risk of losing their own souls.

I shall have more to say about the Cairo and Teheran conferences when I make my report to the Congress in about two weeks' time. And, on that occasion, I shall also have a great deal to say about certain conditions here at home.

But today I wish to say that in all my travels, at home and abroad, it is the sight of our soldiers and sailors and their magnificent achievements which have given me the greatest inspiration and the greatest encouragement for the future.

To the members of our armed forces, to their wives, mothers, and fathers, I want to affirm the great faith and confidence that we have in General Marshall and in Admiral King, who direct all of our armed might throughout the world. Upon them falls the great responsibility of planning the strategy of determining where and when we shall fight. Both of these men have already gained high places in American history, which will record many evidences of their military genius that cannot be published today.

Some of our men overseas are now spending their third Christmas far from home. To them and to all others overseas or soon to go overseas, I can give assurance that it is the purpose of their government to win this war and to bring them home at the earliest possible time.

We here in the United States had better be sure that when our soldiers and sailors do come home they will find an America in which they are given full opportunities for education, and rehabilitation, social security, and employment and business enterprise under the free American system—and that they will find a government which, by their votes as American citizens, they have had a full share in electing.

The American people have had every reason to know that this is a tough and destructive war. On my trip abroad, I talked with many military men who had faced our enemies in the field. These hardheaded realists testify to the strength and skill and resourcefulness of the enemy generals and men whom we must beat before final victory is won. The war is now reaching the stage where we shall all have to look forward to large casualty lists—dead, wounded, and missing.

War entails just that. There is no easy road to victory. And the end is not yet in sight.

I have been back only for a week. It is fair that I should tell you my impression. I think I see a tendency in some of our people here to assume a quick ending of the war—that we have already gained the victory. And, perhaps as a result of this false reasoning, I think I discern an effort to resume or even encourage an outbreak of partisan thinking and talking. I hope I am wrong. For, surely, our first and most foremost tasks are all concerned with winning the war and winning a just peace that will last for generations.

The massive offensives which are in the making—both in Europe and the Far East—will require every ounce of energy and fortitude that we and our allies can summon on the fighting fronts and in all the workshops at home. As I have said before, you cannot order up a great attack on a Monday and demand that it be delivered on Saturday.

Less than a month ago I flew in a big army transport plane over the little town of Bethlehem, in Palestine.

Tonight, on Christmas Eve, all men and women everywhere who love Christmas are thinking of that ancient town and of the star of faith that shone there more than nineteen centuries ago.

American boys are fighting today in snow-covered mountains, in malarial jungles, on blazing deserts; they are fighting on the far stretches of the sea and above the clouds, and fighting for the thing for which they struggle. I think it is best symbolized by the message that came out of Bethlehem.

On behalf of the American people—your own people—I send this Christmas message to you who are in our armed forces:

In our hearts are prayers for you and for all your comrades in arms who fight to rid the world of evil.

We ask God's blessing upon you—upon your fathers, mothers, wives, and children, all your loved ones at home.

We ask that the comfort of God's grace shall be granted to those who are sick and wounded, and to those who are prisoners of war in the hands of the enemy, waiting for the day when they will again be free.

And we ask that God receive and cherish those who have given their lives, and that He keep them in honor and in the grateful memory of their countrymen forever.

God bless all of you who fight our battles on this Christmas Eve.

God bless us all. Keep us strong in our faith that we fight for a better day for humankind—here and everywhere.

Eleventh Annual
Message to Congress

January 11, 1944

An Economic Bill of Rights

This nation in the past two years has become an active partner in the world's greatest war against human slavery.

We have joined with like-minded people in order to defend ourselves in a world that has been gravely threatened with gangster rule.

But I do not think that any of us Americans can be content with mere survival. Sacrifices that we and our allies are making impose upon us all a sacred obligation to see to it that out of this war we and our children will gain something better than mere survival.

We are united in determination that this war shall not be followed by another interim which leads to new disaster—that we shall not repeat the tragic errors of ostrich isolationism— that we shall not repeat the excesses of the wild twenties when this nation went for a joy ride on a roller coaster which ended in a tragic crash.

When Mr. Hull went to Moscow in October, and when I went to Cairo and Teheran in November, we knew that we were in agreement with our allies in our common determination to fight and win this war. But there were many vital questions concerning the future peace, and they were discussed in an atmosphere of complete candor and harmony.

In the last war such discussions, such meetings, did not even begin until the shooting had stopped and the delegates began to assemble at the peace table. There had been no previous opportunities for man-to-man discussions which lead to meetings of minds. The result was a peace which was not a peace.

That was a mistake which we are not repeating in this war.

And right here I want to address a word or two to some suspicious souls who are fearful that Mr. Hull or I have made "commitments" for the future which might pledge this nation to secret treaties, or to enacting the role of Santa Claus.

To such suspicious souls—using a polite terminology—I wish to say that Mr. Churchill, and Marshal Stalin, and Generalissimo Chiang Kai-shek are all thoroughly conversant with the provisions of our Constitution. And so is Mr. Hull. And so am I.

Of course we made some commitments. We most certainly committed ourselves to very large and very specific military plans which require the use of all Allied forces to bring about the defeat of our enemies at the earliest possible time.

But there were no secret treaties or political or financial commitments.

The one supreme objective for the future, which we discussed for each nation individually, and for all the United Nations, can be summed up in one word: security.

And that means not only physical security which provides safety from attacks by aggressors. It means also economic security, social security, moral security—in a family of nations.

In the plain down-to-earth talks that I had with the Generalissimo and Marshal Stalin and Prime Minister Churchill, it was abundantly clear that they are all most deeply interested in the resumption of peaceful progress by their own peoples— progress toward a better life. All our allies want freedom to develop their lands and resources, to build up industry, to increase education and individual opportunity, and to raise standards of living.

All our allies have learned by bitter experience that real development will not be possible if they are to be diverted from their purpose by repeated wars—or even threats of war.

China and Russia are truly united with Britain and America in recognition of this essential fact:

The best interests of each nation, large and small, demand that all freedom-loving nations shall join together in a just and durable system of peace. In the present world situation, evidenced by the actions of Germany, Italy, and Japan, unquestioned military control over disturbers of the peace is as necessary among nations as it is among citizens in a community. And an equally basic essential to peace is a decent standard of living for all individual men and women and children in all nations. Freedom from fear is eternally linked with freedom from want. . . .

If ever there was a time to subordinate individual or group selfishness to the national good, that time is now. Disunity at home—bickerings, self-seeking partisanship, stoppages of work, inflation, business as usual, politics as usual, luxury as usual—these are the influences which can undermine the morale of the brave men ready to die at the front for us here.

Those who are doing most of the complaining are not deliberately striving to sabotage the national war effort. They are laboring under the delusion that the time is past when we must make prodigious sacrifices—that the war is already won and we can begin to slacken off. But the dangerous folly of that point of view can be measured by the distance that separates our troops from their ultimate objectives in Berlin and Tokyo—and by the sum of all the perils that lie along the way.

Overconfidence and complacency are among our deadliest enemies. . . .

Therefore, in order to concentrate all our energies and resources on winning the war, and to maintain a fair and stable economy at home, I recommend that the Congress adopt:

1. A realistic tax law—which will tax all unreasonable profits, both individual and corporate, and reduce the ultimate cost of the war to our sons and daughters. The tax bill now under consideration by the Congress does not begin to meet this test.

2. A continuation of the law for the renegotiation of war

contracts—which will prevent exorbitant profits and assure fair prices to the government. For two long years I have pleaded with the Congress to take undue profits out of war.

3. A cost-of-food law—which will enable the government (a) to place a reasonable floor under the prices the farmer may expect for his production, and (b) to place a ceiling on the prices a consumer will have to pay for the food he buys. This should apply to necessities only; and will require public funds to carry out. It will cost in appropriations about 1 percent of the present annual cost of the war.

4. Early reenactment of the stabilization statute of October 1942. This expires June 30, 1944, and if it is not extended well in advance, the country might just as well expect price chaos by summer. We cannot have stabilization by wishful thinking. We must take positive action to maintain the integrity of the American dollar.

5. A national-service law—which, for the duration of the war, will prevent strikes, and, with certain appropriate exceptions, will make available for war production or for any other essential services every able-bodied adult in this nation.

These five measures together form a just and equitable whole. I would not recommend a national-service law unless the other laws were passed to keep down the cost of living, to share equitably the burdens of taxation, to hold the stabilization line, and to prevent undue profits. . . .

As you know, I have for three years hesitated to recommend a national-service act. Today, however, I am convinced of its necessity. Although I believe that we and our allies can win the war without such a measure, I am certain that nothing less than total mobilization of all our resources of manpower and capital will guarantee an earlier victory, and reduce the toll of suffering and sorrow and blood. . . .

It is our duty now to begin to lay the plans and determine the strategy for the winning of a lasting peace and the establishment of an American standard of living higher than ever before known. We cannot be content, no matter how high that general standard of living may be, if some fraction of our people—whether it be one-third or one-fifth, or one-tenth—is ill-fed, ill-clothed, ill-housed, and insecure.

This Republic had its beginning, and grew to its present strength, under the protection of certain inalienable political rights—among them the right of free speech, free press, free worship, trial by jury, freedom from unreasonable searches and seizures. They were our rights to life and liberty.

As our nation has grown in size and stature, however—as our industrial economy expanded—these political rights proved inadequate to assure us equality in the pursuit of happiness.

We have come to a clear realization of the fact that true individual freedom cannot exist without economic security and independence. "Necessitous men are not free men." People who are hungry and out of a job are the stuff of which dictatorships are made.

In our day these economic truths have become accepted as self-evident. We have accepted, so to speak, a second Bill of Rights under which a new basis of security and prosperity can be established for all—regardless of station, race, or creed.

Among these are:

The right to a useful and remunerative job in the industries or shops or farms or mines of the nation;

The right to earn enough to provide adequate food and clothing and recreation;

The right of every farmer to raise and sell his products at a return which will give him and his family a decent living;

The right of every businessman, large and small, to trade in an atmosphere of freedom from unfair competition and domination by monopolies at home or abroad;

The right of every family to a decent home;

The right to adequate medical care and the opportunity to achieve and enjoy good health;

The right to adequate protection from the economic fears of old age, sickness, accident, and unemployment;

The right to a good education.

All of these rights spell security. And after this war is won we must be prepared to move forward, in the implementation of these rights, to new goals of human happiness and well-being. . . .

I ask the Congress to explore the means for implementing this economic Bill of Rights—for it is definitely the responsibility of the Congress so to do. Many of these problems are already before committees of the Congress in the form of proposed legislation. I shall from time to time communicate with the Congress with respect to these and further proposals. In the event that no adequate program of progress is evolved, I am certain that the nation will be conscious of the fact.

Our fighting men abroad—and their families at home—expect such a program and have the right to insist upon it. It is to their demands that this government should pay heed rather than to the whining demands of selfish pressure groups who seek to feather their nests while young Americans are dying.

The foreign policy that we have been following—the policy that guided us at Moscow, Cairo, and Teheran—is based on the common sense principle which was best expressed by Benjamin Franklin on July 4, 1776: "We must all hang together, or assuredly we shall all hang separately."

I have often said that there are no two fronts for America in this war. There is only one front. There is one line of unity which extends from the hearts of the people at home to the men of our attacking forces in our farthest outposts. When we speak of our total effort, we speak of the factory and the field and the mine as well as of the battleground—we speak of the soldier and the civilian, the citizen and his government.

Each and every one of us has a solemn obligation under God to serve this nation in its most critical hour—to keep this nation great—to make this nation greater in a better world.

RADIO ADDRESS ON THE ANNUAL APPEAL FOR THE NATIONAL FOUNDATION FOR INFANTILE PARALYSIS

January 29, 1944

Tonight, on behalf of the National Foundation for Infantile Paralysis, I wish to express heartfelt thanks to all of you who have contributed your dimes and your dollars to further the fight against a cruel disease—a disease which strikes primarily against little children.

The generous participation of the American people in this fight is a sign of the healthy condition of our nation. It is democracy in action. The unity of our people in helping those who are disabled, in protecting the welfare of our young, in preserving the eternal principle of kindliness—all of this is evidence of our fundamental strength, the strength with which we are meeting our enemies throughout the world.

Early in our history, we realized that the basic wealth of our land is in its healthy, enlightened children, trained to assume the responsibilities and enjoy the privileges of a democracy. The well-being of our youth is indeed our foremost concern—their health and happiness our enduring responsibility. If any become handicapped from any cause, we are determined that they shall be properly cared for and guided to full and useful lives.

How different it is in the lands of our enemies! In Germany and Japan, those who are handicapped in body or mind are regarded as unnecessary burdens to the state. There, an individual's usefulness is measured solely by the direct contribution that he can make to the war machine—not by his service to a society at peace.

The dread disease that we battle at home, like the enemy we oppose abroad, shows no concern, no pity for the young. It strikes—with its most frequent and devastating force—against children. And that is why much of the future strength of America depends upon the success that we achieve in combating this disease.

The dollars and dimes you contribute are the victory bonds that buy the ammunition for this fight against disease—just as the war bonds you purchase help to finance the fight against tyranny.

Tonight, I am happy to receive the report that your generous aid has made possible another year of progress against this dread malady. We are prepared to fight it with the planned strategy of a military campaign—not only because the enemy is a merciless and insidious one, but because the danger of epidemic in wartime makes this fight an actual military necessity.

The tireless men and women working night and day over test tubes and microscopes—searching for drugs and serums, for methods that will prevent and cure—these are the workers on the production line in this war against disease. The gallant chapter workers, the doctors and nurses in our hospitals, the public-health officials, the volunteers who go into epidemic areas to help the physician—these are the frontline fighters.

And just as in war, there is that subtle weapon that, more than anything else, spells victory or defeat. That weapon is morale—the morale of a people who know that they are fighting "the good fight," that they are keeping the faith—the only faith through which civilization can survive, the faith that man must live to help and not to destroy his fellowmen.

We are engaged now in the Fourth War Bond Campaign. The outpouring of American dollars in this campaign will assure that superiority of fighting equipment with which we shall blast our way to Berlin and Tokyo. It will also serve notice that we Americans are irrevocably united in determination to end this war as quickly as possible in the unconditional surrender of our enemies. Every one of us has a chance too to participate in victory by buying war bonds.

Tonight, in the midst of a terrible war against tyranny and savagery, it is not easy for us to celebrate. There cannot be much happiness in our hearts as we contemplate the kind of enemies we face and the very grimness of the task that lies before us.

But, we may thank God that here in our country we are keeping alive the spirit of goodwill toward one another—that spirit which is the very essence of the cause for which we fight.

God speed the spirit of goodwill.

STATEMENT CONDEMNING GERMAN AND JAPANESE WAR CRIMES

March 24, 1944

The United Nations are fighting to make a world in which tyranny and aggression cannot exist; a world based upon freedom, equality, and justice; a world in which all persons regardless of race, color, or creed may live in peace, honor, and dignity.

In the meantime in most of Europe and in parts of Asia the systematic torture and murder of civilians—men, women, and children—by the Nazis and the Japanese continue unabated. In areas subjugated by the aggressors, innocent Poles, Czechs, Norwegians, Dutch, Danes, French, Greeks, Russians, Chinese, Filipinos—and many others—are being starved or frozen to death or murdered in cold blood in a campaign of savagery.

The slaughters of Warsaw, Lidice, Kharkov, and Nanking—the brutal torture and murder by the Japanese, not only of civilians but of our own gallant American soldiers and fliers—these are startling examples of what goes on day by day, year in and year out, wherever the Nazis and the Japs are in military control—free to follow their barbaric purpose.

In one of the blackest crimes of all history—begun by the Nazis in the day of peace and multiplied by them a hundred times in time of war—the wholesale systematic murder of the Jews of Europe goes on unabated every hour. As a result of the events of the last few days hundreds of thousands of Jews, who while living under persecution have at least found a haven from death in Hungary and the Balkans, are now threatened with annihilation as Hitler's forces descend more heavily upon these lands. That these innocent people, who have already survived a decade of Hitler's fury, should perish on the very eve of triumph over the barbarism which their persecution symbolizes would be a major tragedy.

It is therefore fitting that we should again proclaim our determination that none who participate in these acts of savagery shall go unpunished. The United Nations have made it clear that they will pursue the guilty and deliver them up in order that justice be done. That warning applies not only to the leaders but also to their functionaries and subordinates in Germany and in the satellite countries. All who knowingly take part in the deportation of Jews to their death in Poland or Norwegians and French to their death in Germany are equally guilty with the executioner. All who share the guilt shall share the punishment.

Hitler is committing these crimes against humanity in the name of the German people. I ask every German and every man everywhere under Nazi domination to show the world by his action that in his heart he does not share these insane criminal desires. Let him hide these pursued victims, help them to get over their borders, and do what he can to save them from the Nazi hangman. I ask him also to keep watch, and to record the evidence that will one day be used to convict the guilty.

In the meantime, and until the victory that is now assured is won, the United States will persevere in its efforts to rescue the victims of brutality of the Nazis and the Japs. Insofar as the necessity of military operations permit, this government will use all means at its command to aid the escape of all intended victims of the Nazi and Jap executioner—regardless of race or religion or color. We call upon the free peoples of Europe and Asia temporarily to open their frontiers to all victims of oppression. We shall find havens of refuge for them, and we shall find the means for their maintenance and support until the tyrant is driven from their homelands and they may return.

In the name of justice and humanity let all freedom-loving people rally to this righteous undertaking.

Statement Urging the Growing of Victory Gardens

April 1, 1944

I hope every American who possibly can will grow a victory garden this year. We found out last year that even the small gardens helped.

The total harvest from victory gardens was tremendous. It made the difference between scarcity and abundance. The Department of Agriculture surveys show that 42 percent of the fresh vegetables consumed in 1943 came from victory gardens. This should clearly emphasize the far-reaching importance of the victory garden program.

Because of the greatly increased demands in 1944, we will need all the food we can grow. Food still remains a first essential to winning the war. Victory gardens are of direct benefit in helping relieve manpower, transportation, and living costs as well as the food problem. Increased food requirements for our armed forces and our allies give every citizen an opportunity to do something toward backing up the boys at the front.

FIRESIDE CHAT ON THE ALLIES' CAPTURE OF ROME

June 5, 1944

Yesterday on June 4, 1944, Rome fell to American and Allied troops. The first of the Axis capitals is now in our hands. One up and two to go!

It is perhaps significant that the first of these capitals to fall should have the longest history of all of them. The story of Rome goes back to the time of the foundations of our civilization. We can still see there monuments of the time when Rome and the Romans controlled the whole of the then known world. That, too, is significant, for the United Nations are determined that in the future no one city and no one race will be able to control the whole of the world.

In addition to the monuments of the older times, we also see in Rome the great symbol of Christianity, which has reached into almost every part of the world. There are other shrines and other churches in many places, but the churches and shrines of Rome are visible symbols of the faith and determination of the early saints and martyrs that Christianity should live and become universal. And tonight it will be a source of deep satisfaction that the freedom of the pope and the Vatican City is assured by the armies of the United Nations.

It is also significant that Rome has been liberated by the armed forces of many nations. The American and British armies —who bore the chief burdens of battle—found at their sides our own North American neighbors, the gallant Canadians. The fighting New Zealanders from the far South Pacific, the courageous French and the French Moroccans, the South Africans,

the Poles, and the East Indians—all of them fought with us on the bloody approaches to the city of Rome.

The Italians, too, forswearing a partnership in the Axis which they never desired, have sent their troops to join us in our battles against the German trespassers on their soil.

The prospect of the liberation of Rome meant enough to Hitler and his generals to induce them to fight desperately at great cost of men and materials and with great sacrifice to their crumbling eastern line and to their western front. No thanks are due to them if Rome was spared the devastation which the Germans wreaked on Naples and other Italian cities. The Allied generals maneuvered so skillfully that the Nazis could only have stayed long enough to damage Rome at the risk of losing their armies.

But Rome is of course more than a military objective.

Ever since before the days of the Caesars, Rome has stood as a symbol of authority. Rome was the Republic. Rome was the Empire. Rome was and is in a sense the Catholic Church, and Rome was the capital of a United Italy. Later, unfortunately, a quarter of a century ago, Rome became the seat of Fascism— one of the three capitals of the Axis.

For this quarter century the Italian people were enslaved. They were degraded by the rule of Mussolini from Rome. They will mark its liberation with deep emotion. In the north of Italy, the people are still dominated and threatened by the Nazi over-lords and their Fascist puppets.

Our victory comes at an excellent time, while our Allied forces are poised for another strike at Western Europe—and while the armies of other Nazi soldiers nervously await our assault. And in the meantime our gallant Russian allies continue to make their power felt more and more.

From a strictly military standpoint, we had long ago accomplished certain of the main objectives of our Italian campaign— the control of the major islands, the control of the sea lanes of the Mediterranean to shorten our combat and supply lines, and the capture of the airports of Foggia, south of Rome, from

which we have struck telling blows on the continent—the whole of the continent all the way up to the Russian front.

It would be unwise to inflate in our own minds the military importance of the capture of Rome. We shall have to push through a long period of greater effort and fiercer fighting before we get into Germany itself. The Germans have retreated thousands of miles, all the way from the gates of Cairo, through Libya and Tunisia and Sicily and southern Italy. They have suffered heavy losses, but not great enough yet to cause collapse.

Germany has not yet been driven to surrender. Germany has not yet been driven to the point where she will be unable to recommence world conquest a generation hence.

Therefore, the victory still lies some distance ahead. That distance will be covered in due time—have no fear of that. But it will be tough and it will be costly, as I have told you many, many times.

In Italy the people had lived so long under the corrupt rule of Mussolini that, in spite of the tinsel at the top, their economic condition had grown steadily worse. Our troops have found starvation, malnutrition, disease, a deteriorating education, and lowered public health—all by-products of the Fascist misrule.

The task of the Allies in occupation has been stupendous. We have had to start at the very bottom, assisting local governments to reform on democratic lines. We have had to give them bread to replace that which was stolen out of their mouths by the Germans. We have had to make it possible for the Italians to raise and use their own local crops. We have to help them cleanse their schools of Fascist trappings.

I think the American people as a whole approve the salvage of these human beings, who are only now learning to walk in a new atmosphere of freedom.

Some of us may let our thoughts run to the financial cost of it. Essentially it is what we can call a form of relief. And at the same time, we hope that this relief will be an investment for the future—an investment that will pay dividends by eliminating Fascism, by ending any Italian desires to start another war of

aggression in the future. And that means that they are dividends which justify such an investment, because they are additional supports for world peace.

The Italian people are capable of self-government. We do not lose sight of their virtues as a peace-loving nation.

We remember the many centuries in which the Italians were leaders in the arts and sciences, enriching the lives of all mankind.

We remember the great sons of the Italian people— Galileo and Marconi, Michelangelo and Dante—and that fearless discoverer who typifies the courage of Italy, Christopher Columbus.

Italy cannot grow in stature by seeking to build up a great militaristic empire. Italians have been overcrowded within their own territories, but they do not need to try to conquer the lands of other peoples in order to find the breath of life. Other peoples may not want to be conquered.

In the past, Italians have come by the millions into the United States. They have been welcomed, they have prospered, they have become good citizens, community and governmental leaders. They are not Italian-Americans. They are Americans— Americans of Italian descent.

The Italians have gone in great numbers to the other Americas—Brazil and the Argentine, for example—hundreds and hundreds of thousands of them. They have gone to many other nations in every continent of the world, giving of their industry and their talents, and achieving success and the comfort of good living, and good citizenship.

Italy should go on as a great mother nation, contributing to the culture and the progress and the goodwill of all mankind— developing her special talents in the arts and crafts and sciences, and preserving her historic and cultural heritage for the benefit of all peoples.

We want and expect the help of the future Italy toward lasting peace. All the other nations opposed to Fascism and Nazism ought to help to give Italy a chance.

The Germans, after years of domination in Rome, left the people in the Eternal City on the verge of starvation. We and the British will do and are doing everything we can to bring them relief. Anticipating the fall of Rome, we made preparations to ship food supplies to the city, but, of course, it should be borne in mind that the needs are so great, the transportation requirements of our armies so heavy, that improvement must be gradual. But we have already begun to save the lives of the men, women, and children of Rome.

This, I think, is an example of the efficiency of our machinery of war. The magnificent ability and energy of the American people in growing the crops, building the merchant ships, in making and collecting the cargoes, in getting the supplies over thousands of miles of water, and thinking ahead to meet emergencies—all this spells, I think, an amazing efficiency on the part of our armed forces, all the various agencies working with them, and American industry and labor as a whole.

No great effort like this can be a hundred percent perfect, but the batting average is very, very high.

And so I extend the congratulations and thanks tonight of the American people to General Alexander, who has been in command of the whole Italian operation; to our General Clark and General Leese of the Fifth and the Eighth armies; to General Wilson, the supreme allied commander of the Mediterranean theater; to General Devers, his American deputy; to General Eaker; to Admirals Cunningham and Hewitt; and to all their brave officers and men.

May God bless them and watch over them and over all of our gallant, fighting men.

D-DAY PRAYER

June 6, 1944

My Fellow Americans: Last night, when I spoke with you about the fall of Rome, I knew at that moment that troops of the United States and our allies were crossing the Channel in another and greater operation. It has come to pass with success thus far.

And so, in this poignant hour, I ask you to join with me in prayer.

Almighty God: Our sons, pride of our nation, this day have set upon a mighty endeavor, a struggle to preserve our Republic, our religion, and our civilization, and to set free a suffering humanity.

Lead them straight and true; give strength to their arms, stoutness to their hearts, steadfastness in their faith.

They will need Thy blessings. Their road will be long and hard. For the enemy is strong. He may hurl back our forces. Success may not come with rushing speed, but we shall return again and again; and we know that by Thy grace, and by the righteousness of our cause, our sons will triumph.

They will be sore tried, by night and by day, without rest— until the victory is won. The darkness will be rent by noise and flame. Men's souls will be shaken with the violences of war.

For these men are lately drawn from the ways of peace. They fight not for the lust of conquest. They fight to end conquest. They fight to liberate. They fight to let justice arise, and tolerance and goodwill among all Thy people. They yearn but for the end of battle, for their return to the haven of home.

Some will never return. Embrace these, Father, and receive them, Thy heroic servants, into Thy kingdom.

And for us at home—fathers, mothers, children, wives, sisters, and brothers of brave men overseas, whose thoughts and prayers are ever with them—help us, Almighty God, to rededicate ourselves in renewed faith in Thee in this hour of great sacrifice.

Many people have urged that I call the nation into a single day of special prayer. But because the road is long and the desire is great, I ask that our people devote themselves in a continuance of prayer. As we rise to each new day, and again when each day is spent, let words of prayer be on our lips, invoking Thy help to our efforts.

Give us strength, too—strength in our daily tasks, to redouble the contributions we make in the physical and the material support of our armed forces.

And let our hearts be stout, to wait out the long travail, to bear sorrows that may come, to impart our courage unto our sons wheresoever they may be.

And, O Lord, give us faith. Give us faith in Thee; faith in our sons; faith in each other; faith in our united crusade. Let not the keeness of our spirit ever be dulled. Let not the impacts of temporary events, of temporal matters of but fleeting moment —let not these deter us in our unconquerable purpose.

With Thy blessing, we shall prevail over the unholy forces of our enemy. Help us to conquer the apostles of greed and racial arrogancies. Lead us to the saving of our country, and with our sister nations into a world unity that will spell a sure peace—a peace invulnerable to the schemings of unworthy men. And a peace that will let all of men live in freedom, reaping the just rewards of their honest toil.

Thy will be done, Almighty God.

Amen.

STATEMENT ON SIGNING THE G.I. BILL OF RIGHTS

June 22, 1944

This bill, which I have signed today, substantially carries out most of the recommendations made by me in a speech on July 28, 1943, and more specifically in messages to the Congress dated October 27, 1943, and November 23, 1943.

1. It gives servicemen and -women the opportunity of resuming their education or technical training after discharge, or of taking a refresher or retainer course, not only without tuition charge up to five hundred dollars per school year, but with the right to receive a monthly living allowance while pursuing their studies.

2. It makes provision for the guarantee by the federal government of not to exceed 50 percent of certain loans made to veterans for the purchase or construction of homes, farms, and business properties.

3. It provides for reasonable unemployment allowances payable each week up to a maximum period of one year, to those veterans who are unable to find a job.

4. It establishes improved machinery for effective job counseling for veterans and for finding jobs for returning soldiers and sailors.

5. It authorizes the construction of all necessary additional hospital facilities.

6. It strengthens the authority of the Veterans Administration to enable it to discharge its existing and added responsibilities with promptness and efficiency.

With the signing of this bill a well-rounded program of special veterans' benefits is nearly completed. It gives emphatic notice to the men and women in our armed forces that the

American people do not intend to let them down.

By prior legislation, the federal government has already provided for the armed forces of this war: adequate dependency allowances; mustering-out pay; generous hospitalization, medical care, and vocational rehabilitation and training; liberal pensions in case of death or disability in military service; substantial war-risk life insurance, and guarantee of premiums on commercial policies during service; protection of civil rights and suspension of enforcement of certain civil liabilities during service; emergency maternal care for wives of enlisted men; and reemployment rights for returning veterans.

This bill therefore and the former legislation provide the special benefits which are due to the members of our armed forces—for they "have been compelled to make greater economic sacrifice and every other kind of sacrifice than the rest of us, and are entitled to definite action to help take care of their special problems." While further study and experience may suggest some changes and improvements, the Congress is to be congratulated on the prompt action it has taken.

There still remains one recommendation which I made on November 23, 1943, which I trust that the Congress will soon adopt—the extension of social security credits under the Federal Old-Age and Survivors' Insurance Law to all servicemen and women for the period of their service.

I trust that the Congress will also soon provide similar opportunities for postwar education and unemployment insurance to the members of the merchant marine, who have risked their lives time and again during this war for the welfare of their country.

But apart from these special benefits which fulfill the special needs of veterans, there is still much to be done.

As I stated in my message to the Congress of November 23, 1943:

> What our servicemen and women want, more than anything else, is the assurance of satisfactory employment upon their

return to civil life. The first task after the war is to provide employment for them and for our demobilized workers. . . . The goal after the war should be the maximum utilization of our human and material resources.

As a related problem the Congress has had under consideration the serious problem of economic reconversion and readjustment after the war, so that private industry will be able to provide jobs for the largest possible number. This time we have wisely begun to make plans in advance of the day of peace, in full confidence that our war workers will remain at their essential war jobs as long as necessary until the fighting is over.

The executive branch of the government has taken, and is taking, whatever steps it can, until legislation is enacted. I am glad to learn that the Congress has agreed on a bill to facilitate the prompt settlement of terminated contracts. I hope that the Congress will also take prompt action, when it reconvenes, on necessary legislation which is now pending to facilitate the development of unified programs for the demobilization of civilian war workers, for their reemployment in peacetime pursuits, and for provision, in cooperation with the states, of appropriate unemployment benefits during the transition from war to peace. I hope also that the Congress, upon its return, will take prompt action on the pending legislation to facilitate the orderly disposition of surplus property.

A sound postwar economy is a major present responsibility.

STATEMENT ON THE LANDING OF U.S. TROOPS IN THE PHILIPPINES

October 20, 1944

This morning American troops landed on the island of Leyte in the Philippines. The invasion forces, under the command of General Douglas MacArthur, are supported by the greatest concentration of naval and air power ever massed in the Pacific Ocean.

We have landed in the Philippines to redeem the pledge we made over two years ago when the last American troops surrendered on Corregidor after five months and twenty-eight days of bitter resistance against overwhelming enemy strength.

We promised to return; we *have* returned.

In my last message to General Wainwright, sent on the fifth of May 1942, just before he was captured, I told him that the gallant struggle of his comrades had inspired every soldier, sailor, and marine and all the workers in our shipyards and munitions plants. I said that he and his devoted followers had become the living symbol of our war aims and the guarantee of our victory.

That was true in 1942. It is still true in 1944.

We have never forgotten the courage of our men at Bataan and Corregidor. Their example inspired every American in the stern days of Guadalcanal, Tarawa, Salerno, and Normandy. And in every campaign—on battlefront or home front—we remember those men, and their memory spurs us to greater effort.

Nowhere has the desire to avenge their comrades been stronger than among the forces of the Southwest Pacific. Leyte is another rung in the long ladder General MacArthur's men have been climbing for two years.

Starting on the underside of New Guinea in the autumn of 1942 when Australia herself was in danger, pushing over the Owen Stanley Mountains, burning and blasting the Japanese out of Buna and Gona, digging them out of Wewak, starving them at Hollandia—the advance has been a slow, tough struggle by our jungle fighters.

Now they have reached Leyte.

In the six years before war broke out, the Philippine government, acting in harmonious accord with the United States, made great strides toward complete establishment of her sovereignty. The United States promised to help build a new nation in the Pacific, a nation whose ideals, like our own, were liberty and equality and the democratic way of life—a nation which in a very short time would join the friendly family of nations on equal terms.

We were keeping that promise. When war came and our work was wrecked, we pledged to the people of the Philippines that their freedom would be redeemed and that their independence would be established and protected. We are fulfilling that pledge now. When we have finished the job of driving the Japs from the islands, the Philippines will be a free and independent republic.

There never was a doubt that the people of the Philippines were worthy of their independence. There will never be a doubt.

The Filipinos have defended their homeland with fortitude and gallantry. We confidently expect to see them liberate it with courage and audacity.

Under the leadership of President Manuel Quezon whose death came on the eve of his country's liberation, and now under the leadership of their President Sergio Osmeña, the Filipinos have carried on, and are carrying on, with gallantry—even in the midst of the enemy.

We are glad to be back in the Philippines but we do not intend to stop there.

Leyte is only a way station on the road to Japan. It is 700 miles from Formosa. It is 850 miles from China. We are astride the lifeline of the warlords' empire; we are severing that lifeline. Our bombers, our ships, and our submarines are cutting off the ill-gotten conquests from the homeland. From our new base we shall quicken the assault. Our attacks of the last week have been destructive and decisive, but now we shall strike even more devastating blows at Japan.

We have learned our lesson about Japan. We trusted her, and treated her with the decency due a civilized neighbor. We were foully betrayed. The price of the lesson was high.

Now we are going to teach Japan her lesson.

We have the will and the power to teach her the cost of treachery and deceit, and the cost of stealing from her neighbors. With our steadfast allies, we shall teach this lesson so that Japan will never forget it.

We shall free the enslaved peoples. We shall restore stolen lands and looted wealth to their rightful owners. We shall strangle the Black Dragon of Japanese militarism forever.

FOURTH INAUGURAL ADDRESS

January 20, 1945

Mr. Chief Justice, Mr. Vice President, My Friends: You will understand and, I believe, agree with my wish that the form of this inauguration be simple and its words brief.

We Americans of today, together with our allies, are passing through a period of supreme test. It is a test of our courage—of our resolve—of our wisdom—of our essential democracy.

If we meet that test—successfully and honorably—we shall perform a service of historic importance which men and women and children will honor throughout all time.

As I stand here today, having taken the solemn oath of office in the presence of my fellow countrymen—in the presence of our God—I know that it is America's purpose that we shall not fail.

In the days and the years that are to come, we shall work for a just and honorable peace, a durable peace, as today we work and fight for total victory in war.

We can and we will achieve such a peace.

We shall strive for perfection. We shall not achieve it immediately, but we still shall strive. We may make mistakes, but they must never be mistakes which result from faintness of heart or abandonment of moral principle.

I remember that my old schoolmaster, Dr. Peabody, said—in days that seemed to us then to be secure and untroubled, "Things in life will not always run smoothly. Sometimes we will be rising toward the heights—then all will seem to reverse itself and start downward. The great fact to remember is that the trend of civilization itself is forever upward; that a line drawn through the middle of the peaks and the valleys of the centuries always has an upward trend."

Our Constitution of 1787 was not a perfect instrument; it is not perfect yet. But it provided a firm base upon which all manner of men, of all races and colors and creeds, could build our solid structure of democracy.

Today, in this year of war, 1945, we have learned lessons— at a fearful cost—and we shall profit by them.

We have learned that we cannot live alone, at peace; that our own well-being is dependent on the well-being of other nations, far away. We have learned that we must live as men and not as ostriches, nor as dogs in the manger.

We have learned to be citizens of the world, members of the human community.

We have learned the simple truth, as Emerson said, that, "the only way to have a friend is to be one."

We can gain no lasting peace if we approach it with suspicion and mistrust—or with fear. We can gain it only if we proceed with the understanding and the confidence and the courage which flow from conviction.

The Almighty God has blessed our land in many ways. He has given our people stout hearts and strong arms with which to strike mighty blows for freedom and truth. He has given to our country a faith which has become the hope of all peoples in an anguished world.

So we pray to Him now for the vision to see our way clearly —to see the way that leads to a better life for ourselves and for all our fellow men—and to the achievement of His will to peace on earth.

MESSAGE TO CONGRESS URGING ADOPTION OF THE BRETTON WOODS AGREEMENTS

February 12, 1945

In my Budget Message of January 9, I called attention to the need for immediate action on the Bretton Woods proposals for an International Monetary Fund and an International Bank for Reconstruction and Development. It is my purpose in this message to indicate the importance of these international organizations in our plans for a peaceful and prosperous world.

As we dedicate our total efforts to the task of winning this war we must never lose sight of the fact that victory is not only an end in itself but, in a large sense, victory offers us the means of achieving the goal of lasting peace and a better way of life. Victory does not insure the achievement of these larger goals; it merely offers us the opportunity—the chance—to seek their attainment. Whether we will have the courage and vision to avail ourselves of this tremendous opportunity—purchased at so great a cost—is yet to be determined. On our shoulders rests the heavy responsibility for making this momentous decision. I have said before, and I repeat again: This generation has a rendezvous with destiny.

If we are to measure up to the task of peace with the same stature as we have measured up to the task of war, we must see that the institutions of peace rest firmly on the solid foundations of international political and economic cooperation. The cornerstone for international political cooperation is the Dumbarton Oaks proposal for a permanent United Nations. International political relations will be friendly and constructive, how-ever, only if solutions are found to the difficult economic prob-lems we face today. The cornerstone for international economic cooperation is the Bretton Woods proposal for an International Monetary Fund and an International Bank for Reconstruction and Development.

These proposals for an International Fund and International Bank are concrete evidence that the economic objectives of the United States agree with those of the United Nations. They illustrate our unity of purpose and interest in the economic field. What we need and what they need correspond—expanded pro-duction, employment, exchange, and consumption—in other words, more goods produced, more jobs, more trade, and a higher standard of living for us all. To the people of the United States this means real peacetime employment for those who will be returning from the war and for those at home whose wartime work has ended. It also means orders and profits to our indus-tries and fair prices to our farmers. We shall need prosperous markets in the world to ensure our own prosperity, and we shall need the goods the world can sell us. For all these purposes, as well as for a peace that will endure, we need the partnership of the United Nations.

The first problem in time which we must cope with is that of saving life, and getting resources and people back into pro-duction. In many of the liberated countries economic life has all but stopped. Transportation systems are in ruins and therefore coal and raw materials cannot be brought to factories. Many factories themselves are shattered, power plants smashed, trans-mission systems broken, bridges blown up or bombed, ports clogged with sunken wrecks, and great rich areas of farmland inundated by the sea. People are tired and sick and hungry. But they are eager to go to work again, and to create again with their own hands and under their own leaders the necessary physical basis of their lives.

Emergency relief is under way behind the armies under the authority of local governments, backed up first by the Allied military command and after that by the United Nations Relief and Rehabilitation Administration. Our participation in the UNRRA has been approved by Congress. But neither UNRRA nor the armies are designed for the construction or reconstruction of large-scale public works or factories or power plants or transportation systems. That job must be done otherwise, and it must be started soon.

The main job of restoration is not one of relief. It is one of reconstruction which must largely be done by local people and their governments. They will provide the labor, the local money, and most of the materials. The same is true for all the many plans for the improvement of transportation, agriculture, industry, and housing that are essential to the development of the economically backward areas of the world. But some of the things required for all these projects, both of reconstruction and development, will have to come from overseas. It is at this point that our highly developed economy can play a role important to the rest of the world and very profitable to the United States. Inquiries for numerous materials, and for all kinds of equipment and machinery in connection with such projects are already being directed to our industries, and many more will come. This business will be welcome just as soon as the more urgent production for the war itself ends.

The main problem will be for these countries to obtain the means of payment. In the long run we can be paid for what we sell abroad chiefly in goods and services. But at the moment many of the countries who want to be our customers are prostrate. Other countries have devoted their economies so completely to the war that they do not have the resources for reconstruction and development. Unless a means of financing is found, such countries will be unable to restore their economies and, in desperation, will be forced to carry forward and intensify existing systems of discriminatory trade practices, restrictive exchange controls, competitive depreciation of currencies, and other forms of economic warfare. That would destroy all our good hopes. We must move promptly to prevent its happening, and we must move on several fronts, including finance and trade.

The United States should act promptly upon the plan for the International Bank, which will make or guarantee sound loans for the foreign-currency requirements of important reconstruction and development projects in member countries. One of its most important functions will be to facilitate and make secure wide private participation in such loans. The Articles of Agreement constituting the charter of the Bank have been worked out with great care by an international conference of experts and give adequate protection to all interests. I recommend to the Congress that we accept the plan, subscribe the capital allotted to us, and participate wholeheartedly in the Bank's work.

This measure, with others I shall later suggest, should go far to take care of our part of the lending requirements of the postwar years. They should help the countries concerned to get production started, to get over the first crisis of disorganization and fear, to begin the work of reconstruction and development; and they should help our farmers and our industries to get over the crisis of reconversion by making a large volume of export business possible in the postwar years. As confidence returns private investors will participate more and more in foreign lending and investment without any government assistance. But to get over the first crisis, in the situation that confronts us, loans and guarantees by agencies of government will be essential.

We all know, however, that a prosperous world economy must be built on more than foreign investment. Exchange rates must be stabilized, and the channels of trade opened up throughout the world. A large foreign trade after victory will generate production and therefore wealth. It will also make possible the servicing of foreign investments.

Almost no one in the modern world produces what he eats and wears and lives in. It is only by the division of labor among people and among geographic areas with all their varied resources, and by the increased all-around production which specialization makes possible, that any modern country can sustain its present population. It is through exchange and trade that efficient production in large units becomes possible. To expand the trading circle, to make it richer, more competitive, more varied, is a fundamental contribution to everybody's wealth and welfare.

It is time for the United States to take the lead in establishing the principle of economic cooperation as the foundation for expanded world trade. We propose to do this, not by setting up a supergovernment, but by international negotiation and agreement, directed to the improvement of the monetary institutions of the world and of the laws that govern trade. We have done a good deal in those directions in the last ten years under the Trade Agreements Act of 1934 and through the stabilization fund operated by our Treasury. But our present enemies were powerful in those years too, and they devoted all their efforts not to international collaboration, but to autarchy, and economic warfare. When victory is won we must be ready to go forward rapidly on a wide front. We all know very well that this will be a long and complicated business.

A good start has been made. The United Nations Monetary Conference at Bretton Woods has taken a long step forward on a matter of great practical importance to us all. The conference submitted a plan to create an International Monetary Fund which will put an end to monetary chaos. The Fund is a financial institution to preserve stability and order in the exchange rates between different moneys. It does not create a single money for the world; neither we nor anyone else is ready to do that. There will still be a different money in each country, but with the Fund in operation the value of each currency in international trade will remain comparatively stable. Changes in the value of foreign currencies will be made only after careful consideration by the Fund of the factors involved. Furthermore, and equally important, the Fund Agreement establishes a code of agreed principles for the conduct of exchange and currency affairs. In a nutshell, the Fund Agreement spells the difference between a world caught again in the maelstrom of panic and economic warfare culminating in war—as in the 1930s—or a world in which the members strive for a better life through mutual trust, cooperation, and assistance. The choice is ours.

I therefore recommend prompt action by the Congress to provide the subscription of the United States to the International Monetary Fund, and the legislation necessary for our membership in the Fund.

The International Fund and Bank together represent one of the most sound and useful proposals for international collaboration now before us. On the other hand, I do not want to leave with you the impression that these proposals for the Fund and Bank are perfect in every detail. It may well be that the experience of future years will show us how they can be improved. I do wish to make it clear, however, that these Articles of Agreement are the product of the best minds that forty-four nations could muster. These men, who represented nations from all parts of the globe, nations in all stages of economic development, nations with different political and economic philosophies, have reached an accord which is presented to you for your consideration and approval. It would be a tragedy if differences of opinion on minor details should lead us to sacrifice the basic agreement achieved on the major problems.

Nor do I want to leave with you the impression that the Fund and the Bank are all that we will need to solve the economic problems which will face the United Nations when the war is over. There are other problems which we will be called upon to solve. It is my expectation that other proposals will shortly be ready to submit to you for your consideration. These will include the establishment of the Food and Agriculture Organization of the United Nations, broadening and strengthening of the Trade Agreements Act of 1934, international agreement for the reduction of trade barriers, the control of cartels and the orderly marketing of world surpluses of certain commodities, a revision of the Export-Import Bank, and an international oil agreement, as well as proposals in the field of civil aviation, shipping, and radio and wire communications. It will also be necessary, of course, to repeal the Johnson Act.

In this message I have recommended for your consideration the immediate adoption of the Bretton Woods Agreements and suggested other measures which will have to be dealt with in the near future. They are all parts of a consistent whole. That whole is our hope for a secure and fruitful world; a world in which plain people in all countries can work at tasks which they do well, exchange in peace the products of their labor, and work out their several destinies in security and peace; a world in which governments, as their major contribution to the common welfare, are highly and effectively resolved to work together in practical affairs, and to guide all their actions by the knowledge that any policy or act that has effects abroad must be considered in the light of those effects.

The point in history at which we stand is full of promise and of danger. The world will either move toward unity and widely shared prosperity or it will move apart into necessarily competing economic blocs. We have a chance, we citizens of the United States, to use our influence in favor of a more united and cooperating world. Whether we do so will determine, as far as it is in our power, the kind of lives our grandchildren can live.

Address Before
Congress on the
Yalta Conference

March 1, 1945

I hope that you will pardon me for this unusual posture of sitting down during the presentation of what I want to say, but I know that you will realize that it makes it a lot easier for me not to have to carry about ten pounds of steel around on the bottom of my legs; and also because of the fact that I have just completed a fourteen-thousand-mile trip.

First of all, I want to say, It is good to be home.

It has been a long journey. I hope you will also agree that it has been, so far, a fruitful one.

Speaking in all frankness, the question of whether it is entirely fruitful or not lies to a great extent in your hands. For unless you here in the halls of the American Congress—with the support of the American people—concur in the general conclusions reached at Yalta, and give them your active support, the meeting will not have produced lasting results.

That is why I have come before you at the earliest hour I could after my return. I want to make a personal report to you —and, at the same time, to the people of the country. Many months of earnest work are ahead of us all, and I should like to feel that when the last stone is laid on the structure of international peace, it will be an achievement for which all of us in America have worked steadfastly and unselfishly—together.

I am returning from this trip—that took me so far—refreshed and inspired. I was well the entire time. I was not ill for a second, until I arrived back in Washington, and there I heard all of the rumors which had occurred in my absence. I returned from the trip refreshed and inspired. The Roosevelts are not, as you may suspect, averse to travel. We seem to thrive on it!

Far away as I was, I was kept constantly informed of affairs in the United States. The modern miracles of rapid communication have made this world very small. We must always bear in mind that fact, when we speak or think of international relations. I received a steady stream of messages from Washington —I might say from not only the executive branch with all its departments, but also from the legislative branch—and except where radio silence was necessary for security purposes, I could continuously send messages any place in the world. And of course, in a grave emergency, we could have even risked the breaking of the security rule.

I come from the Crimea Conference with a firm belief that we have made a good start on the road to a world of peace.

There were two main purposes in this Crimea Conference. The first was to bring defeat to Germany with the greatest possible speed, and the smallest possible loss of Allied men. That purpose is now being carried out in great force. The German army, and the German people, are feeling the ever-increasing might of our fighting men and of the Allied armies. Every hour gives us added pride in the heroic advance of our troops in Germany—on German soil—toward a meeting with the gallant Red Army.

The second purpose was to continue to build the foundation for an international accord that would bring order and security after the chaos of the war, that would give some assurance of lasting peace among the nations of the world.

Toward that goal also, a tremendous stride was made.

At Teheran, a little over a year ago, there were long-range military plans laid by the Chiefs of Staff of the three most powerful nations. Among the civilian leaders at Teheran, however, at that time, there were only exchanges of views and expressions of opinion. No political arrangements were made— and none was attempted.

At the Crimea Conference, however, the time had come for

getting down to specific cases in the political field.

There was on all sides at this conference an enthusiastic effort to reach an agreement. Since the time of Teheran, a year ago, there had developed among all of us a—what shall I call it?—a greater facility in negotiating with each other, that augurs well for the peace of the world. We know each other better.

I have never for an instant wavered in my belief that an agreement to insure world peace and security can be reached. . . .

When we met at Yalta, in addition to laying our strategic and tactical plans for the complete and final military victory over Germany, there were other problems of vital political consequence.

For instance, first, there were the problems of the occupation and control of Germany—after victory—the complete destruction of her military power, and the assurance that neither the Nazis nor Prussian militarism could again be revived to threaten the peace and the civilization of the world.

Second—again for example—there was the settlement of the few differences that remained among us with respect to the International Security Organization after the Dumbarton Oaks Conference. As you remember, at that time, I said that we had agreed 90 percent. Well, that's a pretty good percentage. I think the other 10 percent was ironed out at Yalta.

Third, there were the general political and economic problems common to all of the areas which had been or would be liberated from the Nazi yoke. This is a very special problem. We over here find it difficult to understand the ramifications of many of these problems in foreign lands, but we are trying to.

Fourth, there were the special problems created by a few instances such as Poland and Yugoslavia.

Days were spent in discussing these momentous matters and we argued freely and frankly across the table. But at the end, on every point, unanimous agreement was reached. And more important even than the agreement of words, I may say we achieved a unity of thought and a way of getting along together.

Of course, we know that it was Hitler's hope—and the German warlords'—that we would not agree, that some slight crack might appear in the solid wall of Allied unity, a crack that would give him and his fellow gangsters one last hope of escaping their just doom. That is the objective for which his propaganda machine has been working for many months.

But Hitler has failed.

Never before have the major Allies been more closely united —not only in their war aims but also in their peace aims. And they are determined to continue to be united with each other— and with all peace-loving nations—so that the ideal of lasting peace will become a reality.

The Soviet, British, and United States Chiefs of Staff held daily meetings with each other. They conferred frequently with Marshal Stalin and with Prime Minister Churchill and with me, on the problem of coordinating the strategic and tactical efforts of the Allied powers. They completed their plans for the final knockout blows to Germany.

At the time of the Teheran Conference, the Russian front was removed so far from the American and British fronts that, while certain long-range strategic cooperation was possible, there could be no tactical, day-by-day coordination. They were too far apart. But Russian troops have now crossed Poland. They are fighting on the eastern soil of Germany herself; British and American troops are now on German soil close to the Rhine River in the west. It is a different situation today from what it was fourteen months ago; a closer tactical liaison has become possible for the first time in Europe—and, in the Crimea Conference, that was something else that was accomplished.

Provision was made for daily exchange of information between the armies under the command of General Eisenhower on the western front, and those armies under the command of the Soviet marshals on that long eastern front, and also with our armies in Italy—without the necessity of going through the Chiefs of Staff in Washington or London as in the past.

You have seen one result of this exchange of information

in the recent bombings by American and English aircraft of points which are directly related to the Russian advance on Berlin. . . .

We made it clear again at Yalta, and I now repeat, that unconditional surrender does not mean the destruction or enslavement of the German people. The Nazi leaders have deliberately withheld that part of the Yalta declaration from the German press and radio. They seek to convince the people of Germany that the Yalta declaration does mean slavery and destruction for them—they are working at it day and night for that is how the Nazis hope to save their own skins, and deceive their people into continued and useless resistance.

We did, however, make it clear at the conference just what unconditional surrender does mean for Germany.

It means the temporary control of Germany by Great Britain, Russia, France, and the United States. Each of these nations will occupy and control a separate zone of Germany—and the administration of the four zones will be coordinated in Berlin by a Control Council composed of representatives of the four nations.

Unconditional surrender means something else. It means the end of Nazism. It means the end of the Nazi party—and of all its barbaric laws and institutions.

It means the termination of all militaristic influence in the public, private, and cultural life of Germany.

It means for the Nazi war criminals a punishment that is speedy and just—and severe.

It means the complete disarmament of Germany; the destruction of its militarism and its military equipment; the end of its production of armament; the dispersal of all its armed forces; the permanent dismemberment of the German General Staff which has so often shattered the peace of the world.

It means that Germany will have to make reparations in kind for the damage which has been done to the innocent victims of its aggression. . . .

Of equal importance with the military arrangements at the

Crimea Conference were the agreements reached with respect to a general international organization for lasting world peace. The foundations were laid at Dumbarton Oaks. There was one point, however, on which agreement was not reached at Dumbarton Oaks. It involved the procedure of voting in the Security Council. I want to try to make it clear by making it simple. It took me hours and hours to get the thing straight in my own mind—and many conferences.

At the Crimea Conference, the Americans made a proposal on this subject which, after full discussion was, I am glad to say, unanimously adopted by the other two nations.

It is not yet possible to announce the terms of that agreement publicly, but it will be in a very short time.

When the conclusions reached with respect to voting in the Security Council are made known, I think and I hope that you will find them a fair solution of this complicated and difficult problem. They are founded in justice, and will go far to assure international cooperation in the maintenance of peace.

A conference of all the United Nations of the world will meet in San Francisco on April 25, 1945. There, we all hope, and confidently expect, to execute a definite charter of organization under which the peace of the world will be preserved and the forces of aggression permanently outlawed. . . .

As the Allied armies have marched to military victory, they have liberated people whose liberties had been crushed by the Nazis for four long years, whose economy has been reduced to ruin by Nazi despoilers.

There have been instances of political confusion and unrest in these liberated areas—that is not unexpected—as in Greece or in Poland or in Yugoslavia, and there may be more. Worse than that, there actually began to grow up in some of these places queer ideas of, for instance, "spheres of influence" that were incompatible with the basic principles of international collaboration. If allowed to go on unchecked, these developments might have had tragic results in time. . . .

We met in the Crimea, determined to settle this matter of

liberated areas. Things that might happen that we cannot foresee at this moment might happen suddenly—unexpectedly—next week or next month. And I am happy to confirm to the Congress that we did arrive at a settlement—and, incidentally, a unanimous settlement.

The three most powerful nations have agreed that the political and economic problems of any area liberated from Nazi conquest, or of any former Axis satellite, are a joint responsibility of all three governments. They will join together, during the temporary period of instability—after hostilities—to help the people of any liberated area, or of any former satellite state, to solve their own problems through firmly established democratic processes.

They will endeavor to see to it that the people who carry on the interim government between occupation of Germany and true independence will be as representative as possible of all democratic elements in the population, and that free elections are held as soon as possible thereafter.

Responsibility for political conditions thousands of miles away can no longer be avoided by this great nation. Certainly, I do not want to live to see another war. As I have said, the world is smaller—smaller every year. The United States now exerts a tremendous influence in the cause of peace throughout all the world. What we people over here are thinking and talking about is in the interest of peace, because it is known all over the world. The slightest remark in either house of the Congress is known all over the world the following day. We will continue to exert that influence, only if we are willing to continue to share in the responsibility for keeping the peace. It will be our own tragic loss, I think, if we were to shirk that responsibility.

The final decisions in these areas are going to be made jointly; and therefore they will often be a result of give-and-take compromise. The United States will not always have its way 100 percent—nor will Russia nor Great Britain. We shall not always have ideal answers—solutions to complicated international problems, even though we are determined continuously to strive toward that ideal. But I am sure that under the agreements reached at Yalta, there will be a more stable political Europe than ever before. . . .

One outstanding example of joint action by the three major Allied powers in the liberated areas was the solution reached on Poland. The whole Polish question was a potential source of trouble in postwar Europe—as it has been sometimes before—and we came to the conference determined to find a common ground for its solution. And we did—even though everybody does not agree with us, obviously.

Our objective was to help to create a strong, independent, and prosperous nation. That is the thing we must always remember, those words, agreed to by Russia, by Britain, and by the United States: the objective of making Poland a strong, independent, and prosperous nation, with a government ultimately to be selected by the Polish people themselves.

To achieve that objective, it was necessary to provide for the formation of a new government much more representative than had been possible while Poland was enslaved. There were, as you know, two governments: one in London, one in Lublin—practically in Russia. Accordingly, steps were taken at Yalta to reorganize the existing provisional government in Poland on a broader democratic basis, so as to include democratic leaders now in Poland and those abroad. This new, reorganized government will be recognized by all of us as the temporary government of Poland. Poland needs a temporary government in the worst way—an ad interim government, I think is another way of putting it.

However, the new Polish Provisional Government of National Unity will be pledged to holding a free election as soon as possible on the basis of universal suffrage and a secret ballot.

Throughout history, Poland has been the corridor through which attacks on Russia have been made. Twice in this generation, Germany has struck at Russia through this corridor. To insure European security and world peace, a strong and independent Poland is necessary to prevent that from happening again.

The decision with respect to the boundaries of Poland was, frankly, a compromise. I did not agree with all of it, by any means, but we did not go as far as Britain wanted, in certain areas; we did not go so far as Russia wanted, in certain areas; and we did not go so far as I wanted, in certain areas. It *was* a compromise. The decision is one, however, under which the Poles will receive compensation in territory in the north and west in exchange for what they lose by the Curzon Line in the east. The limits of the western border will be permanently fixed in the final peace conference. We know, roughly, that it will include—in the new, strong Poland—quite a large slice of what now is called Germany. And it was agreed, also, that the new Poland will have a large and long coastline, and many new harbors. Also, that most of East Prussia will go to Poland. A corner of it will go to Russia. Also, that the anomaly of the Free State of Danzig will come to an end; I think Danzig would be a lot better if it were Polish.

It is well known that the people east of the Curzon Line—just for example, here is why I compromised—are predominantly white Russian and Ukrainian—they are not Polish; and a very great majority of the people west of the line are predominantly Polish, except in that part of East Prussia and eastern Germany, which will go to the new Poland. . . .

I am convinced that the agreement on Poland, under the circumstances, is the most hopeful agreement possible for a free, independent, and prosperous Polish state.

The Crimea Conference was a meeting of the three major military powers on whose shoulders rested chief responsibility and burden of the war. Although, for this reason, France was not a participant in the conference, no one should detract from the recognition that was accorded there of her role in the future of Europe and the future of the world.

France has been invited to accept a zone of control in Germany, and to participate as a fourth member of the Allied Control Council of Germany.

She has been invited to join as a sponsor of the International Conference at San Francisco next month.

She will be a permanent member of the International Security Council together with the other four major powers.

And, finally, we have asked that France be associated with us in our joint responsibility over all the liberated areas of Europe.

Agreement was reached on Yugoslavia, as announced in the communiqué; and we hope that it is in process of fulfillment. But, not only there but in some other places, we have to remember that there are a great many prima donnas in the world. All of them wish to be heard before anything becomes final, so we may have a little delay while we listen to more prima donnas.

Quite naturally, this conference concerned itself only with the European war and with the political problems of Europe— and not with the Pacific war.

In Malta, however, our combined British and American staffs made their plans to increase the attack against Japan.

The Japanese warlords know that they are not being overlooked. They have felt the force of our B-29s, and our carrier planes; they have felt the naval might of the United States, and do not appear very anxious to come out and try it again. . . .

It is still a long, tough road to Tokyo. It is longer to go to Tokyo than it is to Berlin, in every sense of the word. The defeat of Germany will not mean the end of the war against Japan. On the contrary, we must be prepared for a long and costly struggle in the Pacific.

But the unconditional surrender of Japan is as essential as the defeat of Germany. I say that advisedly, with the thought in mind that that is especially true if our plans for world peace are to succeed. For Japanese militarism must be wiped out as thoroughly as German militarism.

On the way back from the Crimea, I made arrangements to meet personally King Farouk of Egypt; Haile Selassie, the emperor of Ethiopia; and King Ibn Saud of Saudi Arabia. Our conversations had to do with matters of common interest. They will be of great mutual advantage because they gave me, and a good many of us, an opportunity of meeting and talking face to face, and of exchanging views in personal conversation instead of formal correspondence.

For instance, on the problem of Arabia, I learned more about that whole problem—the Moslem problem, the Jewish problem —by talking with Ibn Saud for five minutes, than I could have learned in the exchange of two or three dozen letters.

On my voyage, I had the benefit of seeing the army and navy and the air force at work.

All Americans, I think, would feel as proud of our armed forces as I am, if they could see and hear what I saw and heard.

Against the most efficient professional soldiers and sailors and airmen of all history, our men stood and fought—and won.

This is our chance to see to it that the sons and the grandsons of these gallant fighting men do not have to do it all over again in a few years. . . .

The Crimea Conference was a successful effort by the three leading nations to find a common ground for peace. It ought to spell the end of the system of unilateral action, the exclusive alliances, the spheres of influence, the balances of power, and all the other expedients that have been tried for centuries—and have always failed.

We propose to substitute for all these a universal organization in which all peace-loving nations will finally have a chance to join.

I am confident that the Congress and the American people will accept the results of this conference as the beginnings of a permanent structure of peace upon which we can begin to build, under God, that better world in which our children and grandchildren—yours and mine, the children and grandchildren of the whole world—must live, and can live.

And that, my friends, is the principal message I can give you. But I feel it very deeply, as I know that all of you are feeling it today, and are going to feel it in the future.